TRANSCENDENCE IN RELATIONSHIP

EXISTENTIALISM AND PSYCHOTHERAPY

FRONTIERS IN PSYCHOTHERAPY

Edward Tick, *Series Editor*

Angela Browne-Miller•*Gestalting Addiction: The Addiction-Focused Group Therapy of Richard Louis Miller*

Angela Browne-Miller•*Transcending Addiction and Other Afflictions: Lifehealing*

James Flosdorf•*My Father Was Shiva*

John Gagnon•*Wounded Healer*

Alexander Jasnow•*Freud and Cézanne*

Michele Ritterman•*Hope Under Siege State Terror vs. Family Support in Chile*

Edward W. L. Smith•*Gestalt Voices*

William S. Taegel•*The Many-Colored Buffalo*

Steve Trimm•*Walking Wounded*

Robert J. Willis•*Transcendence in Relationship: Existentialism and Psychotherapy*

TRANSCENDENCE IN RELATIONSHIP EXISTENTIALISM AND PSYCHOTHERAPY

ROBERT J. WILLIS

ABLEX PUBLISHING CORPORATION
NORWOOD, NEW JERSEY

Cover art and design by Pamela LaRegina

Printed in the United States of America

Library of Congress Cataloging-in-Publication Data

Willis, Robert J.
Transcendence in relationship / Robert J. Willis.
p. cm. — (Frontiers in psychotherapy series)
Includes bibliographical references and index.
ISBN 1-56750-073-0 (cloth). — ISBN 1-56750-074-9 (pbk.)
1. Existential psychotherapy. I. Title. II. Series.
RC489.E93W55 1994
616.89'14—dc20 94-28155
CIP

Ablex Publishing Company
355 Chestnut Street
Norwood, New Jersey 07648

THREE WOMEN SHAPE MY LIFE:
MIKE BORE AND NURTURED A BOY;
GERMAINE GUIDED A BOY TO
INDEPENDENT ADULTHOOD;
PAT WALKS ALONGSIDE HER MAN.
MAY THIS CREATION OF MINE
CELEBRATE THEIR GIFT OF LOVE.

CONTENTS

INTRODUCTION

I left La Jolla in 1972. Carl Rogers had been a fine mentor and I enjoyed my colleagues at the Center for Studies of the Person, but I needed to move on. As our car sped toward the East Coast, I had only a vague inkling about something missing in my years there. I now know it was transcendence.

Carl developed independence in people. He knew how to cherish others right out of dependency. His nonjudgmental listening and clear communicating brought them, often for the first time, into direct contact with their inner selves. In an uncanny fashion, he could hone in on the least flicker of struggling life, call attention to its desire for growth, and then delight in watching it blossom. I still picture him today as a kind father wanting nothing less for his sons and daughters than the fullness of independent adulthood.

However, I always experienced him as shy. For all his emphasis on relationships, I did not see him relating easily to others. Clearly, he valued others and could be unselfishly present to their experience, but he appeared to do so from an independent, detached stance. When he chose to be present, his attention was bestowed undividedly. However, he could just as readily choose not to be present. Neither professionally nor personally did I find in the kind of relating he espoused the mutuality that comes from lives touching, influencing, and shaping one another—not only in the moment, but continually. When I said goodbye to La Jolla, I was searching for interdependence.

During that period, the Transpersonal Psychology movement was spreading. That movement, which arose out of the writings and research of Abraham Maslow, emphasized self-actualization *and* transcendence. It turned academic and scientific skills to the task of understanding nonordinary communication and experience. In a reaction to the perceived controlling stances and spiritual sterility of much of Christianity, it for the first time brought to the Western world an in-depth examination of the spiritual psychologies of the East. Here followers of the movement found transcendence realized through a disciplined interiority and without dogmatic or bureaucratic subservience.

As I studied and read, thought and meditated, I realized afresh that I was looking not simply for transcendence but for *transcendence in relationship.* I wanted to concentrate my scholarly skills in articulating a sound basis for intersubjectivity. This could, then, more consistently inform my psychotherapeutic encounters with my clients.

In the writings of Rollo May, I first encountered the thinking of such European analysts as Ludwig Binswanger and Medard Boss, who were attempting to apply the phenomenological methodology of Edmund Husserl and Martin Heidegger to psychoanalysis. They also were markedly influenced by the existentialist writers who came into prominence after the end of the Second World War. Although still clearly in the psychoanalytic tradition, they noticeably parted from Freudian orthodoxy.

Following their lead, James Bugental attempted to construct an Existential–Analytic system of therapy in the mid-1960s. Although he denominated its final phase as one of transcendence, he did not develop it as a therapeutic model. Indeed, the first phase, psychotherapy, seemed to me to be more analytic than existential.

When Irvin Yalom's exhaustive volume on *Existential Psychotherapy* appeared in 1980, I hoped to find there the equivalent of Bugental's attempt, but one more clearly based in the tradition of interpersonal psychotherapy. Although he does emphasize the power of the relationship in therapy, his work dealt more with the four major existential anxieties (death, meaninglessness, isolation, and freedom) than with a systematic presentation of psychotherapy.

Although it has become a kind of existentialist dogma in American psychological writings to speak about an "existentialist approach" and to decry the possibility of developing a system of psychotherapy based firmly on existentialist principles, I decided to see for myself if such a system was possible. I thought of myself as an "existentialist psychotherapist," so what did I mean by that and how was I practicing it?

The first problem I encountered stemmed from the fact that existentialism itself does not exist as a coherent school. The term applies simply to a varied group of European thinkers and writers who, in the public consciousness, somehow stand under the same umbrella.

However, they often did not seem to share the same picnic! For example, the group composed of Friedrich Nietzsche, Jean-Paul Sartre, Simone de Beauvoir, Franz Kafka, and Albert Camus espoused philosophical nihilism and atheism, while the likes of Gabriel Marcel, Maurice Merleau-Ponty, Karl Jaspers, and such literary giants as Tolstoy, Dostoevsky, and Rilke did not identify with either of these grim positions. However, in the ordinary consciousness of college-educated Americans, existentialism has become much more associated with the former than the latter group.

I soon realized that I could not do what the existentialists themselves despaired of doing—constructing a coherent philosophy ascribed to by all the so-called existentialists. I, therefore, had to identify for myself some central principles in existentialist writings with which I could agree and which held the promise of supplying a basis for a systematic approach to psychotherapy. My search through their works finally distilled six such principles; they constitute the core of this book's first part.

Given my desire to spell out a process of therapy of relational interdependency, I necessarily chose transcendence as one of these principles. In so doing, I locate myself on the theistic and optimistic side of existentialist thinking. However, my task as a psychologist would be to point to givens in our experience that justify taking such positions.

Across whatever spectrums, most existentialists affirm that for human beings their "being" is a "being-with." This does place transcendence deep within us, for "to be human" is "to be in relationship." Here, indeed, one could philosophically ground a psychotherapy of *transcendence in relationship*.

Human community does not essentially derive from the work of the intellect but rather from emotional contact. Thus, it became obvious to me that in writing about existential psychotherapy I had to touch potential readers with other means than just intellectual argumentation or analysis if I were to be true to myself as a being-with. In addition, transcendence happens through our imaginative and intuitive powers. If reading this book is to be a transcendental experience, then I must engage its readers' imagination as well as satisfy the intellect.

In an endeavor to meet these existentialist requirements, I have purposely chosen the following literary devices. First, I have proposed to be with you, the reader, by sharing pertinent experiences in my personal life and in my psychotherapeutic practice. In this I am practicing the relational vulnerability I preach. Secondly, I have carefully chosen a teaching story to introduce each chapter. In so doing I hope to give you a feel for what I am describing. It may also help to bring your imagination into enhanced contact with the material. Finally, I am including numerous vignettes from my practice so that you may also bring your feelings and imagination to bear on the actual experience of existential psychotherapy.

I do not intend, however, to shortchange the intellect's legitimate quest for knowledge. I have, therefore, striven to present in unusual fullness for a work in psychology the philosophical principles undergirding this kind of psychotherapy. I have also brought together a wide spectrum of psychological theory and research that touch upon the topic at hand. It is hoped that the extensive bibliography will whet some readers' appetites to pursue particular avenues simply introduced by this book. By including others' witnessing, I also intend to buttress my argument that both a relational and an existential psychotherapy exist firmly within the professional landscape of today's American psychology.

By the time you have completed your reading, I trust that I will have demonstrated to you the following:

- Existential psychotherapy is more than an "existential approach";
- Neither nihilism nor atheism define existentialism; they, therefore, need not be part of existential psychotherapy;
- In stressing relationship, this kind of therapy builds on the work of interpersonal, humanistic psychologists; in recognizing human transcendence in immanence, it furthers the investigations of transpersonal psychologists;
- An interpersonal psychotherapy, not just an analytic one, may flow from existential philosophical principles.

As you will undoubtedly grasp more fully at the conclusion of the existential journey that you have shared with me and my clients, I leave you with this fervent message: If you do not find pleasure here, I am sorry; nevertheless, I wish you joy.

ACKNOWLEDGMENTS

Grateful acknowledgment is made to the following for permission to quote from copyrighted material:

Ballantine Books, New York, New York;

Humanities Press International, Atlantic Highlands, New Jersey;

Project Innovation, Chula Vista, California;

Random House, New York, New York;

Sounds True Recordings, Boulder, Colorado;

Arthur Deikman;

Wilson Van Dusen.

Excerpts from the following:

A Way of Being by Carl Rogers, page 142. Originally appeared in *The Counseling Psychologist*, 5(2), pp. 2–10;

Escape from Freedom by Erich Fromm. Copyright © 1941, 1969 by Erich Fromm. Reprinted by permission of Henry Holt and Company, Inc.;

How to Meditate by Lawrence LeShan. Copyright © 1974 by Little, Brown, & Company. Reprinted by permission.

"Perspective and Engagement in Counseling and Psychotherapy: The Phenomenological Approach" by Douglas Snyder. Originally appeared in the *International Journal for the Advancement of Counseling*, 5, pp. 99–100. Reprinted by permission of Kluwer Academic Publishers;

Psychoanalysis and Daseinanalysis by Medard Boss. Copyright © 1963 by Basic Books, Inc. Reprinted by permission of Basic Books, a division of HarperCollins Publishers, Inc.;

On Becoming a Person by Carl Rogers. Copyright © 1961. Used by permission of Houghton Mifflin Company;

Shaking of the Foundations by Paul Tillich. Copyright © 1948 by Charles Scribner's Sons; copyright renewed 1976 by

Hannah Tillich. Reprinted by permission of Charles Scribner's Sons, an imprint of Macmillan Publishing Company;

Stalking the Wild Pendulum by Itzhak Bentov. Reprinted with permission from Destiny Books, One Park Street, Rochester, Vermont;

Tales of the Hasidim: The Early Masters by Martin Buber. Copyright © 1947, 1948, and renewed 1975 by Schocken Books, Inc. Reprinted by permission of Schocken Books, published by Bantam Books, a division of Random House, Inc.;

The Courage to Be by Paul Tillich. Copyright © 1969. Used by permission of Yale University Press;

"The founding of a tradition," from *Tales of the Dervishes* by Indries Shah. Copyright © 1967 by Indries Shah. Used by permission of the publisher, Dutton, an imprint of New American Library, a division of Penguin Books USA, Inc.;

The Way of the Sufi by Indries Shah. Copyright © 1968 by Indries Shah. Used by permission of the publisher, Dutton, an imprint of New American Library, a division of Penguin Books USA, Inc.

PART I

EXISTENTIALISM

Life is nothing until it is lived; but it is yours to make sense of, and the value of it is nothing else but the sense that you choose. Therefore, you can see that there is a possibility of creating a human community.

Jean-Paul Sartre in Kaufmann, p. 309

1

THE CALL OF BEING

I was reading on a summer's day. The sun sparkled on the lake and only an occasional fly disturbed the calm.

An old fellow, rod in hand, ambled by. I nodded, neighbor-like. In return, he smiled, lifted up his rod and, in brief explanation, grunted, "Goin' fishin'."

"Good luck," I said.

Many pages and much contentment later, I watched the seasoned fisherman's homeward journey. When he was abreast of me, he paused. "Nice day," he reckoned.

"Sure is," I returned. "How many did you catch?"

A brief cloud darkened his face. Then, facing me squarely and shaking his head somewhere between bewilderment and disgust, he corrected me:

"Young man, I said I was goin' fishin'; I didn't say I was goin' to catch fish."

Off he moved. I went back to my reading and slapping an occasional fly.

BEING WITH

Many years ago, a Filipino psychologist, Jaime Bulatao, S.J., startled me. In the midst of a discussion about human growth and development, he quietly but firmly declared: "The problem with Western psychology lies in its goal of individual independence. In the East, we know that makes only half the journey."

As I recited to myself oft-repeated phrases about becoming an adult, I clearly recognized this goal of independence: "Be a man";

"grow up"; "stand on your own two feet"; "pull yourself up by your own bootstraps"; "be self reliant"; "he's a 'self-made man'"; "a man owes nothing to anyone." I was most disturbed, however, as I found myself unable to imagine just as clearly the path lying beyond independence. I knew well the "I" as separate, as "ego"; my awareness of myself being truly myself only in relationship had, through the pressures of growing up, been stored away in the treasure house of memorable moments.

Through his groundbreaking work on human subjectivity, *I and Thou*, Martin Buber brought light to my search. Growing up as I did in the years following World War II, I naturally joined in my generation's lust for "experience." I thought that through experience one attained the fullness of adulthood. Buber challenged that expectation.

We humans do relate to the world of things through experience: "As experience the world belongs to the primary word *I-It*" (Buber, 1958, p. 6). Our connection with things "is comprised in *experiencing*, which continually reconstitutes the world, and *using*, which leads the world to its manifold aims, the sustaining, relieving and equipping of human life" (p. 38). In our complex modern world, education focuses heavily on developing our ability to deal quickly and effectively with the world of objects. As we broaden our experience and through trial and error sharpen our abilities to influence situations for our own purposes, we eventually may outgrow the need for teachers. We also may receive the rewards for work well done—money, a home, a secure job, personal and financial independence. Thus do most of us walk the road from childhood to adulthood.

But we do so not without risk, for "the development of the ability to experience and use comes about mostly through the decrease of man's power to enter into relation—the power in virtue of which alone man can live the life of the spirit" (pp. 38–39). We risk becoming individuals who may differentiate ourselves from others through our ability to manipulate reality, including them, to our advantage. As individuals over against others we become, as we think, a subject. Such a subject "acquires no substance, but remains a functional point, experiencing and using, no more. None of its extensive and manifold defined being and none of its zealous 'individuality' can help it to win substance" (p. 64). Each of us may, in a word, act as a *subject* but have no *subjectivity*. Or, as Buber warns, "hear this: without *It* man cannot live. But he who lives with *It* alone is not a man" (p. 34). How, then, does one become "a man"?

Granted the necessity of learning how to "experience and use" objects, "I become through my relation to the *Thou*; as I become *I*, I say *Thou*. All real living is meeting" (p. 11). The key to becoming a person may be found in this meeting, not as a subject over against and separate from some object, but as a person directly connected with an other.

The qualities of this meeting are directness ("Every means is an obstacle. Only when means have collapsed does the meeting come about," p. 12), the experience of oneself ("The existence of *I* and the speaking of *I* are one and the same thing," p. 4), and unity ("When *Thou* is spoken, the speaker has no *thing*; he has indeed nothing. But he takes his stand in relation," p. 4). In it we alone exist as a present to each other, in a present that transcends time and space (pp. 13–14), as present. As *we* meet, the *I* and the *Thou* as separate beings fade to the edges of awareness as the existence of both happens in the living energy of the relationship (p. 87).

Such meetings may happen in three spheres: our life with nature, with other persons, and with spiritual beings. Let us consider examples of each.

In his novel *Nausea* (1964), Jean-Paul Sartre paints a vivid picture of a "meeting" with a tree, an interaction that changed the tree from an object to a presence:

> I was in the park just now. The roots of the chestnut tree were sunk in the ground just under my bench. I couldn't remember it was a root any more. The words had vanished and with them the significance of things, their methods of use, and the feeble points of reference which men have traced on their surface. I was sitting, stooping forward, head bowed, alone in front of this black, knotty mass, entirely beastly, which frightened me. Then I had this vision.
>
> It left me breathless. Never, until these last few days, had I understood the meaning of "existence." I was like the others, like the ones walking along the seashore, all dressed in their spring finery. I said, like them, "The ocean *is* green; that white speck up there *is* a seagull," but I didn't feel that it existed or that the seagull was an "existing seagull"; usually existence hides itself. . . . It had lost the harmless look of an abstract category: it was the very paste of things, this root was kneaded into existence. On rather the root, the park gates, the bench, the sparse grass, all that had vanished: the diversity of things, their individuality, were only an appearance, a veneer. This veneer had melted, leaving soft,

> monstrous masses, all in disorder—naked, in a frightful, obscene nakedness.
>
> . . . But faced with this great wrinkled paw, neither ignorance nor knowledge was important; the world of explanations and reasons is not the world of existence. A circle is not absurd, it is clearly explained by the rotation of a straight segment around one of its extremities. But neither does a circle exist. This root, on the other hand, existed in such a way that I could not explain it. Knotty, inert, nameless, it fascinated me, filled my eyes, brought me back unceasingly to its own existence. In vain to repeat: "This is a root"—it didn't work any more. (pp. 170–171, 172, 174)

As the tree becomes present to this man, we can feel his horror at the connectedness, a presence that could not be avoided through some intellectual distancing. We can almost hear the cry of each: "I exist!"

But where lies the mutuality of this meeting? Does the tree have some consciousness similar to the man's? When speaking about his encounter with another tree, Buber (1958) answered these questions this way:

> Of that I have no experience. But do you wish through seeming to succeed in it with yourself, once again to disintegrate that which cannot be disintegrated? I encounter no soul or dryad of the tree, but the tree itself. (p. 8)

Contrast that vivid encounter with the following: Imagine yourself lying on a quiet beach. The sun strokes your body; the warm sand molds around you, offering little resistance to your weight; the steady pounding of the surf caresses your ears and your soul. In the womb of nature you drift away from yourself, somewhere. You "are" but not as an aware person. Though still awake, you don't think or feel, remember or see. In the disappearance of time and space, you, too, dissolve into a non-reflective nothingness. Like Sartre's character you could no longer objectify this natural world by giving it names. It surrounds you, cutting all else out. For you a soothing pleasure takes the place of his disgust.

But you encounter your world with a quite different kind of energy. He met the tree in a flash of personal encounter; you are meeting the earth in "a purely natural combination, bodily interaction and flowing from the one to the other, just like a child in a mother's womb" (Buber, 1958, p. 25). In this moment, as in the dark embrace of sleep, you are slipping back into "the womb of the great mother, the undivided primal world that precedes form" (p. 25). You are seeking that state of original connectedness that "is the *a priori* of relation, *the inborn Thou*" (p. 27). To meet the other, to relate as a person requires the vulnerability of transcendence, not the annihilation of oneself through absorption. Indeed *you* will reappear on that beach only when your friend calls your name.

In the summer of 1958, I was attending classes at a small Jesuit university in the Pacific Northwest. My fellow students included a sizable number of religious sisters from many congregations. In that pre-Vatican II era, the variety of medieval outfits revealed clearly their orders' origins and differences. On July 4th, our only holiday, a friend borrowed a school bus to offer a tour of the city to those sisters who lived on campus and did not have cars. At his request, I accompanied him.

I sat next to a petite woman some years my senior, a member of a Canadian group. Though a rather quiet and serene person, she straightforwardly engaged me in conversation. Soon, the usual sharing of facts "out there" changed. In the energy of her presence, I felt special and secure. As I began to talk about myself, to open up an inner world long kept secret, the busload of happy people and shifting landscapes of the tour faded out of my awareness. For me only *we* existed. In *no* time but in a time that today, 34 years later, still exists, we pulled up to the women's dorm, and amid many thanks the sisters disembarked. That night, as I still lived in the amazement of that meeting, I knew I had changed. Today I recognize that moment as the time when my *self* was born.

I wondered if this might simply be infatuation: she is a lovely woman. But no, somehow this meeting surpassed feelings. As Buber (1958) might have told me:

> Feelings are "entertained"; love comes to pass. Feelings dwell in man; but man dwells in his love. That is no metaphor, but the actual truth. Love does not cling to the *I* in such a way as to love the *Thou* only for its "content," its object; but love is *between I* and *Thou*. (Buber, 1958, p. 14)

Moreover, she had left me a different person. No chance encounter or planned date had so affected me previously. I could sincerely affirm what Buber says of such interactions:

> In this chronicle of solid benefits the moments of the *Thou* appear as strange lyric and dramatic episodes, seductive and magical, but tearing us away to dangerous extremes, loosening the well-tried context, leaving more questions than satisfaction behind them, shattering security—in short uncanny moments we can well dispense with. (p. 34)

I had spent many years, rather successfully at that, becoming an individual. Through discipline and work, I had detached myself from the world in order to control it. Previous to that Independence Day, I did not know, however, that "A person makes his appearance by entering into relationship with other persons" (p. 62).

That "person," indeed, may be spiritual in form. In the Native American tradition, the Vision Quest took a major role in the ritual movement from boyhood to manhood within the tribe. At the moment indicated by his elders, the boy, fasting and alone, equipped only with his ingenuity, went off into the wilderness. There he stayed, waiting, watching, until he encountered some helper from the spirit world who would both point him toward his manly destiny and signify acceptance of the role of assisting him in its prosecution.

James Thom (1989), in his novel *Panther In The Sky*, offers his vision of the Shawnee boy, Tecumseh, being given his fate:

> It was the time of morning when there should have been the sound of many birds. But he was struck by the silence, it was as if he had awakened deaf.
>
> And while he was thinking in wonder of that, he heard one sound, one sound only:
>
> "*Coo-ah, coo, coo, coo.*"
>
> There not four paces in front of him, as if it had formed itself from the drifting mist around its own mournful call, was a dove, its left side toward him, one eye seeming to watch him. But its color was not the dove's familiar ruddy gray; it was white, the faintly bluish white of snow in shadow. Tecumseh long ago had dreamed of a white bird. A white animal of any race was rare and considered to be a chief of that race. This would be the chief of the doves. When animals spoke to people, it was usually through their chiefs, the white ones like this. Tecumseh was certain that this was the form of his Spirit Helper, and he watched it intently for its message. . . .

> The dove did not call again, but from it was coming, instead of sound, something else, something like a pressure in the air. When this enveloped him, Tecumseh suddenly felt warm, and his despair was gone. Then he could open himself again to receive the messages.
>
> They did not come as words or as thoughts or even as images. But they came and filled him with understandings. First, that this was indeed his Spirit Helper. And that it would return at proper times. That it was to aid him with the needs of the People. That it would guide him, that it would alert him to signs, that it would cause him to have dreams in which would be answers. That he was for the People, and that the white dove was for him. That someday, when the People's needs were most dire, the way would be clear.
>
> All this comprehension diffused into Tecumseh during the time he sat looking at the dove. He did not know how long that was. It seemed like a moment or like always. When the dove finally dissolved into mist again, Tecumseh was refreshed and strong . . . grateful but humbled, feeling as weightless as a spirit, he set off down a path for the trail toward Chillicothe, toward food, to the embrace of the tribe and his family. (pp. 164, 167)

Whatever our personal beliefs may be concerning the existence of a spirit world and the possibilities of our interaction with such beings, the histories of people of every civilization record such visitations. And there appear to be some common elements about them.

This meeting usually takes place in solitude, in a time and place far removed from experiencing and using objects (Buber, 1958, pp. 203–204). Although nothing can make the meeting happen because "the *Thou* confronts me" (p. 77), prayer and sacrifice as a purification and focusing prepare us for it (pp. 82–83, 89). Aside from that, we must be ready to exclude everything except the relation, should it occur (p. 78). For just as the spirit chooses to relate to us, so we must also choose to relate to the spirit. This requires from us an active reception—an intense hospitality ready for relationship (p. 77). During and after the meeting strong feelings may be aroused, but they "are a mere accompaniment to the metaphysical and metapsychical fact of the relation, which is fulfilled not in the soul but between *I* and *Thou*" (p. 81). This meeting happens through a mutuality of action, not through some absorption of us by the spirit (p. 89). On the spirit's part, nothing like ordinary speech occurs, yet meaning is transferred in and through the disclosure of the relationship; we, indeed, may reply through speech or action (p. 106). Finally, the spirit's message aims at assisting us to live our lives more fully, with depth and integrity, for the benefit of ourselves *and* our world (p. 107).

In order to attain the fullness of adulthood, then, we must "be with" other persons, primarily, but the worlds of nature and of spirit may also enter into the ongoing creation of our person. For us, "to be" is "to be with," not only in the minimal sense of needing a human context in which to become human, but also as the *only* path to personal existence.

Such a position filters through the reflections of philosophers who otherwise take quite diverse existential stances. "Quoting St. Exupery, Merleau-Ponty says that 'man is but a network of relations, and these alone count for him'" (Bannan, 1967, p. 137). Heidegger (1962, p. 281) succinctly declares that the human being "is essentially Being with Others." Marcel (1951, p. 18), in asking "under what conditions I become conscious of myself as a person," emphatically maintains that "it must be repeated that those conditions are essentially social." Jaspers (Kaufmann, 1966, p. 147) takes as his thesis that "The Individual cannot become human by himself. Self-being is only real in communication with another self-being." Kierkegaard, the individual who desired only "the individual" (1969, p. 121) to mark his tombstone, maintains anyway that "the fact is that the individual is himself and the race" (1944, p. 26). Even Sartre (1947, p. 60), who despairs that "Hell is—other people!", at the same time asserts that "The other is indispensable to my existence, and equally so to any knowledge I can have of myself" (1966, p. 303).

Given that litany, however, Buber reigns as *the* philosopher of "being with." For him the human being lives authentically as the "creature of the between" (1965, p. xx).

BEING IS BECOMING

Thinking back to the Jesuit's challenge about individual independence being "only half the journey," I now see how we live authentically only as interdependent beings. But what constitutes "the journey"? Where does it begin, how does it proceed, wherein lies its destination?

Troubled by the unstable world of Heraclitean flux, the Greek philosophers sought refuge in the essence of things. Taking rational dialogue as a given experience, Plato argued back to an unchanging world of ideas and to an absolute Good. Aristotle, accepting the need for a secure ground for human existence, asserted that all material beings are composed of essence (an unchanging principle that bestows meaning and stability) and existence (the principle that allows growth and change). Human perfection for him is found, indeed, in the rational contemplation of the absolute One.

Western civilization, Judæo–Christian in its philosophy and Greco–Roman in its political structure, baptized Plato and enthroned Aristotle. After the philosophers discovered essence, civil and religious leaders set about defining the "laws of nature," explaining "the natural law," describing "human nature," and establishing "the Holy Roman Empire." As the philosophers deduced from the One, the rulers proclaimed the Truth from above, while theologians pontificated about God's Will. Security and certainty reigned in a well-ordered universe.

With the economic–political demise of medieval feudalism, the cultural liberation of the Renaissance, and the theological pressure of the Reformation, the well-defined world of essence began to split apart. Immanuel Kant challenged our philosophical certainty by demonstrating how even if *das ding an sich* exists, given the categories of our minds, we can know this supposedly objective world only subjectively. A determined band of American colonists confronted a political world secured by the Divine Right of Kings. In their wake, empires tumbled and the ordered disorder of citizen government scattered across the globe. Even Newton fell. Einstein introduced Relativity, Heisenberg argued for Indeterminancy, particle physicists demonstrated the Quantum Leap.

The inevitable backlash happened: We humans don't give up certainty and security without a fight! Darwinian evolutionary theory sought to explain material development; Social Darwinism strove to order society hierarchically; biological and behavioral determinism offered to make us all understandable, if not predictable. Then, in the name of cultural purity and Aryan perfection, civilized Germany flung its armies across Europe in the name of a modern Caesar. Indeed, only in the ovens of the Third Reich did the fool's gold of essence melt away for many of us. The various forms of rationalism, be they political or philosophical, stood nakedly revealed in all their nonhumanness. As the cry for a human reality rose in millions of throats, existentialism was born.

In the uncompromising light of experience, rational certainty, the legacy of essentialism, now stands before the bar of history. What, truly, do we know for certain about ourselves as human beings? Camus (1955) answers:

> Of whom and of what indeed can I say: "I know that!" This heart within me I can feel, and I judge that it exists. This world I can touch, and I likewise judge that it exists. There ends all my knowledge, and the rest is construction. For if I try to seize this self of which I feel sure, if I try to define and to summarize it, it is nothing but water slipping through my fingers. I can sketch one by one all the aspects it is able to assume, all those likewise that have been attributed to it, this upbringing, this origin, this ardor or these silences, this nobility or this vileness. But aspects cannot be added up. This very heart which is mine will forever remain indefinable to me. Between the certainty I have of my existence and the content I try to give to that assurance, the gap will never be filled. Forever I shall be a stranger to myself. In psychology as in logic, there are truths but not truth. (p. 14)

We know we are living; we admit that we cannot account for living in this time and place among this people; we recognize that we came into this life brimming with potentialities and seized by an inbuilt task of giving them actuality; in this inner drive to create ourselves, we experience a force more powerful than any momentary desire or whim; we claim this particular existence as our own. These truths we may hold as certain in the immediacy of our experience, but no others. The darkness of birth and death shrouds the "why" and the "whither" of our lives. "What" and "how" we are appear and disappear with each breath, with the newness of each passing moment, with the registering of *this* experience. Certainty attaches itself to the "that" of existence, and that alone. Aside from that "I am nothing but an empty void; for, still, I can affirm nothing about myself which would be really myself; nothing, either, which would be permanent; nothing which would be secure against criticism and the passage of time" (Marcel, 1951, p. 16).

What happens, you inquire, to the essence of being human? Sartre (1957) maintains that instead of its anticipating existence, it follows upon it:

> What is meant by saying that existence precedes essence? It means that, first of all, man exists, turns up, appears on the scene, and, only afterwards, defines himself. If man, as the existentialist conceives him, is indefinable, it is because at first he is nothing. (p. 15)

Heidegger (1962, p. 274) responds that essence *is* existence. As beings whose "essence is made up of existence," we cannot by our very nature grasp ourselves as a given (p. 276). We are "*constantly something still to be settled*" (p. 279); we may only be defined as an "ahead-of-itself-Being-already-in (the world) as Being-alongside entities which we encounter (within-the-world)" (p. 293). Instead of beings already fashioned who now live out of some predetermined format, we exist from the beginning as potentiality-for-Being (pp. 322, 435).

Given that point of departure, life's journey unfolds through action. "Become what thou art," counsels Zarathustra, and "Let it not be your honor henceforth whence ye came, but whither ye go! Your will and your feet will seek to surpass you—let these be your new honor" (Nietzsche, 1883–91, pp. 226, 265). "How many things are still possible! So *learn* to laugh beyond yourselves! Lift up your hearts, ye good dancers, high! higher! And do not forget the good laughter" (p. 332)! Life's worth rests not in the creator, but in the creation; its meaning depends on the creating, not the receiving. "Man is nothing else than his plan; he exists only to the extent he fulfills himself; he is therefore nothing else than the ensemble of his acts, nothing else than his life" (Sartre, 1957, p. 31). Indeed, our very reality is our freedom to create ourselves.

What possibility for existing lies before us?

Western science has been brilliantly successful in constructing a modern world in which personal independence stands not only as life's *desideratum*, but even as a reality for increasing numbers of people. And capitalism has enshrined the "self-made man," such as the entrepreneur or the professional, as its hero.

Much of this success is attributable to scientific victories over the forces of disease and death. As the biological sciences prevent a variety of death-dealing plagues, as the medical sciences develop ever more sophisticated methods of diagnosis and repair, infant mortality rates fall, longevity rates rise. This battle against the evil forces of Death fits admirably well our Western urge for independence. By their close attention to detail, through rational control, with the predictable ordering of resources, independence and success await the talented and the industrious.

So goes the theory. But even the independent shall die, often at their own hands, as they behold the next generation, striving for *their* independence, taking advantage of their elders' diminishing vitality and increasing age. And long before death, how often does the momentary lord of the mountain complain, in the words of a popular song, "Is that all there is?" Having made it to the top, with no place further to go, one's being becomes boredom. "When there is nothing to do, human liberty—which for the existentialist *is* human reality—is smothered" (Bannan, 1967, p. 173). The independent one may be standing firmly on his or her own two feet, but now flat-footed, stuck, and purposeless, there is nothing left to do but die. Science inevitably bows before death.

In a brilliant article in *ReVision* (1980), the philosopher-psychologist Ken Wilber pointed out the short-sightedness of this view of life. He argued that in confusing the "Prepersonal" and the "Transpersonal" we westerners have effectively blocked ourselves from "half the journey." Following a developmental philosophy "represented most effectively by Hegel in the West and Aurobindo in the East . . . and developmental psychology . . . epitomized by Baldwin and Piaget in the West and Kundalini yoga in the East" (p. 51), he proposed that two movements characterize human growth: the first, from the prepersonal to the personal, corresponds with our Western drive toward individual independence; the second, from the personal to the transpersonal, offers a way to a transformative unity. The dual movement may be illustrated as shown in Figure 1.1.

Our task of self-creation requires a move past independence to interdependence. We must be able to choose not only separateness but also unity. The key to human development is this: the flat-footed stance of independence must be complemented by balancing on one's tiptoes so as to be off-balance in a direction. Being is becoming; being is not fulfilled by having made it. To have made

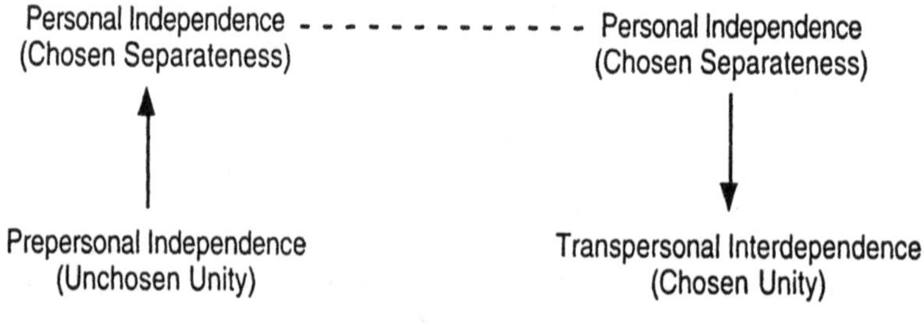

FIGURE 1.1 Complementary Processes of Human Growth

it means death. Life says, "Behold . . . I am that *which must ever surpass itself*" (Nietzsche, 1883–91, p. 125).

Religion has through its spiritual masters illuminated this complementary movement from separateness to unity. It recognizes that Science's interaction with Death is doomed because it takes account of only half the truth. Consider Figure 1.2.

The left-hand side of the figure demonstrates the scientific stance vis-à-vis Death. It fights for Life, the unqualified good; it struggles against the enemy, Death. For a time, Science may win, may keep Death at bay. Final defeat, however, lurks inevitably, somewhere, some time.

The opposite side of the figure offers the recognition that life sustains itself not by clinging to what it has or has become (life–), but rather by letting go of these in order to grow (death+). The actual must make room for the potential, essence must cede to existence, certainty in the name of living must give way to risk. Independence, indeed, may not be maintained nor interdependence attained except through the daily relinquishing of control. When death+ in the form of risk and change joins Life+, personal and interpersonal growth results.

In attempting to describe the "emerging person" Carl Rogers (1969) emphasized the passionate embracing of becoming as an identifying hallmark in the "new revolution":

> He is a person who is aware that he is continually in process—always changing. In this process he is spontaneous, vitally alive, willing to risk. His likes and dislikes, his joys and his sorrows are passionate and are passionately expressed. His adventuresomeness has an almost Elizabethan quality—*everything* is possible, *anything* can be tried. . . . I

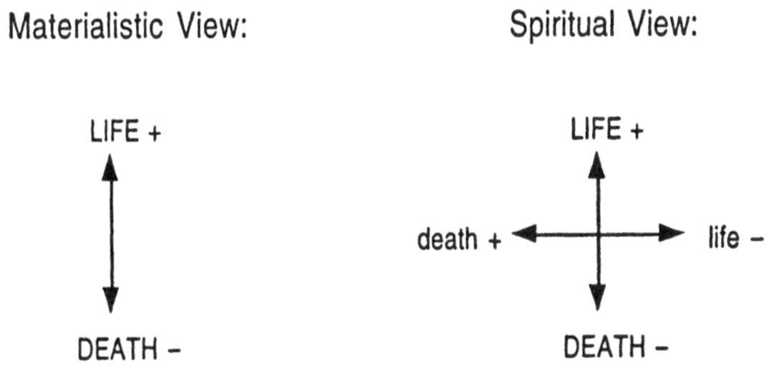

FIGURE 1.2 Interaction Between Life And Death Forces

> believe he is the first instance in history of man being fully aware that changingness is the one constant of life. (p. 19)

As he meditated about life and death, Dostoevsky (1864/1974) recognized the danger of holding on to anything—a belief in God, a certitude about essence, the accumulating of achievements, victories over death—as a substitute for living:

> And who knows (no one can vouch for that), perhaps the only goal toward which mankind is striving on earth consists of nothing but the certainty of a process of achieving—in other words, of life itself, and not the goal proper which, naturally, must be nothing but two times two is four—in other words, a formula; and two times two, gentlemen, is no longer life but the beginning of death. (p. 38)

The old fellow who once upon a summertime admonished me knew that also. Being a fisherman, like becoming a person, has little to do with counting one's catch; it has, indeed, everything to do with entering enthusiastically into the world of fish!

2

THE CHALLENGE TO BE

There was a professor taking a sea voyage in a little boat and one night he goes up to an old sailor and says, "Hey, old man, what do you know about oceanography?" The old sailor didn't even know what the word meant. The Professor said, "You've wasted a quarter of your life! Here you are, sailing on the sea, and you don't even know any oceanography."

The next night the Professor goes up to the old man and says, "Hey, old man, what do you know about meteorology?" Again the old sailor had never heard of the word. "The science of the weather." "Ah, I don't know anything about that." "Oh, you've wasted half your life!"

The next night the Professor goes up to the old man. "What do you know about astronomy?" "Nothing." "Here you are, out on the sea, and you need the stars to navigate, and you don't know anything about astronomy. You've wasted three quarters of your life!"

The next night the old sailor comes rushing up to the Professor and says, "Professor, what do you know about swimology?" The Professor says, "Oh, nothing. I've never learned to swim." "Ah, too bad, the boat is sinking. You've wasted all your life!"

It's the swimology which is important. (Goldstein, 1976, p. 2)

BEING AND NOTHINGNESS

In his introduction to *Nausea* by Jean-Paul Sartre, Hayden Carruth (1964) proclaims that "By concentrating all attention on this nothing within himself and underlying the objective surface of reality, he [Sartre] gradually transforms nothing into the concept of Nothingness, one of the truly great accomplishments of human sensibility" (p. viii). In our capitalistic world we are used to celebrating the entrepreneur who from nothing becomes someone; what possibly could raise cheers about making nothing over into Nothingness? Consider each concept in turn.

Imagine yourself finishing off the absolutely last mouthful of an over-generous Thanksgiving dinner. As you push yourself with determination away from the table, you actually ache from fullness. While loosening your clothes around an overpacked midsection, you declare firmly that you'll never eat again. You don't want to see any more food, smell any more food, or even talk about food. For you, at this moment, food holds no allure. It has become nothing to you. Fullness generates nothing. It stirs no motivation, raises no questions, prompts no exploring of options.

You know the ad, "What do you give the man who has everything?" How often have you agonized over what to give Dad—Dad who needs and wants nothing for his birthday! So what finally happens? You give him a "nothing" tie in at least some kind of nod to ritual. Everything generates nothing and takes the joy out of giving because there exist no options among which to explore.

Now take yourself back in time to your hurried preparations for that Thanksgiving feast. Before your guest arrived the house had to be cleaned, the table had to be decked out in fine array, the dinner had to be ready for presentation on call. Finally, with ten minutes to spare, you're all ready. You sit down in your living room . . . to wait.

As you pretend to read the nearest magazine, your senses become hyper-alert for any indication of an arriving guest. You hear every car turning on to your street and straightaway speculate over its identity: "Is that Bill's Pontiac? No, sounds like a Ford." With each slam of a car door, a myriad of questions rise up in you: "Is that Bill? Does he usually slam his door that way? Should I look out the window? Oh, am I sure I've prepared everything?" As footsteps echo along the street, they sound incredibly clear. More questions abound: "Is that his walk? Does he shuffle like that? Is that person in a hurry?" All of this happens because of your emptiness as a host or hostess. You wish to be one, but you may become so only through the action of receiving your guest.

Previous to his arrival, relative to hosting, your state is one of nothingness.

What generates nothingness?—emptiness and the freedom to question. As the first car drove slowly by, your question "Is that Bill's Pontiac?" indicated that you were free, not stuck to the being of that particular vehicle, that you were able to say either "yes" or "no" relative to its being something for you. And as you say a resolute "no," that car not only moves on down the street, it also loses all meaning for you and fades away into nothingness for you. In this way, the questioner introduces nothingness into the world.

Sartre (1965) explains the process this way:

> Thus insofar as the questioner must be able to effect in relation to the questioned a kind of nihilating withdrawal, he is not subject to the causal order of the world; he unsticks himself from being. This means that by a double movement of nihilation, he nihilates the thing questioned in relation to himself by placing it in a *neutral* state, between being and non-being—and that he nihilates himself in relation to the thing questioned by wrenching himself away from being in order to be able to bring out the possibility of non-being. Thus in posing a question, a certain negative element is introduced into the world. We see nothingness making the world iridescent, casting a shimmer over things. But at the same time the question emanates from a questioner who in order to motivate himself in his being as one who questions, disengages himself from being. This disengagement is then by definition a human process. Man presents himself at least in this instance as a being who introduces nothingness into the world. . . . (p. 115)

As human beings we have the freedom to focus our attention on whatever we will. In so doing we invest something with meaning for us, bring it into relationship to us, make it stand out in our world as a figure against a not-so-important ground. As for the unattended-to background, we locate it somewhere between being and non-being, between something and nothing. An existentialist calls that somewhere "nothingness" (Sartre, 1965, p. 113).

For the Professor oceanography and meteorology and astronomy held general interest; for the old sailor they did not. As the Professor was met with the recurrent "no," relative to the discussion of these sciences, for him the ignorant sailor faded into the background, into a state of nothingness. Only when he was faced with the pressing need for "swimology" did the Professor relegate those other sciences to that same state of nothingness.

As human beings we always have the option of meeting ourselves in each of these three modes: as *some*-thing, *no*-thing, and nothingness. How does this happen?

Imagine yourself at work. The boss runs the place like a boot camp. Unquestioning and immediate obedience is expected and alone guarantees continued employment. So you put on your best face and play the game according to his rules. Indeed, after a while you even cease being angry inside as you and the compliant role you have assumed become one. You may exist "in yourself," you still are a being, but you no longer exist "for yourself" as you exist only for him (Sartre, 1956, pp. lxii–lxvii). At work you have become *no one*; you exist only as *some thing*, like a table or a book, to be used according to another's whim.

Only at night, when you come home, do you allow yourself to feel. At first you rage at him; then you rage at yourself over your cowardice. But rage soon turns to frustration as you examine your helpless state: you need the job, other jobs aren't available, so you're trapped. At that point, out comes the bottle of vodka and another night of drinking yourself into oblivion begins. If you can't be a person living for yourself, then, at least, you can escape from being his slave by filling yourself with liquor to the point when you pass out, when you move from *some-thing* to *no-thing*.

Until you hit bottom. When your wife is threatening divorce, when your kids won't speak to you, when your friends no longer visit, when your doctor has given you dire warnings about the liquor's effect on your liver, and when you find yourself becoming increasingly incapable of maintaining yourself at work according to *his* demands, *then* you may finally come face to face with the terrible responsibility of nothingness. Perhaps the boss hasn't assigned you a role; perhaps you fashioned it yourself. Could it be that he didn't trap you but that you trapped yourself? Have all your options truly vanished or have you just used that as an excuse for avoiding the risk of standing up for yourself? Might you not be blaming him for your helpless state when, in reality, you are employing him as a handy way of relinquishing your responsibility for making yourself *some one*? As you look inside yourself, as you uncompromisingly question your motives and scrutinize your personal options, you now have become, finally, the nothingness that is your being.

We all would on occasion, almost reflexively, like to blame someone or something for our pain. And if no suitable candidate may be found, then, at least, we can make our very humanity with all its imperfection the villainous source of our discomfort. Or may we be deceiving ourselves here also? Listen to Gabriel Marcel (1951):

> Burdened with myself, plunged in the disturbing world, sometimes threatening me, sometimes my accomplice, I keep an eager look-out for everything emanating from it which might either soothe or ulcerate the wound I bear within me, which is my ego. . . . What then is this anguish, this wound? The answer is that it is above all the experience of being torn by a contradiction between the all which I aspire to possess, to annex, or, that after all I am nothing but an empty void; for still, I can affirm nothing about myself which would be really myself; nothing, either, which would be permanent, nothing which would be secure against criticism and the passage of time. (p. 16)

How are we as matter and spirit "nothing but an empty void"?

Before modern science introduced us to the subatomic particle world of quantum physics, we could hold firmly the commonsensical position that material things, tangible reality, constituted a solid bulwark against nothingness. Now, however, we are confronted with the strange behavior of particles that tend to appear, now here, now there, blinking in and out of material existence like a congregation of fireflies on a sultry summer night. Indeed, underneath it all our "solid" world may exist "for us only as long as there is movement, and when the movement stops, matter and solid reality become diffuse and disappear" (Bentov, 1977, p. 40). Light comes to us both as a wave and as a particle; matter and energy are convertible; scientists hunting for the ultimate building block of matter have so far found only energy.

Itzhak Bentov (1977) confronts us brilliantly with the radical emptiness of matter by applying the Principle of Indeterminancy to our everyday experience of a pendulum:

> We have heard about Heisenberg's principle of uncertainty. This principle states that in trying to measure two parameters of a particle—for instance, its momentum and its position—we find that the more accurately we can mea-

> sure its momentum, the less we can know about its position and vice versa. (Momentum simply means: mass x velocity.)
>
> If we want to measure either the momentum or the position of a particle, we can measure precisely only one of these quantities. If we know the exact momentum of a particle, then its position is completely indefinite or unknowable, and vice versa. This is an example of those strange ways in which particles of atomic size or smaller behave.
>
> We know that at rest, when the pendulum is changing direction, its velocity is zero. But the momentum, at low speeds at least, is equal to *velocity* multiplied by *mass*. However, if we multiply any quantity by a zero, we get zero. Thus, we have now established that the momentum of the pendulum at that point is zero, that is, we know its value very precisely: *It's zero*. But we have said before that if we know precisely the momentum of a particle, then its position becomes diffuse and completely indefinite. That is, the pendulum can be just about any place, even at the end of the universe. Yes, but it has very little time to get there because this whole event occurs in zero time. So there we go again. The pendulum has to disappear in all directions at infinite velocity. It will have to expand very rapidly into space, like a balloon, and then collapse just as rapidly.
>
> Having done this, it comes back, picks up speed, and goes about its usual good-hearted business as if nothing had happened. None of us would suspect the leisurely pendulum of doing such a wild thing when no one is looking! But then again, one cannot rely on appearances. (p. 38)

Undoubtedly, in our daily lives we experience tangible reality as solid, consistent, and predictable. Our intellect and our senses need these qualities for understanding, activity, and growth. They, therefore, organize our world for us in that fashion. We see things through the lenses of our subjectivity; we choose lenses that give promise of meeting our needs and goals of the ordinary moment. In that sense we get the reality we create.

But as Lawrence LeShan argues in *Alternate Realities* (1976), "reality" exists in different ways. The nonordinary realities of the quantum physicist, or the psychic healer, or the mystic (LeShan, 1974b) are not less real than sensory reality or "due to some aberration or other" (LeShan & Margenau, 1982, p. 12). Indeed, LeShan (a psychologist) and Margenau (a physicist) draw this conclusion from their examination of "reality":

> We therefore no longer ask which construction of the cosmos, which state of consciousness is the correct one in that, when using it, we are perceiving and reacting to reality. We only ask which construction and which state of consciousness is most effective in helping us attain which goal. The concept of a "correct" or "normal" state of consciousness is one we will have to put on the crowded and dusty shelf marked "outmoded ideas: ingest at your own risk." . . . There is no "correct" state of consciousness that will reflect "reality," but only a number of states useful or useless for specific human purposes. (p. 213)

In the real world of subatomic particles, the quantum physicist beholds nothingness in the very core of matter. How does nothingness dwell at the center of the human spirit?

Put yourself in this imaginary situation: Because of your status in society you have been invited by the Queen of England to attend a formal ball at Buckingham Palace. When the time comes, you are outfitted most properly and your demeanor is impeccably correct. You do all in your power to present yourself as a person worthy to mix with royalty. New acquaintances will later describe you as pleasant and courteous, attentive and knowledgeable. You publicly portray yourself as a self-assured, quite proper gentleman or lady. You wear the persona, the mask of respectability, well.

But this mask changes with the situation. The wild you has been observed at less formal parties with friends sometimes to drink too much, talk too loudly, poke too much fun at others' foibles, and even tell an occasional off-color joke. What happened on those occasions to the "respectable" you? It vanished into nothingness. You are not the role you play, and you may play many roles that blink on and off, just like subatomic particles.

Moreover, during that evening with royalty you at times feel quite shy and even fearful, especially when you are being introduced to the cream of English society. You find yourself silently wishing that you had stayed home; you long for the security of the familiar and the anonymous. In such moments you fall quiet, tend to fade into the crowd, and accept any excuse to move out of the uncomfortable engagement. The facade of the self-assured you gives way to the personality patterns that for a lifetime have been your best line of defense when you feel threatened. In the grip of fear your public face crumbles to reveal the child searching frantically for safety.

Are you, therefore, really just a trembling child? No, for you also have been known to fly into a rage when your family or friends appear to be slighting you or otherwise disregarding your feelings. And, no, for you have also paid your societal dues by marching bravely in protests decrying a variety of social injustices. So just as you may don diverse public faces, so too you may choose different modalities for defending yourself. Again, the diverse defenses move in and out of nothingness depending on your choices.

On your flight back home, you think about yourself and your life. How did *you* ever get to that gathering in London anyway! You came from a German Lutheran family of Midwest farmers. After attending a private school, you became the first in your family to get a college education. You picked the big city, Chicago, went to Northwestern, majored in communications. After graduation, you took a series of television jobs until you moved with your family to Pittsburgh to settle into your current position as a senior vice president for PBS.

So, who are you? You're well-educated, hardworking, religious, a product and representative of Middle America. You love your family, enjoy your friends, contribute your talents to worthwhile community projects. You like to think of yourself as independent, but you recognize yourself as needing acceptance and validation from others. Your life aspirations now revolve mainly around raising your family, providing for their education, passing on the values you and your spouse hold dear. And some day, when you both have retired, you'll enjoy traveling together to experience other peoples, other cultures, at your leisure.

You have become the product of your life's journey with its values and needs, experiences and decisions, relationships and aspirations. These have stamped your human nature, your essence, with a special uniqueness. When you say "I am," your identity or the "real you" (the "ego") is much more complex than the persona that waltzed with royalty, much more stable than the occasional insecure child awestruck by others' fame and fortune.

But you could have been different. When you were born, a multitude of potential "you's" awaited your call. With each decision, no matter how insignificant or grand, one "you" blinked stronger—like the celebrating firefly—while one or other "you" faded or even ceased to be. As a free being you have had the anguishing task of being your own creator. You have daily exercised the decisions of life and death as you have molded and shaped yourself out of nothingness.

Again, listen to Sartre's (1965) comments on the task of freedom:

> Freedom, manifesting itself through anguish, is characterized by a constantly renewed obligation to remake the *self* which designates the free being. As a matter of fact, when we showed earlier that my possibilities were agonizing because it depended on *me* alone to sustain them in their existence, that did not mean that they derived from a *Me* which to itself, at least, would first be given and would then pass in the temporal flux from one consciousness to another consciousness. The gambler who must realize anew the synthetic apperception of a *situation* which would forbid him to play, must re-invent at the same time the *self* which can evaluate that situation, which "is in situation." This *self* with its *a priori* and historical content is the essence of man. Anguish as the manifestation of freedom in the face of self means that man is always separated by a nothingness from his essence. (p. 123)

Existentialists do not deny that human beings possess a human essence. Moreover, they recognize an ego identity that endures over time. Contrary to the essentialistic tradition, however, they do assert that this essence or ego "is not an antecedent structure which, when disclosed by reflection, will provide a causal explanation of why I am doing what I am doing." And they further maintain that "to the extent that I construe as an explanatory principle the self or character of which I am conscious through reflection, my self-consciousness is self deception" (Barnes, 1956, p. 8). You owe yourself to yourself alone. All praise, and all blame, rests with you.

But let us continue our imaginary journey from Pittsburgh to London and back.

After a long plane ride, home looks better than ever! Gradually, as you share the week's highlights with your family, the accumulated stress of being a public person begins to dissolve. Bags unpacked, a familiar dinner enjoyed, you settle back into the welcoming embrace of your regular life.

That night in the arms of your partner the past week fades further away. As your attention narrows to the one you love, as the tension of the coming together rises, time and space collapse to this moment . . . here . . . now. And as the living energy flows massively between you, your persona and personality—those long-practiced ways of being distant—dissolve too. At some point even your ego sinks into the background as the self-reflective and self-observing you is swept away in the immediacy of living. Indeed, you and your partner in the strongest moment of living contact both seem to join the movement into nothingness so that only the vital vibration of the relating continues to exist.

What is happening? Taking a clue from Fritz Kunkel (Sanford & Lough, 1988, p. 67), consider Figure 2.1.

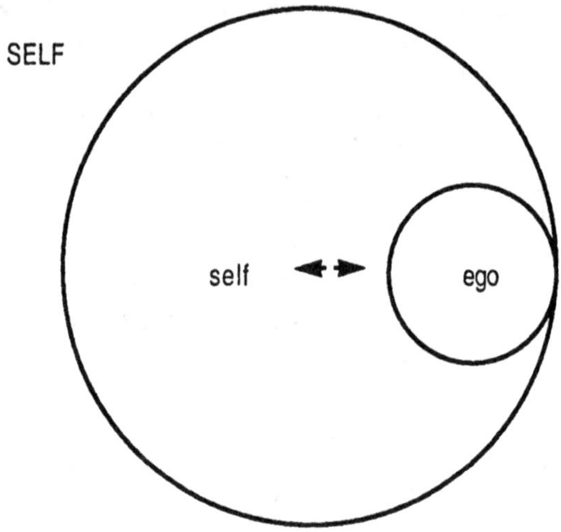

FIGURE 2.1 Healthy Interaction Between The Ego And The Self

The self is depicted here both as the large circle and as the central dot. The ego with open boundaries is contained in the self and receives the self's living energy through drawing close to, observing, and interacting with the self's internal focusing point.

In your loving encounter with your spouse, your ego serves as a focusing mechanism similar to the lens of a camera. In the first instance it brings this special other person into focus, creating that one as figure and reducing all else to the ground of nothingness. As that focus intensifies and narrows, the loving energy flowing from the central core of the self floods the ego. This flooding prompts the ego itself to move aside so as to remove any egocentric block to the living contact. Thus does the ego also fade into nothingness. When that happens all the enormous life of the Self rushes through the core of the self. Time, space, separateness evaporate. What alone remains is Life living the contact that you have become. In that timeless instant you are absorbed into an Infinity in which existence alone is.

However we may name that experience afterward, this encounter can be described only as transcendent. Rilke (1947), speaking about religion as spirituality, catches its flavor, when he says:

> Religion is something infinitely simple, simple-souled. It is not knowledge, not the content of feeling (for every kind of content is admitted at the outset when a man enters into collusion with life), it is not duty and not renunciation, it is not a limitation: but, within the perfect amplitude of the universe it is—a direction of the heart. (p. 336)

And, let us add, that direction happens most totally as the spirit of the self becomes nothingness in the living energy of the Self.

FREEDOM AND RESPONSIBILITY

I once heard about an incident, real or fanciful, that well illustrates the dilemma of freedom.

On a wintry day a beggar asked a gentleman for his loose change to get a steaming bowl of soup. The gentleman, in a fit of mercy, opened his wallet, selected a crisp twenty-dollar bill, and offered it to the fellow. After a long look, the beggar shook his head, and turned away muttering to himself: "If I took that, I couldn't be no beggar no more."

With every choice made, with each new potentiality realized, new horizons open up that call us to the responsibility for creating our lives. Sometimes being trapped—by joblessness or ill health, little education or less motivation—affords some seeming protection against the task of freedom. The existentialist, however, would challenge this stance for, as Rollo May (1990) well points out,

> The existentialist's central proclamation was this: No matter how great the forces victimizing the human being, man has the capacity to *know* that he is being victimized, and thus to influence in some way how he will relate *to* his fate. There is never lost that kernel of the power to take some stand, to make some decision, no matter how minute. This is why the existentialists hold that man's existence consists, in the last analysis, of his freedom. (p. 270)

In his chilling play, *The Flies*, Sartre (1947) presents this telling dialogue between Zeus and Aegistheus, the tyrannical king of Argos:

Aegistheus: I have no secret.
Zeus: You have. The same as mine. The bane of gods and kings. The bitterness of knowing men are free. Yes, Aegistheus, they are free. But your subjects do not know it, and you do. (p. 69)

However, one person, Orestes, the son of murdered Agamemnon, has returned to Mycenae as a free man. Zeus continues:

Zeus: Orestes knows he is free.
Aegistheus: (Eagerly) He knows he's free? Then, to lay hands on him, to put him in irons, is not enough. A free man in a city acts like a plague-spot. He will infect my whole kingdom and bring my work to nothing. Almighty Zeus, why stay your hand? Why not fell him with a thunderbolt?
Zeus: (Slowly) Fell him with a thunderbolt? (A pause. Then in a muffled voice) Aegistheus, the gods have another secret.
Aegistheus: Yes?
Zeus: Once freedom lights its beacon in a man's heart, the gods are powerless against him. It's a matter between man and man, and it is for other men, and for them only, to let him go his gait, or to throttle him. (p. 135)

Although even the gods cannot deprive human beings of their freedom, its burden weighs heavily for no god may save them from freedom either. Orestes grimly states this in his closing conversation with Zeus:

Orestes: Why, since it is their [people of Argos'] lot, should I deny them the despair I have in me?
Zeus: What will they make of it?
Orestes: What they choose. They're free; and human life begins on the far side of despair. (p. 160)

We enter life incomplete. This incompleteness manifests itself primarily in our very way of existing; that is, our existence precedes our essence (Heidegger, 1962, p. 276) in the sense that we are an indefinable nothing until we begin to define ourselves through our chosen actions (Sartre, 1957, p. 15). As beings living in this world we are at the core "potentiality-for-Being" (Heidegger, 1962, p. 322, 435).

Because of our dependent condition from birth, we tend to fill up our incompleteness by taking on the way of existing of those about us, particularly our family. As we model ourselves on others, obediently following their choices, we are relieved of the burden of choosing, we get carried along in the lives of others, and we lose ourselves. In fact, we exist more as a "potentiality-for-Being-one's-self" than a "potentiality-for-Being" (Heidegger, p. 312). But authentic existence demands, at some point, that we find ourselves by making up for our past failing to choose. We do this by deciding to make the choice in freedom to create ourselves (p. 313).

To accept this task, however, means to risk:

> In the uncertain, that marks the phenomenality of true future, there inheres as a positive constituent the quality of unprotectedness as a *conditio sine qua non* of freedom; freedom, indeed, is a *willing* exposure of the self to whatever is ordained to turn into its presence. (Sonnemann, 1954, p. 276)

With each choice we take *this* path, not *that* one. And each path chosen inevitably leads to a new crossroads where we must risk being ourselves again.

At the end, we finally must choose death, for to be oneself, to be free to be whole, means to be free for death as the point of human completeness. As Heidegger (1962) straightforwardly says:

> . . . *death, as in the end of Dasein, is Dasein's ownmost possibility—non-relational, certain, and as such indefinite, not to be outstripped. Death is*, as *Dasein's* end, in the Being of this entity *towards* its end. (p. 303)

We are a Being-towards-death (p. 310). "Human life on the far side of despair" that accepts this fact and embraces it in freedom.

As historical beings we exercise our freedom within the limits of the possibilities presented us by our heritage and our fate. We may only choose what we deem valuable; we only perceive as valuable those choices that fit the self we are: in this family and nation, in this time and place, in this personal history. And in the face of threat, real or imagined, our values may become far less influential than anxiety or fear.

We all run painfully into these limits on our freedom. I did so, fatefully, in the seventh grade.

My mother had recently moved me from a protected but over-crowded private grade school to a large public junior high school. The unfamiliar setting with its relative lack of personal and interpersonal structures felt exciting and terrifying. And nascent puberty added to my insecurity.

These all converged when Barbara, a girl I had spied eyeing me for days, invited me to a Halloween party. "It's a hayride out at Jerry's farm. Everybody's going. It'll be fun. Will you come?" She wasn't threatening me, but I was afraid. And the combinations of bashfulness, an unfamiliar activity, and a rush of new and uncomfortable emotions raised anxiety levels unbearably. I solved it all when I blurted out: "Thank you, but I can't go. My folks don't like hayrides!"

In the face of the burden of freedom, I opted for the safety of pretending I had no choice. My parents' strict sexual mores plus anxiety over the unknown overruled my desires as I chose not to choose. Only later would I realize that the combination of an unsought-for opportunity that raises both excitement and anxiety calls for a choice that risks freedom to be in relationship. I *did* have a choice but I could not make a decision for "Only he who knows relation and knows about the presence of the *Thou* is capable of decision" (Buber, 1958, p. 51).

In that boyhood flirtation with sexuality, I tried to avoid responsibility by placing the burden of decision on my parents. Because of the possibility of some vague harm, I opted not to be me. Indeed, as Gelven (1970) observes:

> The moral responsibility involved in a serious decision, for example, has far greater existential significance than the subsequent facts resulting from the actual choice made. To suggest that the simple chronicling of actual events can reflect what it means to be is to overlook the most important characteristic of existing—responsibility. (p. 157)

Faced with the possibility of some unimaginable sexual transgression, in the name of responsibility I pretended both to myself and to Barbara that I had no responsibility in this situation, not to her and especially not to myself.

But, finally, life offers no place to hide. As Sartre (1956) ominously points out:

> Nothing can insure me against myself, cut off from the world and from my essence by this nothingness which I *am*. I have to realize the meaning of the world and of my essence; I make my decision concerning them—without justification and without excuse. . . . In anguish I apprehend myself at once as totally free and as not being able to derive the meaning of the world except as coming from myself. (p. 129)

None of us may achieve personhood except by assuming responsibility for our acts and for the decisions we make that lead us into action.

Nor does the responsibility stop there. We all, each and every one of us, stand before the bar of civilization as co-creators of humanity. Consider the following example.

At the outbreak of the Persian Gulf War, many American citizens supported the Administration's decision to attack the Iraqi forces; many did not. We are accustomed by extension to praise or blame supporters of an activity as assuming some responsibility through their encouragement. We do not ordinarily include nonsupporters in this attribution. As a bumper sticker on a Massachusetts car proudly proclaimed during Nixon's Watergate troubles, "Don't blame me: I voted for McGovern!"

But do negative votes about a particular policy absolve dissenters from responsibility? Politically, *any* vote keeps our government in power; economically, *any* consumption of energy resources makes us fuel-dependent; socially, *any* interaction with our neighbors helps to weave us into a people creating its own destiny; morally, *any* aggressive action in the face of opposition fashions human reality as a violence-responding one. And whenever we fall away from our true selves, or "lose ourselves in the crowd" to deny our fate and shirk our task of resolutely embracing our finitude, or let fear and anxiety close us against realizing our potentialities, we are shaping human reality as one inauthentically striving to measure itself by its objective accomplishments.

Jesus long ago challenged the Pharisees' dissenting from a lonely woman's life of adultery: "You without sin cast the first stone." Indeed, who among us may not find in the scenes of the dismembering of Iraq his or her own reflection? As Sartre (1957, p. 54) observes,

> There are no *accidents* in a life, a community event which suddenly bursts forth and involves me in it does not come from the outside. If I am mobilized [even just emotionally] in a war, this war is *my* war; it is in my image and I deserve it.

The anguish of human existence lies in our responsibility not only to create ourselves but also humanity (p. 16).

> And every man ought to say to himself, "Am I really the kind of man who has the right to act in such a way that humanity might guide itself by my actions?" And if he does not say that to himself, he is masking his anguish. (p. 20)

Our freedom makes us responsible for the human race we are co-creating, and, by extension, for the meaning of the world of all living and nonliving beings. As the only self-reflecting creatures on earth, we alone can say back to the earth its meaning and its worth (Sartre, 1956, p. 129).

As we face squarely the awful task of human existence, we inevitably experience guilt. It flows from the demands of our being in three ways.

Guilt as failure rises readily to consciousness. If we, each one of us, must shape human life and our world from our actions, if we may not shift this burden off on to any form of determinism, if we cannot authentically place the blame for the misery of existence on some "other," then we stand condemned.

In the 1800s Thoreau commented that "most men lead lives of quiet desperation"; in 1914 Rilke wrote to friends that "distress and disaster are perhaps no more prevalent than before, only more tangible, more active, more visible. For the misery in which mankind has lived daily since the beginning of time cannot really be increased by any contingency" (1947, p. 249). As we today skirt a homeless man sleeping on a sidewalk grate, or quickly flip the pages of *Time* past images of starving African children, or in lurid fascination follow smart bombs to their antiseptic devastation, we may attempt to deny our participation. But we have failed and are failing to create a humane world. For most of us, this guilt reflects noninvolvement rather than involvement, inaction rather than action, omission rather than commission. Denial of the reality of our responsibility for the world's misery shapes our guilt.

It should be said that this guilt does not simply originate in owing something to others over which they exercise a claim, like paying off a debt. Nor do we deserve guilt because we are causing or even are being the occasion for some evil. Such "moral guilt" gives rise to "guilt feelings." As existential guilt our distress lies rather in a "failure to satisfy some requirement which applies to one's existent Being with others" (Heidegger, 1962, p. 327). As co-creators of humanity, we must summon each other and ourselves to the fullness of being. We are failing to meet this responsibility.

We may also experience guilt in our refusal to accept the reality of our being:

> As thrown, Dasein has been delivered over to itself and to its potentiality-for-Being, but as *Being-in-the-world*. As thrown, it has been submitted to a "world," and exists factically with others. Proximally and for the most part the Self is lost in the "they." It understands itself in terms of those possibilities of existence which "circulate" in the "average" public way of interpreting Dasein today. (p. 435)

Every time we objectify ourselves or others, every time we measure ourselves or them solely by the rule of actual accomplishments, every time we forget who we are as potentiality-for-Being and fail to strive resolutely to maximize that potential, we are living inauthentically. Guilt flows from inauthenticity (Gelven, 1970, p. 170).

Finally, by our very existence we are guilty. "This does not mean, of course, that Dasein has always done something for which it is ashamed, but rather that as long as Dasein is, it *is* in such a way as to be the ground of not being in such a way" (p. 169). We exist as a potentiality-for-Being that remains incomplete till death. Our completeness lies in the future, outside of ourselves. We may refuse to accept our way of being, deny the reality of our finitude, and fail to strive resolutely to realize our potential. As *incomplete* and *responsible*, we introduce not-being and the possibility of not-being into the world. "Dasein as such is guilty . . . Being-the-basis of a nullity" (Heidegger, 1962, p. 331).

This existential guilt does not depend on specific actions. Moreover, "Being-guilty is more primordial than any *knowledge* about it" (p. 332). This flies in the face of the traditional version of moral guilt "which usually insists that one cannot be guilty without first knowing about it. But, ontologically speaking, one is capable of notness before one need be explicitly aware of deviation from what ought to be" (Gelven, 1970, p. 169). For the human being, "to be" existentially is "to be guilty."

The vague awareness that nonbeing exists within our very being gives rise to anxiety (Tillich, 1969, p. 35). In the first place we *shall* die; our death opens up the possibility of our then ceasing to exist. Secondly, with every decision made, every path taken or refused, we irreversibly call into existence a particular version of ourselves and just as certainly deny existence to other possible ones. And finally, we know quite painfully our incompleteness and the awesomeness of our self creation. As finite beings, "the threat of nonbeing cannot be eliminated. It belongs to existence itself" (p. 38).

We experience this anxiety not when we are being threatened by a definite person or thing, but rather when the world "says" nothing to us in such a way that we are thrown back upon our own nothingness (Heidegger, 1962, p. 383). How often have we heard our children complain, "Mom, there's *nothing* to do" and watched them either explode into restlessness or sink into depression. And no matter what we may suggest—a book to read, a letter to write, a friend to call, a game to play—the alternatives fall upon deaf ears. Nothing works as nothing appeals. Indeed, the very fact of these possibilities' existing but not drawing the children's attention and involvement makes them feel worse. Being in a world of non-desire and non-action simply increases their emptiness.

The anxiety of such moments lies in

> the dizziness of freedom which occurs when the spirit would posit the synthesis, and freedom then gazes down into its own possibility, grasping at finiteness to sustain itself. In this dizziness, freedom succumbs. (Kierkegaard, 1944, p. 55)

The freedom to take hold of one's life in the moment and the responsibility for doing so, one that may not be avoided, causes anxiety. While ordinarily some person or thing or situation may save one from oneself, in these moments only the call of the self in and through anxiety may be heard. Indeed, for all the pain, such moments are adventures

> that every man has to affront if he would not go to perdition by not having known dread [anxiety] or sinking under it. He therefore who has learned rightly to be in dread has learned the most important thing. . . . Dread is the possibility of freedom. (p. 139)

Faced only with themselves some adolescents commit suicide, some retired sink into senility, some widows shrivel up and die for no apparent physical reason. They have not learned "rightly to be in dread" but rather succumb by "sinking under it." Other adolescents emerge wiser from their depression, knowing now that no one can save them from their own lives. Some retirees come out of their agitated withdrawal, accept the guilt of their attempt to escape responsibility, and turn to activities that more truly express their spirit. And some widows, confronted with the possibility of dying before their time, grab hold of their lives and love others more deeply for having weathered the possibility of not loving. These people have "rightly learned to be in dread" and now live more freely.

By confronting responsibly in and through anxiety "the possibility of freedom," we learn three most valuable truths about life: in the first place, no matter how heavy reality weighs or how frightening it may appear, the weight of the possibility of nonbeing, with the terror of annihilation, makes reality's burdens relatively light (p. 140); secondly, as the seductive pull of the external world recedes, in snatching out of the dizzy whirl of possibilities this particular choice for action, we discover the interiority of spirit (p. 134); finally, no one may save us from the task of self creation, and only actions freely contributing to this endeavor enjoy lasting value.

A concluding word should be said about the relationship of anxiety and fear. As anxiety flows from the whirl of possibility, so fear arises from a definite reality. Nonbeing elicits anxiety; being inspires fear. Whereas in anxiety the world of things and people and situations recedes into irrelevance, in fear the external world bears down on one with terrible relevance. The fearful person becomes externally focused and loses an internal sense of self; indeed this state is marked by a backing away from oneself in bewilderment as one lurches, now here, now there, after what ways one may ward off an intruder. The anxious person, on the contrary, loses any meaningful relationship to the external situation and is forced mercilessly into an interior world of nothingness. Fear calls for a choice that makes some protection present in anticipation of an attack; anxiety demands a choice that repeats one's self creation and thrusts one resolutely toward the realization of one's fate (Heidegger, 1962, pp. 392–393).

Given a choice, the anxious person would, on reflection, gladly avoid the responsibility of anxiety by changing it into fear.

3

THE POSSIBILITY OF BEING

[A famous rabbi] was coming to visit a small town in Russia. It was a very great event for the Jews in the town and each thought long and hard about what questions they would ask the wise man. When he finally arrived, all were gathered in the largest room and each was deeply concerned with the questions they had for him. The Rabbi came into the room and felt the great tension in it. For a time he said nothing and then he began to hum softly a Hasidic tune. Presently all there were humming with him. He then began to sing the song and soon all present were singing with him. Then he began to dance and soon all were deeply involved in the dance, all fully committed to it, all just dancing and nothing else. In this way, each one became whole with himself, each healed the splits within himself which kept him from understanding. After the dance went on for a time, the Rabbi gradually slowed it to a stop, looked at the group, and said, "I trust that I have answered all your questions." (LeShan, 1974a, pp. 36–37)

BEING AND TIME

Son: "What time is it?"
Mother: "It's time to get up."
Son: "Oh, I've plenty of time."
Mother: "You say that every morning, but you know how time flies. . . . Now get up!"

We are surrounded by time. Dialogues like the one above have accompanied us ever since we had a mother to keep track of time for us! Yet for all its everydayness, like well-worn and comfortable shoes, we easily leave it unexamined, expecting it simply to continue familiarly on. An existentialist philosophy directs us to a dialogic shift from "what time is it?" to "what is it—time?"

Daily experience expressed in familiar phrases reveals how we treat time as an object, like those old shoes, an object we possess. We claim time for ourselves ("This is my time to relax") or cede control over it to others ("Take your time"). We own it ("I have time now") or we lament its disappearance ("I just don't have any time left"). We parcel it out ("I'll have some time to see you at three") because we've found a ready supply ("I'll have plenty of time then"), or because we recognize its diminishing availability ("My time will run short after four"). We share this commodity generously with others ("Take all the time you need") or we apologize for our thoughtlessness ("I'm sorry that I can't see you now; I simply lost track of time"). We guard our time, bestow our time, hoard it and even sell it. To hear us talk we could easily place it among our most valued possessions.

How we act with this possession depends, at least in part, on the kind of time we are experiencing. A phone call from a salesman will merit a different response at night time or during our leisure time than it will during our daytime working hours. After all, we expect people to approach us at the right, not the wrong, time. Indeed, we treat our little children differently when it's daylight saving time ("You can play after dinner till 9:00 because it's so light out"), and we tell their adolescent siblings to be in at "a reasonable time." In our conversations we often reminisce about the "good old times" and speculate about what opportunities or misfortunes future times hold for us. We also regale each other with the strange goings-on in our dream time, of both the day and nighttime varieties. And we wonder what the curved time of space revealed to us in Einstein's relativity theory would be like for human beings exploring the furthest reaches of our universe in space time.

As we live in these various times, we experience them quite differently. Sometimes time flies, other times it drags. It seems empty ("What a boring time!") or full ("What an exciting time we had!"), heavy ("We spent a depressing time at the hospital") or light ("It was a carefree time"), peaceful ("My retreat was such a quiet time") or agitated ("We had a frantic time in the city"). It may take forever to get to our summer cottage or we may be back home in "no time at all." When we are enjoying ourselves time invariably speeds up, but it slows to a snail's pace during life's more painful times. We have good times and bad times, happy times and sad times. Time, indeed, stands ready to carry the ever-changing complexity of our momentary feelings, our daily moods.

How do we measure this possession of ours? It depends on the situation. If we should be monitoring an examination, we do so exactly ("Stop! Your time is up"). And the examinees are expected to start and stop at a specific time; we will not allow them to come at "any old time" or to stop whenever "the time feels right for you." But when we have tickets for a Broadway play, we know that the announced time (8:00 P.M.) and the curtain time (8:15 P.M.) will give us some leeway before we miss the opening curtain. Or when we are invited to a dinner party at a friend's home at 7:00 P.M., we'll arrive at a polite time, say 7:10 P.M. And should that dinner be anywhere south of the border, heaven help us if we expect our hostess to be prepared for us according to North American time! Mexican time, as any true Mexican knows, is measured by the rule of *mañana!*

Whatever we expect relative to exactitude and specificity, we ordinarily measure time broadly by the movement of the sun and the ongoing flow of lightness and darkness, specifically by the calibrated, exact movement of a pointing second hand as it travels predictably around the face of a clock. Whether we judge the time by the light/dark stream or the successive disconnected jumps of a pointer, we commonly divide time into the parameters of present (now), past (no longer), and future (not yet).

Aristotle straightforwardly enunciates this commonsensical experience of time when he says, "But when we perceive a distinct before and after, then we speak of time; for this is just what time is, the calculable measure or dimension of motion with respect to before-and-afterness" (*Physics* IV, 219a, 11. 32ff).

Heidegger (1962), the existentialist philosopher who considered time to be the very ground of human experience and who placed it at the heart of his philosophical examination, echoes Aristotle in this existential-ontological interpretation:

> This time is that which is counted and which shows itself when one follows the travelling pointer, counting and making present in such a way that this making present tempor-

> alizes itself in an ecstatical unity with the retaining and awaiting which are horizontally open according to the "earlier" and "later." (p. 473)

As seems obvious, this "echo" contains a much richer explanation of time than does Aristotle's abstract definition. Let us continue our examination of time, now, by moving away from the everyday experience to the existential understanding of time. By our discussion's conclusion, the nuances of Heidegger's statement should be more readily available for our continued deliberation.

If we look closely at our ordinary understanding of present, past, and future, we may uncover some rather startling conclusions.

In the first place, if "now" alone stands as present to us, then life turns into a successive series of ongoing happenings. Following our clock's lead, our "now" most recently did not exist as it was a "just been not-yet-now" and it will "forthwith be no-longer-now" (p. 474; Buber, 1958, p. 12). In this way, the past dissolves into nothingness and the future has not yet been called into existence. And even if we uncomfortably forsake the clock's jerky account of time and embrace the sun's more flowing rendition, we still find the same disconcerting fact: the sun at high noon, directly above us, has this time around forever abandoned its rising, and its setting exists only in our expectations. This course of time is still composed of "nows" that come out of nowhere, wink on, only to disappear forever. We enjoy the sun only at one position at a time, now, and nowhere or no time else.

Such an account certainly violates the everyday experience of our lives. Therefore, we must be treating time falsely in this accounting. And further examination points up even more serious problems flowing from this commonsensical approach on time.

If only "now" exists, then what happens to our cherished memories, say of a childhood home? Do they live on only "in our memory," fragmentary relics that we happen to recall and somehow re-experience in the fleeting "now"? Has the life and energy of those times faded forever away only to be rekindled in the moment's pseudo-presence of a hard-working imagination? Perhaps so . . . but we would hate to accept that.

But perhaps not. We have been treating time as an object, like the large rock we can see in the distant corner of our backyard. It just sits there; we don't want to take the effort to move it; we've accepted its presence. But it concerns us not a whit. The familiar saying "out of sight, out of mind" fits our relationship to that thing quite nicely. And should we wake up some day to its disappearance, we would not mourn its passing.

But do we really equate our childhood home and our past experiences there with that rock? Both have been present, both could be past, but only the former has been invested with our concern. We have never been involved with that granite boulder; we have been intimately involved in and shaped by those past times in our old hometown. In Heidegger's terminology, the rock has, as regards us, been a "present-at-hand," a thing; our home and our life there are "ready-at-hand" (Gelven, 1970, p. 57). The former belongs fittingly in the neutrality of "now time" or "passing time"; the latter lives on in "world time" or "personal time."[1]

"Personal time" constitutes itself through human involvement with objects or situations in such a way that they live on in us as repetitive possibilities. As we formerly surveyed, acted, and were open to realizing our potential through involvement in the world of tools or equipment, those things intimately woven into our life's experience, so we are, if we allow it, throughout our life called back to ourselves by them in the nonfading, ongoing reality of personal time (Buber, 1958, p. 14).

Reflect back on the Hasidic tale that opened this chapter. Do you think that the rabbi's effect on that congregation belongs only in the realm of reminiscences? Would you not expect that for some of those people, when they find themselves in other situations of tension and they need to find answers, that the memory of the dance that heals still lives on? They originally hoped that their many questions would be answered by another in such a way that life would become easier for them. Instead, they were guided inside themselves to the truly important confrontation with their own lives. In personal time life is not a problem to be solved but rather a mystery to be explored (Marcel, 1951, p. 35).

What has been said about personal time as past holds equally for personal time as future. For one who has expended time, effort, creative imagination on a path to a distant goal, like fin-

---

[1] These terms, translations of Heidegger's German text, strike our ears awkwardly. Therefore, throughout the following discussion, "passing time," which is the most significant quality of "now time," will replace it; "personal time" will substitute for the easily misunderstood "world time." (Cf. Buber, 1958, p. 12)

ishing college or building a home or starting a new business or completing a book, that desired objective exists as a strong call. Just as the childhood home is more than a memory, so this destination is more than a dream. The former fuels life through the possibility of repetition; the latter energizes it through the anticipation of further realizing one's potentialities. In both instances personal time hinges on that "moment of vision" today that leads to decision and action (Gelven, 1970, p. 186; Heidegger, 1962, p. 357).

When we conceive of time as only "passing time," we deprive our actions of personal significance (Heidegger, 1962, pp. 114–122). This does not deny, certainly, the worth of our accomplishments as external to us, such as a picture taken, developed, and beautifully framed. This object may well show itself as important art. But the significance for us *as artists* rests in the ongoing possibility of our artistry, a potential publicly revealed in some "now" of this completion and exhibition, but personally continuing as a quality flowing from our past into our future. The art work is completed in one "now" and no other; the artistry as potential lives on as a significant call till our life completes itself in death. To identify ourselves with our accomplishments, business successes, political popularity, clever children, or artistic productions places our worth and significance outside of ourselves and in past moments that no longer exist for us (p. 574). Personal significance, understood as that which inheres in our being, always rests in our potential for striving "to be all we can be" and not in actual deeds accomplished (Gelven, 1970, p. 185).

Moreover, passing time alone strips life of datability (Heidegger, 1962, p. 574). We assign dates to particular times not because of the moment itself, but because at that moment some personally relevant event occurred. The time of your birth, say in 1940, is dated by "on that former occasion when" you were born; you do not celebrate it simply as a point "now" no longer existing. Similarly, you may look forward to a future time, to a "then when" you will, for example, pay off the mortgage. That red letter day signifies not just the completion of a financial requirement but also a new reality of financial freedom. And when that day shall finally arrive, "now that" you have less indebtedness, "now" is the day "that" you shall put down money for that trip to Africa you have dreamed about and worked so hard to make happen. Passing time as a succession of unrelated "nows" knows nothing about "then when," "on the former occasion when," and "now that." And since we assign dates only to the times that relate importantly to us, we need the memorable involvement of personal time in order to realize datability.

Passing time shapes present, past, and future very differently from the life they assume in the connectedness of personal time. Let us consider this by contrasting the opposing pairs.

In passing time the present functions primarily as a space for "making present" some action. Through that action something becomes actual (before dinner you were hungry; then you ate a big meal; now you are full). Importance rests here on actions taken and on the objective realized. Actuality counts for everything.

The present in personal time serves as the arena for awakened awareness of one's personal possibility, for Heidegger's "moment of vision":

> This term must be understood in the active sense as an ecstasis. It means the resolute rapture with which Dasein [the human being as human] is carried away to whatever possibilities and circumstances are encountered in the Situation as possible objects of concern, but a rapture which is *held* in resoluteness. (1962, p. 387)

The present assumes importance only as calling the person to attend to his or her potential and to move forward to the ongoing realization of that potential. Its worth lies primarily in the future, secondarily in the past, and only finally in itself as the place of recognizing the call of each. The present accomplishments of passing time offer nothing to rest upon (Gelven, 1970, p. 185).

For one dwelling in the past of passing time, this past serves as a repository of objects, be they recollections of events or personal accomplishments or cherished memorabilia. This past moment has disappeared, its action has been quieted, and the one who formerly acted has been displaced by the action's product. Indeed, that actor with various abilities, diverse motivations and some decisiveness has faded away with time into the mists of forgetfulness.

While we all may readily fall out of ourselves so as to become lost in the everyday world of objects and activities, the past of personal time acts as a counterweight. At some past moments we knew ourselves as grounded in ourselves—with all the possibility of realizing our own futures. In the face of the siren call to "lose ourselves in the crowd" (as did the Jews anxiously waiting for the rabbi's appearance), we listened instead to our inner being (as did those meditative dancers). And we made choices and took actions, not because of the allure of others' acceptance, but rather because they fit the truth of our being. Those past moments of integrity have not disappeared; on the contrary, they constantly summon us back to ourselves. We *may* return home; we may *choose again* to be ourselves; we may *repeat* the actions that will authentically express us and that will lead us toward our self-creating personal future (Heidegger, 1962, p. 388).

Turning finally to the future, in passing time we stand passively awaiting its arrival. As it does not yet exist, we may not call it nor shape it nor force its appearance. We may expect it, we may await its coming, we may prepare ourselves to receive it, but we cannot act on it. As an object not yet actual it eludes us.

As the ground of our human wholeness, the future in personal time insistently calls us toward ourselves. We interact with it constantly as we act in the present for the sake of the being whom we may someday become. The future exists as potentiality; we anticipate its realization as we strive resolutely to actualize it. And each future moment so actualized simply opens up other futures, offers new options, reveals previously unseen possibilities, challenges with yet a different life's completeness.

Personal time concerns itself with our own possibilities and our decisiveness in striving for our own being; passing time considers the possibilities only of those objects—things, tools, affairs—that will touch our lives at some future moment (Heidegger, 1962, pp. 385–389). As Gelven, commenting on Heidegger's conception of these two futures, notes, " . . . one might say that authentic understanding (anticipation) lies in Dasein *going toward* the future, whereas inauthentic understanding (awaiting) lies in the future *coming toward* Dasein" (p. 192).

To summarize the differences between these two kinds of time: passing time functions as an object, external to us, which has worth in its actuality and to the extent we may manipulate it to our advantage. It emphasizes the present, remembers the past, and awaits the future. Personal time functions as a conscience (Heidegger, 1962, p. 322), interior to us, which has worth in its summoning us to our ownmost possibilities as finally bounded only by our death. It emphasizes anticipatory resoluteness in seeking future wholeness, responding repetitively to former moments of integrity, and acting decisively in moving toward the ongoing realization of our potentialities.

Before we conclude this examination of time, we must consider one other kind of time, "historical time."

As human beings we are born into a world and exist as beings in a world of other human beings. We interact with each other; we use some things and situations to further ourselves; we simply cohabit the earth with other things. This world serves as a context, as a ground out of which we may express ourselves. As such, it in some ways defines the possibilities of our existence. Our potentialities may be recognized in, and striven for realization only within, our world.

The past of historical time touches us as *heritage* (Heidegger, 1962, p. 435). By heritage is meant "that historical awareness of one's tradition as significantly determining to some extent the makeup of the 'world' that one is 'in' as Being-in-the-world" (Gelven, 1970, p. 212).

Our ancestors conceived of themselves and their potentialities for the fullness of living in a particular way. Within that conception they created a world in which they decided and acted. Their actions flowed from the limits of the possibilities they saw for themselves in interacting with others, with the things they used, and with the things around them. To facilitate their actions, they came to perceive their world in a constant fashion. To maintain that constancy they established personal guidelines (roles) and community guidelines (rules). Then they celebrated those fellow citizens who preserved the People while expanding the possibilities of living, both for the People and for individuals. In story and song they recounted the moments of decision and the decisive actions of their heroes as guiding lights for themselves and as wisdom for their descendants.

Succeeding generations may receive this heritage in two vastly different ways. By joining historical time with passing time, heritage becomes a handing down of facts and objects, rules and roles, heroes and a world that either no longer exists but should be remembered out of respect, or that should be faithfully reproduced out of loyalty. As such, heritage limits possibilities by the actualities of the past.

But historical time as personal time delivers to us the integrity of our ancestors, not their accomplishments. It summons us to consider their inner truth and their process of translating that truth through their actions into the fullness of living. It furnishes us with models of people who lived the values that formed them and the vision that called them. And it charges us to do the same. Indeed, we too will structure our world as they structured theirs; but we shall act respectfully and loyally only to the extent that our structure helps us realize the potentialities of ourselves and our People. Take from the past whatever facts you wish, our ancestors say, as memorabilia, but you must preserve the integrity of existence to which we all are summoned.

Through fate we experience historical time as future (Heidegger, 1962, p. 435). As human beings we exist in a world fenced in by birth and death. Given this finitude we enjoy only limited possibilities of existing. No matter what we may wish or decide or do, as historical beings we *shall* die. This is our fate.

On receiving this death sentence we may stop living and assume the position of the condemned resignedly waiting for the executioner's blow. In so doing we would actually die before the end of our lives. Or we may deny this fate by surrounding ourselves with past accomplishments that have taken on some objective reality and give some promise of enduring. Or, finally, we may pour ourselves out in present activities so as to lose ourselves and any sense that we exist separately from these well-executed endeavors. In all these ways we actually reject any fate to which we may respond.

But should we accept this human fate as our own, it becomes an "awareness of one's *limited possibilities* and the ensuing *significance* of one's choices and decisions made in the flux of these possibilities" (Gelven, 1970, p. 213).

When the ancient Roman sage counseled *carpe diem* ("seize the moment"), he was calling our attention to the limited opportunities that the expectation of our death affords us for acting decisively in a way that will influence our own lives and those of others. His fellow citizen, Caesar, took his counsel. Standing with his victorious legions outside Rome, he decided to challenge Rome's current rulers. Facing the likelihood of death, he courageously led his countrymen across the Rubicon River, seizing both the moment and his fate. In so doing he significantly shaped the history of Western civilization. Our death, while limiting our possibilities, at the same time acts as an urgent stimulus to grab hold of the lives we do have, and to realize the potentialities for life we do enjoy, so as to expand our lives into the wholeness that human existence as an interaction between life and death may attain.

As beings in a world with humans also bounded by birth and death, we share fate with them in the form of *destiny* (Heidegger, 1962, p. 436). Families have a destiny ("We are destined to settle here"), and so do nations ("We Americans were destined to triumph finally in the Cold War"). Even races and civilizations claim such entitlement: the Southern slaveowner cited destiny as the reason for their African slaves' subjugation; the European colonialist seized African and Asian territory as part of the destiny of Christianity; a "Manifest Destiny" justified the U.S. government's systematic requisitioning of "our land" from all intruders—the British, the Spanish and French, and, incredibly, especially the Indians.

In the face of destiny, we may respond with either expectation or resignation. The winners in this cosmic lottery usually justify their conquests by understanding their destiny as a predetermined plan issuing from some power superior to human negotiations. Thus, for example, in God's name were thousands of rural ("pagan") women practicing nonlicensed pharmacology burned as witches by "good Christians." And the ones "favored by God" usually find it an unexplainable affront that others should resist this hegemony. They should, whether they fight back as Sioux or Viet Cong, bow to the destiny of their rightful superiors and take themselves to the reservations prepared for them. Throughout human history many have taken that route, and, in so doing, they have lost both their hearts and their destinies.

This view of destiny as historical passing time stresses the past as entitlement, the future as expectation, and the present as power. And the nondestined ones are treated as objects to be manipulated and used for the advancement of their masters.

Within an existentialist framework of historical personal time, destiny presents itself differently. As future it forces peoples and nations to confront their finitude, to accept the boundary that death places upon human beings, and it requires them to strive resolutely for the sake of human wholeness within these limits. As past it calls them back to themselves, to an inner world of conscience that demands that they employ humanity's limited freedom to realize the possibilities of human existence for all people. As present it faces them with guilt, with the objectifying of people, animals and other living beings, and the physical environment. This guilt lies in our being seduced by the actual; it also stems from our limited ability to be co-creators of a human world (Heidegger, 1962, pp. 436–437).

Destiny becomes a *superior power*, the power of its finite freedom (p. 436), by being free for death. This freedom happens only as family or nation or People communicate about, and struggle with, the task of human existence: the realizing of human potentialities within a world initiated by birth and completed in death. The present of destiny is communication, not power; its past is change, not entitlement; and its future is not expectation, but creation.

BEING AND TRANSCENDENCE

In a charming book of stories about, and reflections on, the human condition, Sheldon Kopp (1972, pp. 40–41) compares the life of the human being to that of a mayfly. He concludes, almost offhandedly, that both occur for no apparent reason, neither has any special purpose in existing, and after a momentary earthly appearance both fade back into the nothingness from which they unaccountably emerged. That is simply how it is.

Whether one agrees with Kopp or not, his disarmingly light comparison does not reveal the seriousness and anguish with which the question of transcendence has perennially engaged human beings.

Leo Tolstoy (1887/1991) poignantly opens up the depth of this struggle for meaning. He states the problem succinctly:

> The question is this: What will come of what I do today and tomorrow? What will come of my entire life?
>
> Expressed differently, the question may be: Why should I live? Why should I wish for anything or do anything? Or to put it differently: Is there any meaning in my life that will not be destroyed by my inevitably approaching death? (p. 154)

As he wrestled with the purpose for being, Tolstoy at one point exclaimed: "What is the meaning of my life? It has none. Or: What will become of my life? Nothing. Or: Why does everything that is exist, and why do I exist? Because it exists" (p. 156).

At that stage in his struggle, his conclusion coincides with that proposed by Kopp. Instead of any kind of stoic acceptance of this fate, Tolstoy, however, concluded further that "All is vanity. Happy is he who has never been born; death is better than life; we must rid ourselves of life" (p. 156). Given this conviction, while he continued his frantic search, he also endured an intensified struggle against the appeal of suicide.

Kopp's position echoes faithfully that taken by Jean-Paul Sartre (1964). In *Nausea*, his novel about the meaninglessness of existence, Sartre's anti-hero, Antoine Roquentin, reflects to himself:

> And it was true, I had always realized it. I hadn't the right to exist. I had happened by chance, I existed like a stone, a plant or a microbe. My life put out feelers toward small pleasures in every direction. Sometimes it sent out vague signals; at other times I felt nothing more than a harmless buzzing.

Later on in a conversation with the Self-Taught Man he laughingly comments:

> I was just thinking . . . that here we sit, all of us, eating and drinking to preserve existence and really there is nothing, nothing, absolutely no reason for existing. (p. 112)

Toward the tale's end, Roquentin simply concludes that "Every existing thing is born without reason, prolongs itself out of weakness and dies by chance" (p. 133).

Sartre takes this position about human existence because of the declared nonexistence of God (1966, pp. 290–291). However, just as no one can demonstrate God's existence (Buber, 1958, p. 137), so neither can one disprove it. But that matters little, for

> Existentialism is not atheist in the sense that it would exhaust itself in demonstrations of the non-existence of God. It declares rather, that even if God existed that would make no difference from its point of view. Not that we believe God does exist, but we think that the real problem is not that of existence; what man needs is to find himself again and to understand that nothing can save him from himself, not even a valid proof of the existence of God. (Sartre, 1966, p. 311)

Sartre proposes to ground human existence firmly in itself. We exist as finite beings that have appeared on the world scene. Once here we fashion our life's plan, go about striving to follow it, and finally exist only as the ensemble of all the acts which constitute our life (1957, pp. 31–33). We alone stand responsible for our life and "It is therefore senseless to think of complaining since nothing foreign has decided what we feel, what we live, or what we are" (p. 53).

Prior to Sartre, Friedrich Nietzsche in *Thus Spake Zarathustra* (1883–91, p. 6) announced the death of God, and for much the same reason. The existence and question of God only assume importance to the extent that they draw humankind away from itself:

> I conjure you, my brethren, *remain true to the earth,* and believe not those who speak unto you of super-earthly hopes! Poisoners are they, whether they know it or not. (p. 6)
>
> What is the great dragon which the spirit is no longer inclined to call Lord and God? "Thou shalt," is the great dragon called. But the spirit of the lion saith, "I will." (p. 24)
>
> A new pride taught me mine ego, and that teach I unto men: no longer to thrust one's head into the sand of celestial things, but to carry it freely, a terrestrial head, which giveth meaning to the earth. (p. 30)

With this declaration, Nietzsche was striving to shift the basis of human transcendence from an infinite to a finite perspective. In the Judæo-Christian tradition, theologians found human worth, meaning, and purpose in relationship to God: thus the necessity of proving God's existence and proclaiming God's love for humankind. Throughout the Middle Ages western philosophers also tended to secure human meaning in the Absolute. More recently, Kant placed stability in the moral imperative, the immediate grasp of what *ought to be,* while Hegel clung stubbornly to the rational intuition of the Absolute Idea. As Gelven (1970) clearly explains:

> Nietzsche's point, then, is not that there can be no logical possibility of an infinity, but that the values and functions of human activity and reason cannot be formulated from an infinite and hence "other" perspective. Transcendence is still necessary; but the stepping-beyond is *not* from the finite human perspective to the infinite of God, but from the finite perspective of man to the still finite but transcendent view of the overman. . . . (p. 231)

These existentialist critics of the generally accepted Judæo-Christian Western worldview leave us with a strong challenge:

place the basis of transcendence and the ground of meaning in human experience.

Heidegger (1962), accepting that task, found human transcendence in the temporality of human existence (p. 232). As we closely examined in the first part of this chapter (Being and Time), human reality "exists" always outside of itself in being "potentiality-for-Being."

We certainly experience being taken out of ourselves and being released from the bonds of space and time. How often as "we come back to our senses" after listening to a concert or being swept up in a pageant or glorying in a sunset do we exclaim, "where did time go!" or "I feel like I've been in another world!" Moreover, we instantly know that our imagination pays little attention to sense boundaries as we may be strolling on a moonlit Caribbean island or stepping on to the moon in a timeless and spaceless leap.

This ordinary ability to transcend the immediate has been scientifically documented by generations of parapsychologists. We possess indisputable evidence that psychic phenomena—for example, telepathy, psychokinesis, or psychic healing—are human potentialities. Indeed, to exercise these we need simply to alter our consciousness through the use of our imagination to enter an "alternate reality" that obeys laws of reality quite different from those of our ordinary reality (LeShan, 1976). Marcel (1963) personally attests to the validity of such out-of-the-ordinary experiences:

> It must be said that the metaphysical—today we would more likely say parapsychological—experiments which I personally made during the Winter of 1916–1917 and which I cannot retrace here in detail, although they had really disturbing aspects, convinced me once and for all of the reality of the phenomena which only ignorance and a wilful self-deception would permit me to doubt. (p. 42)

Marcel would clearly agree with LeShan and Margenau (1982) when they declare that any intellectual denial of alternate states of reality is a position that "we will have to put on the crowded and dusty shelf marked 'outmoded ideas: ingest at your own risk'" (p. 12).

I recently spent a night in the Adirondack Mountains as a Sioux medicine man led our group in a sweat lodge ritual. Four cycles, each one consisting of chanting through intense waves of heat generated by water hitting red-hot stones, ended with the flaps being opened and reflections shared through prayer and conversation.

During the first cycle, which seemed to least about forty-five minutes, I wanted to flee from the cruel heat. I lay as close to the ground as possible; I placed a towel on my head and over my face; I prayed for the heat to diminish; I gasped aloud as the steam seared my nose, throat, and lungs.

As the second cycle grew in intensity, my experience altered dramatically. Though the heat still blasted me, I found myself moving my attention and my sense of myself deeply inside. Suddenly, this inner journey terminated in a point, a quiet and peaceful location far removed from the heat-filled confines of the lodge. There I rested—free. Barely did I seem to be there, when the cycle ended. And the subsequent cycles simply flew by as I found this place of transcendence deep within.

As I write these words, I recall Eliot's description in *Four Quartets* (1943):

> At the still point of the turning world. Neither flesh nor fleshless;
> Neither from nor towards; at the still point, there the dance is,
> But neither arrest nor movement. And do not call it fixity,
> Where past and future are gathered. Neither movement from nor towards,
> Neither ascent nor decline. Except for the point, the still point,
> There would be no dance, and there is only the dance.
> I can only say, *there* we have been: but I cannot say where.
> And I cannot say, how long, for that is to place it in time.
> (pp. 15–16)

How explain this experience? As the transcending of ego and the touching of the self that is spirit.

Ulrich Sonnemann (1954), although speaking in another context, describes this experience of transcendence with remarkable exactness:

> the timelessness of radical self-transcendence means . . . a cleansing of time from the negativity of its ordinary power to destroy (in the sense of undo) by its *passing*; it is therefore

> a suspension of the past as such, a state which phenomenally occurs as a unique simultaneity of the future and the past and hence as a widening of the present. "Simultaneity" and "widening," of course, do not refer to clock time. . . . Its content is rather a perceptual one, namely *the presence in time per se of being as a standing center.* This discovery of its phenomenal content explains at once the vanishing of all anxiety so inherent in the experience: as the "standing center" of the horizon of time, *being* "knows itself" as just as little subject to the power of time to *undo* as dependent any longer on what corresponds to that power on the side of the "subject." What corresponds to it on the side of the "subject," in turn, is nothing "real," but only the most persistent of *images*: that perishable little *ego*, in one word, which existence in its inauthentic if most ready self-identification of the everyday alleges obstinately, if never quite satisfactorily, to be its *who.* (p. 254)

One need not seek out extraordinary situations to experience transcendence. Love from which ego has retired and that shares the life of the self is "one among all elementary situations of the human person that allows of the fullest most engaging *factual* transcendentness of the self." So concludes the existential anthropologist Ludwig Binswanger (Sonnemann, p. 149). As love deepens, it moves from the exchanging of ideas and perceptions at an intellectual level to a sharing of body and soul at a feeling level. But it finds its fullness as an energizing and freeing self-transcendence at a spiritual level. As Buber (1958) points out:

> The significance of the effect is not so obvious in the relation with the *Thou* spoken to men. The act of the being which provides directness in this case is usually understood wrongly as one of feeling. Feelings accompany the metaphysical and metapsychical fact of love, but they do not constitute it . . . love is *between I* and *Thou.* The man who does not know this, with his very being know this, does not know love; even though he ascribes to it the feelings he lives through, experiences, enjoys, and expresses. (pp. 14–15)

Such a possibility of a joining of spirits happens only when one dares the interior movement away from the ordinary sensory world to that silent place where self and spirit and existence become one. From that spot and in its power one knows "the existential imperative of self transcendence or love that alone can break that isolation" (Sonnemann, 1954, p. 299). Indeed, existential psychiatrist Medard Boss has a "central contention that all sexuality, regardless of the specificity of its aims, strives to return to a primordial totality of being in its absoluteness, and hence must transcend itself into that affirmation of the absolute value of the other which is the world-transparency of love" (1963, p. 301).

Once we have experienced the ecstatic joy of spirit, through the pleasures of love or the pains of our individual sweat lodges, we know human transcendence that is based not in the infinite, but in the finite. From that point, then, we may seek for the meaning of this self-transcending human being.

Soren Kierkegaard (1849/1989) offers one answer:

> The human being is spirit. But what is spirit? Spirit is the self. But what is the self? The self is a relation which relates to itself, or that is the relation which is its relating to itself. . . . Faith is: that the self in being itself and in wanting to be itself is grounded transparently in God. (pp. 43, 114)

Leo Tolstoy (1887/1991) rises from his despairing fall toward suicide when he understands that

> Faith is the force of life. If a man lives, then he must have faith in something. If he did not believe that he had something he must live for, then he would not live. If he fails to see and understand the illusory nature of the finite, then he believes in the finite; if he understands the illusory nature of the finite, then he must believe in the infinite. . . . "He is there, the one without whom there could be no life." To know God and to live come to one and the same thing. God is life. (pp. 157, 158)

And, finally, Karl Jaspers (1991) finds human meaning not in an answer but in the very experience of transcendence:

> It is the silence in the face of being. Speech ceases in the presence of that which is lost to us when it becomes object.
>
> The ultimate can be attained only in the transcending of all thought. It cannot itself be transcended. Before it lies contentment with one's lot and the extinction of all desire.

> Here is a haven and no fixed home. Here is a repose that can sustain us and the inevitable unrest of our wanderings in the world.
>
> Here thought must dissolve into radiance. Where there is no further question, there is also no answer. In the philosophical transcending of question and answer we arrive at the limit, at the stillness of being. (p. 149)

As we watch the "Mayflies . . . those dainty insects with lacy wings and slender trailing tail," we need not conclude that "There is no point: That's just the way it is" (Kopp, 1972, pp. 40–41). And, moreover, we humans exist for more than one day.

PART II

EXISTENTIAL PSYCHOTHERAPY

Existentialism restores man to his central place in man's own experience and grants us the possibility of realizing our fondest and most extreme imaginings about the human condition, if only we will have the courage and perseverance to see them through.

James F. T. Bugental

4

THE PERSON AS CLIENT

Once upon a time there was a town composed of two parallel streets. A dervish passed through one street into the other, and as he reached the second one, the people there noticed that his eyes were streaming with tears. "Someone has died in the other street!" one cried, and soon all the children in the neighborhood had taken up the cry.

What had really happened was that the dervish had been peeling onions.

Within a short space of time the cry had reached the first street; and the adults of both streets were so distressed and fearful (for each community was related to the other) that they dared not make complete inquiries as to the cause of the furor.

A wise man tried to reason with the people of both streets, asking why they did not question each other. Too confused to know what they meant, some said: "For all we know there is a deadly plague in the other street."

This rumor, too, spread like wildfire, until each street's population thought that the other was doomed.

When some measure of order was restored, it was only enough for the two communities to decide to emigrate to save themselves. Thus it was that, from different sides of the town, both streets entirely evacuated their people.

Now, centuries later, the town is still deserted; and not so far away are two villages. Each village has its own tradition of how it began as a settlement from a doomed town, through a fortunate flight, in remote times, from a nameless evil. (Shah, 1970, p. 70)

We, too, like traditions, are born. In some mysterious fashion we show up at this moment in history, the offspring of these parents, members of this family. From conception, genetic and social influences shape the potential for life that we are. The more fortunate among us find ourselves surrounded by loving people who are concerned for our well being and attentive to our needs. In such families self-expression is encouraged as the indispensable means of growth and the necessary condition for each one's self-creation. As Tillich (1969) remarks:

> I refer above all to his [Sartre's] proposition that "the essence of man is his existence." This sentence is like a flash of light which illuminates the whole Existentialist scene. One could call it the most despairing and the most courageous sentence in all Existentialist literature. What it says is there is no essential nature of man, except in the one point that he can make of himself what he wants. Man creates what he is. Nothing is given to him to determine his creativity. The essence of his being—the "should-be," "the ought-to-be"—is not something which he finds; he makes it. Man is what he makes of himself. And the courage to be as oneself is the courage to make of oneself what one wants to be. (pp. 149–150)

In the best of interpersonal environments, however, no one may be perfectly sensitive to every barely recognized and only haltingly expressed infantile need. Moreover, parental needs clamor for some attention too. Inevitably, therefore, every human of whatever age and whatever family will have experienced some abandonment, at times will have felt alone and vulnerable. Thus does the necessity of self-protection enter the tiniest of worlds. Even the blessed child knows some threat.

We all—children and adults alike—live on separate streets. Try as we may to express ourselves to some other, we will be understood only imperfectly, only insufficiently responded to by even the most loving person. And so we begin to construct our own separate and secure towns, to build strong walls against painful intruders. With each success we also tell ourselves how we managed to ward them off, congratulate ourselves on our ingenuity, and reinforce our preferred way of handling all threatening "others."

EXISTENTIAL ANXIETY

Although we may readily understand how threat and self-protection must be part of every human's story, we need to explore how they may be integrated into the ongoing realization of our life potential. I will begin this analysis with a personal example.

My wife and I have ordered tickets for an evening performance at the Yale Repertory Theater. She is obtaining them from the box office while I am attempting to park the car, no small endeavor as New Haven is overrun with students' families this Parents' Weekend in October. Indeed, I finally must settle down on an unfamiliar and dark parallel street if I am not to miss the opening curtain.

A group of young men is lounging about under a street light near where I park. Feeling threatened, I choose to walk down the tree-lined avenue to the next corner before turning toward the well-lighted and populated campus.

I've walked barely fifty yards when a tall, black fellow in his 20s steps out of the darkness. He wants money. I shake my head and brush by him. He follows. Now also frightened I increase my pace hoping to make it to the next corner without an incident. He increases his speed and clearly now is pursuing me. As he draws nearer, I realize he will probably use force to get what he wants. I suddenly feel quite alone and confused. What should I do? Should I run, yell out?

Seeing what appears to be a short cut, I dart down a driveway. It's a dead end. I turn around just as he grabs at my coat. In a kind of fascination I watch his right hand flexing around something he is holding. Then my face explodes with pain and light. I find myself on the ground; he is pummeling me as I try to cover my head from his blows. Then I seem to come to, start yelling for help, and begin struggling with him. As people rush out of their homes, he grabs my wallet and runs off into the night. Soon, I'm in an over-lighted emergency room. My jaw and nose are broken, and I can barely walk from the severe bruises on my legs and feet.

Stop now and consider Figure 4.1. It summarizes the psychological dynamics of this experience.

When I saw the laughing crowd, I had a present experience of threat and spontaneously chose to defend myself by avoiding it. This threat expanded into fear after my encounter with the black beggar and his initial pursuit of me. From past experience of violence as well as other pain-filled situations, I knew my danger was real. This intensified my fear and my desperate need to flee. But I could not readily shake him off. The closer he approached, the lonelier and more confused I became until I made what could have been a fatal mistake. In the moment preceding the beating, I stood horrified in my isolation as I confronted the possibility of a senseless death in which I was an unwilling yet participating actor. Only when the initial shock had passed away and I continued to be alive did my way of defending myself switch to attacking my attacker directly.

In situations of threat we must either fight or flee. We are immediately assisted in this attempt by physiological changes that we recognize emotionally as anger or fear. Moreover, as historical beings we remember; our memories of other hurtful times help to fuel our present attempts to protect ourselves. These memories consist essentially of those moments when we are torn apart from others or from ourselves. We clearly know that to remain in such a divided state would ultimately mean our death. Therefore, we must do everything possible to strive for unity and wholeness.

Some clients seek therapeutic assistance in the aftermath of situations that have thrown them painfully up against the

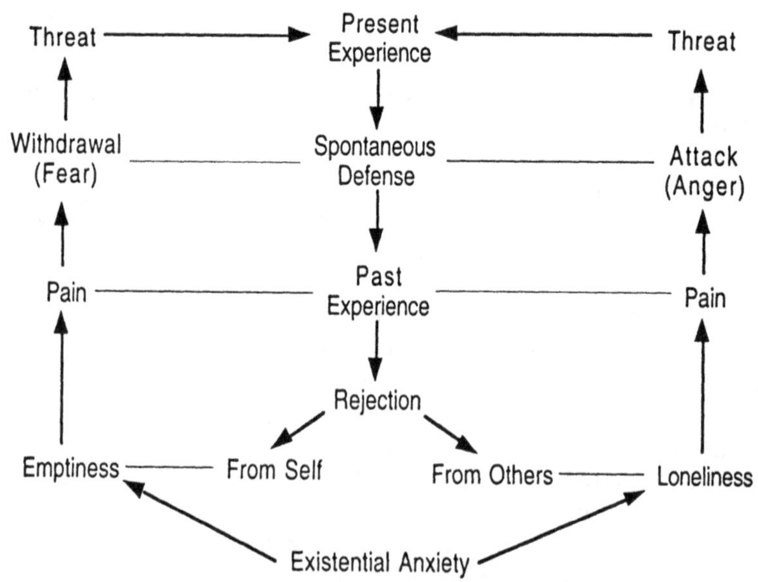

FIGURE 4.1 Dynamics of Existential Anxiety

human condition: the breakup of a relationship, the death of a child, the loss of a job, the trials of physical illness. They require a safe place in which they may express the lingering uncomfortable emotions and in which they may experience healing with another and within themselves. But most deeply they desire to integrate into themselves and into their lives the raw reality of nonbeing. Tillich (1969) states this succinctly:

> Immediately seen, anxiety is the painful feeling of not being able to deal with the threat of a special situation. But a more exact analysis shows that in the anxiety about any special situation anxiety about the human situation is implied. It is the anxiety of not being able to preserve one's own being which underlies every fear and is the frightening element in it. . . . The basic anxiety, the anxiety of a finite being about the threat of nonbeing, cannot be eliminated. It belongs to existence itself. (p. 38)

Such people do not necessarily exhibit any pathology; what they bring to the therapist is the human reality and the anxiety inevitably attached to it. The tragic situation will have, indeed, served the purpose of calling them back to the whole truth of themselves, a truth that includes the awful responsibility of living one's life in the ever-present milieu of isolation, doubt, and death. Tillich (1969) calls all therapists to this realization when he challenges the psychiatric profession to accept this existential anxiety as normal:

> The psychiatrist who asserts that anxiety is always pathological cannot deny the *potentiality* of illness in human *nature*, and he must account for the facts of finitude, doubt, and guilt in every human being; he must, in terms of his own presupposition, account for the universality of anxiety. He cannot avoid the question of human desire since in practicing his profession he cannot avoid the distinction between health and illness, existential and pathological anxiety. This is why more and more representatives of medicine generally and psychotherapy specifically ask for cooperation with the philosophers and theologians. (p. 71)

Existential anxiety requires no cure; it seeks only recognition and acceptance. As long as we live as human beings on this earth, we may be joined to others and may be whole within ourselves only in rare moments. Even then we will have lurking in the background the specters of isolation and death. Healthy existence demands the resolute embracing of lives fulfilled ultimately in and through death.

PATHOLOGICAL ANXIETY

Other clients are suffering, however, under the cross of pathological anxiety. How does it differ in kind from its existential reflection? Consider with me the aftermath of my violent encounter in New Haven.

After some pain-filled days in the hospital, I finally return home to recuperate. I also must adjust to obstructed breathing, eating, and talking as my nose is packed and my jaw wired shut. Aside from the restlessness during sleep, I am progressing as expected in body and spirit until my wife returns to work. Then I am alone.

I notice right away that I have little inclination to get up and move about; I would much rather stay within the defined and secure boundaries of my bed. I feel at home there. As my physical condition strengthens, I do dress, but I am uncomfortable with even the thought of going outdoors. Indeed, one day I nearly panic when I realize that I need milk for lunch, and that I would have to drive to the neighborhood market to obtain it. Driving feels terribly dangerous; meeting other people seems in my vulnerable state both embarrassing and frightening. As I recognize my present inability to meet such perfectly ordinary and normal demands of life, I go back to bed, depressed and guilty.

Some days later I simply must seek out an optician as my glasses have been bent almost beyond the possibility of use. Moreover, I need to replace my stolen automobile driver's license. The former task I soon manage with some normalcy; the latter sends me into panic. When I enter the Department of Transportation building, the service area is teeming with people. Although I know better, I feel them staring at me, especially the black people who seem to be pressing in on me from all sides. As perspiration soaks me and my breaths come in gulps, I struggle between terror and guilt. A phrase keeps searing my mind: "A conservative is a liberal who has been mugged." Could that now be me?

With time I return to work. But each new task requiring another move further from home and from the present sphere of comfort and security stimulates the same confusing clamor of feelings. At their extremes they fluctuate between panic and guilt; in their quieter moments they bring loneliness and confusion. Gradually, the extremes become less frequent until they virtually disappear; loneliness, however, even today still lingers on in a threatening universe no longer simply my home.

I have recounted in some detail this mugging and its effect upon me in order to illustrate as vividly as I may the diverse experiences of existential and pathological anxieties. An existential psychotherapy must differentiate them in order to treat each appropriately. Let us now look more analytically at the dynamics of pathological anxiety. It may be useful to follow this discussion by referring to Figure 4.2.

This anxiety begins with some perceived threat that requires the erecting of a psychological defense. But since this threat is generalized, no specific object presents itself from which one may flee or against which one may hurl himself or herself.

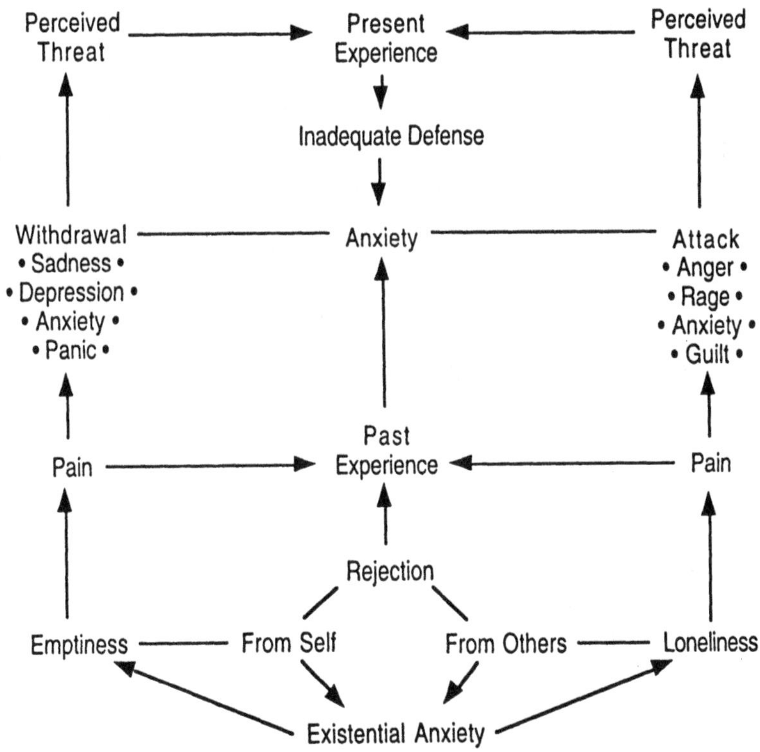

FIGURE 4.2 Dynamics of Pathological Anxiety

Therefore, no matter the defensive maneuvers, they prove inadequate to the task. As it grows inside, this pathological anxiety soon becomes a greater source of discomfort than the original perceived threat. In order to quiet its pain, other stronger emotions must now be generated. This happens through a fight or flight tactic directed against the anxiety.

If one chooses to fight, then anger immediately rises within and spills out indiscriminately upon others. As these innocent folks do not constitute the threat nor cause the anxiety, this anger fails to do the job. The troubling anxiety remains firmly entrenched. Rage then replaces anger as it may in its intensity block out the anxious feelings. But as the rage takes hold and itself threatens to capture the enraged person, it boils into a new well of anxiety. In desperation now the sufferer has only one clear object left to attack—one's self. By turning all this fragmentary anxiety and anger and rage into a laser beam of guilt, at least one may enjoy the illusion of success. If nothing else, the self as intruder may be attacked and, one hopes, be subdued.

Sadly, this ploy fails also. The self did not cause the guilt; the ego did. The ineffectual guilt may now enlist the opposing tactic of flight.

As one flees the anxiety, fear does not take over, for no specific object may be focused upon as the source of fear. Instead one experiences sadness. It rises up as one's ordinary life activities are curtailed. But just as anger could not snuff out the anxiety, so neither can sadness quench it. A stronger feeling must be enlisted. And so one sinks now into the arms of depression. As the slough of depression engulfs and threatens to drown the person in its dark depths, it causes its own anxiety. "My God, I may never get out of this . . . I may die!" As that realization settles in, anxiety becomes the context of the person's every waking moment. Again, relief may only come through making oneself into the feared object. And so panic now sweeps over one and threatens even the extremes of death. The panicked person now becomes, finally, a welcome object of fear.

Of course, flight from anxiety and the metamorphosis of self into the threatening object, as with the mirroring tactic of attack, does not succeed. Indeed, it may simply now follow the pendulum shift into a renewed round of anger to rage to anxiety to guilt . . . and on and on.

This pathological anxiety is further fueled by past rejections. When others have failed to furnish us with the degree of respectful attention we require, we feel lonely. As we struggle to understand the reasons for their lack of love, we may easily judge ourselves as being unworthy. This opens up a chasm of self-rejection between the self-affirming voices of our life and the self-negating ones of our death. Indeed, as we comprehend more fully our human condition inevitably bounded by death and inexorably torn by separation, these negative voices are strongly reinforced by the anxiety flowing naturally from this existential situation. As human beings, we must somehow come to accept as our lot some degree of loneliness and interior emptiness.

The grip of pathological anxiety may be broken in three ways:

1. The perceived threat must be examined in the light of the generally accepted reality within one's community.
2. The perceived threat must be taken out of generalities and made specific.
3. The specific threats must be dealt with one at a time and directly.

Clients will accomplish this task only as past experiences of rejection are healed. Such healing will come about as a loving therapist sets a context in which loneliness may give way to a solid therapeutic alliance supported by a genuine relationship. Within that bond a person may gather the interior wholeness and sense of self that will ground the ongoing struggle against the pathological forces of anxiety.

Moreover, they—and we—must also come to terms with the fragile state of human reality. This means believing in the worth of life in spite of certain death, accepting ourselves in spite of evident imperfection, and loving others in spite of our limited capacity for sustaining interpersonal unity. In Chapter 8 I will address at some length how the experience of spiritual transcendence becomes part of the client's struggle against the forces of pathological and existential anxiety.

Think back to the story that opened this chapter. If the one wise man had been able to convince the threatened population to hold a town meeting, it would soon have been apparent that their panic stemmed from pathological anxiety. Should the onion-loving dervish, now contented and all smiles, have joined them, the specific threat would have vanished. And after some embarrassed laughter about how they had been ready even to abandon their homes because of an onion, they would have settled back down into their routine lives. But, one suspects, their flirtation with pathological anxiety would leave them not only wiser but also with a more sensitive recognition of humanity's vulnerable condition. Existential anxiety would, after this scare, be more difficult to deny.

CLIENT ASSUMPTIONS

When people step into a therapist's office, they bring along some anxiety that has become problematic for them. Unable to handle their present troubling life experience, they seek someone with more expertise who may perform some magical operation, offer some healing explanation that may solve their problems and dissolve their anxiety. As if consulting with a physician, they expect that their task lies in recounting in some detail their present symptoms and the relevant life histories that have brought them to this pass. In the telling they may light upon some overlooked facts or change their perspectives just enough that they may now clearly see what must be done. The therapist will assist them in this endeavor by indicating what should be related, by asking astute questions, and, ultimately, by pointing out the preferred solution.

In this scenario we may recognize three major unspoken assumptions. In the first place, the anxious clients most immediately and most tellingly assume that their presently experienced pain is bad. Perhaps unwittingly, they are subscribing to the modern pursuit of material comfort and personal pleasure that have come to be regarded as *the* significant measures of a worthwhile life. It should be pain free, marked by ongoing contentment, punctuated by increasingly frequent pleasurable moments, and generally be under rational control. Effort, strain, pressure: these must be borne only as requisite accompaniments of achievement; from an ideal life, however, these would be banished also. Indeed, even the pain of ecstasy should be experienced only within tightly prescribed limits.

Fifty years ago, when Nazi forces were systematically assaulting civilized existence, Erich Fromm (1967) warned us about Western Civilization's determined *Escape From Freedom.* Faced with the anxiety of living, we have striven unceasingly for control. Fromm notes that the

> mechanism of escape which is of the greatest social significance . . . is the solution that the majority of normal individuals find in modern society. To put it briefly, the

> individual ceases to be himself; he adopts entirely the kind of personality offered to him by cultural patterns; and he therefore becomes exactly as all others are and as they expect him to be. The discrepancy between "I" and the world disappears and with it the conscious fear of aloneness and powerlessness. (pp. 208–209)

This vision of conformity releasing people from pain and maximizing pleasure was painted in its extremity by Aldous Huxley (1932/1969). In his *Brave New World* interiority is banished, pleasure is technologically available everywhere, and relationships are programmed. And should anything approaching emotion, let alone ecstasy, intrude, "soma pills" may expeditiously transform both into a drugged state of heavenly pleasure.

Clients searching for such a pain-free world mistakenly consider health to be a life without tension. Viktor Frankl (1984) directly challenges this notion:

> Thus it can be seen that mental health is based on a certain degree of tension, the tension between what one has already achieved and what one still ought to accomplish, or the gap between what one is and what one should become. . . . I consider it a dangerous misconception of mental hygiene to assume that what man needs in the first place is equilibrium or, as it is called in biology, "homeostasis," i.e., a tensionless state. What man actually needs is not a tensionless state but rather the striving and struggling for a worthwhile goal, a freely chosen state. (p. 110)

In order to escape from life's tension and the responsibility of freedom, clients act out another assumption about psychotherapy: when they cannot maintain a satisfying and relatively disturbance-free life through conformity, then they may obtain it by giving themselves over to the control of the therapist. This wise person will listen to them, analyze their problems, indicate desirable solutions, and direct their corrective efforts.

When Fromm (1967) is detailing the ordinary methods in our modern society of avoiding freedom, he puts authoritarianism in a prominent position. He describes it as

> the tendency to give up the independence of one's self with somebody or something outside of oneself in order to

> acquire the strength which the individual self is lacking. (p. 163)

This maneuver may be played out quite easily in psychotherapy when clients flee from themselves into the arms of a saving therapist:

> The reasons why a person is bound to a magic helper are, in principle, the same as we have found at the root of the symbiotic drives: an inability to stand alone and to fully express his own individual potentialities. In the sadomasochistic strivings this inability leads to a tendency to get rid of one's individual self through dependency on the magic helper—in the milder form of dependency I am discussing now it only leads to a wish for guidance and protection. The intensity of the relatedness to the magic helper is in reverse proportion to the ability to express spontaneously one's own intellectual, emotional, and sensuous potentialities. In other words, one hopes to get everything one expects from life, from the magic helper, instead of by one's own actions. The more this is the case, the more is the center of life shifted from one's own person to the magic helper and his personifications. The question is then no longer how to live oneself, but how to manipulate "him" in order not to lose him and how to make him do what one wants, even to make him responsible for what one is responsible oneself. (pp. 198–199)

An existential psychotherapist must never forget that therapy does not consist in the therapist doing something to the client; rather clients must walk along their own therapeutic paths, make their own life decisions, and take responsibility for their own growth and development. The therapist functions best as a facilitator of and a companion on this journey.

The final assumption portrays health and happiness as the products of intellectual knowledge. Clients look to the therapeutic expert for answers. Their obsessive search to know why they act as they do even to their own distress becomes their first request: "Tell me why." Once given logical reasons, they may then turn to correcting how they are living. As they look at their life's complexities, they expect an expert opinion about the most felicitous strategy for solving this puzzle and the most effective tactics for carrying it out. Knowledge about causes, information about possible solutions, directions about right actions—these form the necessary and sufficient basis of personal change. Therapy in such a model becomes a species of problem solving, an intellectual plumbing for the correct answers. Health is supposed to follow automatically upon receiving from the therapist the "why" of the illness, and then the "what" and "how" of possible ameliorative actions.

This Platonic conception of health wrongly asserts that not only virtue but also health follow upon knowledge. Neither intellectual deficiency nor lack of information keep the majority of clients from living healthy lives. They do not require of another person clever answers, brilliant interpretations, or creative solutions. Rather, they must find the courage to risk living. This means exchanging security for vulnerability, replacing certainty with trust, and forsaking control for the excitement of discovery. These personal qualities flow not from a well-functioning intellect, but from an indomitable spirit. Life must become a passionate endeavor resolutely striving for fullness in spite of the human reality of death. Therapy is the joining of spirits, not the collusion of intellects.

Besides the previously described anxieties and assumptions, clients manifest a layered defensive structure. In the remainder of this chapter let us consider, first, their personal defenses; then let us shift our attention to the principal ways in which they act out those defenses interpersonally.

PERSONAL DEFENSIVE STRUCTURE

We all wear masks. As we move about in our routinized world, a tapestry woven from daily demands and stresses, we habitually present ourselves in a predictable fashion. We have learned, primarily from our family, secondarily from companions at school and colleagues at work, to assume acceptable roles. They guarantee to others expected patterns of interaction contributing to personal and social stability. As we meet these expectations our compliance earns for us the acceptance we feel we must have from the significant people in our lives.

We live these roles so readily and easily we give little thought to them. Only rarely do we question their continuance. Indeed, most of our acquaintances simply equate our identity with this public self. To them we are the "boss" or the "rebel," the "hero" or the "fall guy," the "savior" or the "martyr," the "brain" or the "playboy," the "perfectionist" or the "clown." They relate to us through such roles and expect us to act them out consistently. Ordinarily, we oblige because assuming a well-practiced role requires little extra effort and pays off in ego-boosting responses from others.

Some years ago, I received a frantic phone call from a distraught mother. Her teenage son was acting so strangely she was concerned for his sanity. I agreed to see the parents and son for an evaluative session.

When I first met them in the waiting room, the mother was sitting alone weeping, her son was gazing fixedly out into the dark night, her husband was reading an article in *Life* magazine. In my office we positioned ourselves around a rectangular table, I on one side, the son directly across from me sitting between his parents. Our conversation began this way:

Therapist: (as an opener) Well, how are you?

Father: (immediately) Oh, just fine! (His wife is dabbing at her red eyes with a wet handkerchief; his son is staring straight ahead and with no expression.)

Therapist: (to the boy) Well, did you hear what your father just said? I wonder if that's how you experience life in your family.

Son: There are storms on the sea some times.

Therapist: I see. For you life is not always just the gentle sailing that your father indicated.

Son: (long lapse) The moon sets over the Adriatic.

Therapist: Yes. Too much light so early on could raise a lot of anxiety. I hear you. I'd better back off some. Thanks.

In this opening vignette I recognized the family members' routine roles: the father played the "protector" who denied problems and pretended normality; the mother fretted and fussed out of her long-suffering martyr's position; the son, the identified patient, was the "vanishing one" who concretized his father's emotional distance and his mother's loneliness. This emotionally estranged couple needed their son's illness as an emotional glue binding them all together. Until the couple could directly address their relationship dying from repressed anger and festering emotional wounds, the son would have to supply them with the only passion left in the family. From the beginning I recognized that my task would be to challenge these habitual roles, to pierce through this first layer of defense. This family kept up a public facade of relating to one another; in reality even the glow of an Adriatic moon would reveal its emptiness.

Behind the facade of conventional relating lie personality patterns, our ingrained methods of handling stress. Like automatic psychological reflexes, they spring into place when our public face is challenged. The shift to this level of defense plays itself out on two interrelated continua: pleasure–pain and togetherness–separation. Figure 4.3 illustrates a healthy interaction between them when tension gives a call to growth that disturbs our present psychological state.

We all seek out for ourselves some satisfying compromise between unity with others and our own independence. In ordinary circumstances we will emphasize our place in community (quadrant #1) or our stance as a self-responsible person (quadrant #2). Either position, however, may be confronted with changes in our current life situation. A new job, a move to another part of the country, chronic illness, the approach of death: these and other human realities disrupt the accustomed expression of fulfilling relationships. The assumption of new or more demanding responsibilities at home, at work, in the community may require increased interaction with others and decreased time for personal activities. In either case this forces a repositioning of ourself on the togetherness–separation continuum. However, if peace is to be maintained and a new level of growth

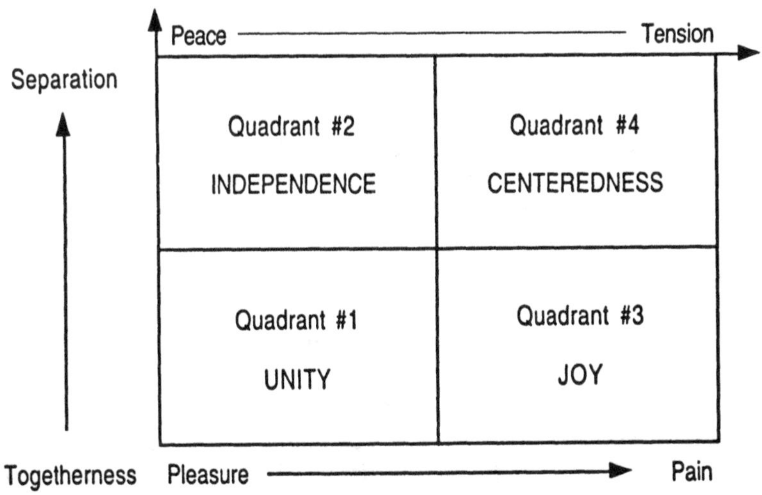

FIGURE 4.3 Healthy Response to Tension

attained, this movement must be accompanied by an integration of the pain associated with the new situation.

Pain flowing from unity disrupted or broken through physical separation may be integrated by love. Love does not depend upon material presence for contact. As we discussed in Chapter 3, it readily transcends the isolation resulting from distance. On one level, we may grieve for the loss of loved ones and experience the pain of forced separation; at the same time and in the midst of this pain we may also experience the joy of transcendence (quadrant #3). Though physically apart, we shall exist in spirit always together. No shift in material space can alter the place (*locus*) the other has in our self nor force our love to change its relational position (*situs*).

As responsibilities narrow the boundaries of our personal space and encroach upon our precious moments of privacy, we may well experience the pain of intrusion. This pain may be incorporated by purposefully turning inward to that center of the self where quiet and stillness remain even in the midst of diverse activities and the insistent summons of the crowd (quadrant #4). Though these consume much of our passing time, they cannot touch the transcendent reality of our personal time. As we mourn the loss of physical independence and feel its pain, we may recognize that in the depths of the spirit-self we still stand alone. For just as unity is retained through the immanent transcending of space, so independence remains inviolate through the immanent transcending of time.

Almost invariably, people find their way to the therapist's office when shifting circumstances are causing them unaccustomed pain. The healthier ones simply require a time and space in which to mourn and assistance in integrating the pains of separation and intrusion into a changed life. The therapist with these clients strives to facilitate their finding of joy and centeredness in the midst of pain. Less healthy clients, however, manifest a quite different psychological profile and require much more complex intervention.

Figure 4.4 presents the form their defensive personality patterns have assumed in the search for pleasure joined with security. It highlights the principal differences in their customary stances and in their pain-filled responses to threat, especially when these are compared with the stances and responses of their healthier counterparts. Most significantly, for them togetherness and the pleasures of community have been turned into enmeshment and symbiotic dependency. And rejection and isolation have replaced separation and independence. This has happened through the equating of pleasure with security, rather than recognizing pleasure as the result of interpersonal love and personal wholeness.

As long as people feel secure in their chosen position, be that one of exaggerated dependency on others or one of excessive protection of themselves from others, they will experience some degree of pleasure. However, this pleasure does not issue so much from a freely chosen position taken vis-à-vis self or others; it rather signals the maintenance of the status quo and the absence of threat and pain. Pleasure here tends to be more a sense of satisfaction than a feeling of happiness.

When such people experience a serious threat to their secured relationship (quadrant #1), they tend to pursue their partner to the point of suffocation (quadrant #2.). In so doing they are desperately striving to regain the previous symbiotic attachment. Should this tactic be successful, their mutually dependent lives will settle back down into a reinforced closed system, one now even more impervious to potentially disruptive forces. But their pursuit may generate instead an even deeper emotional chasm as the other flees the intensified enmeshment. At that point a painful loneliness (quadrant #3) overwhelms the pursuer. It drives him or her at one moment into torrents of rage, at another into orgies of guilt and cascades of promises. Couples' therapy

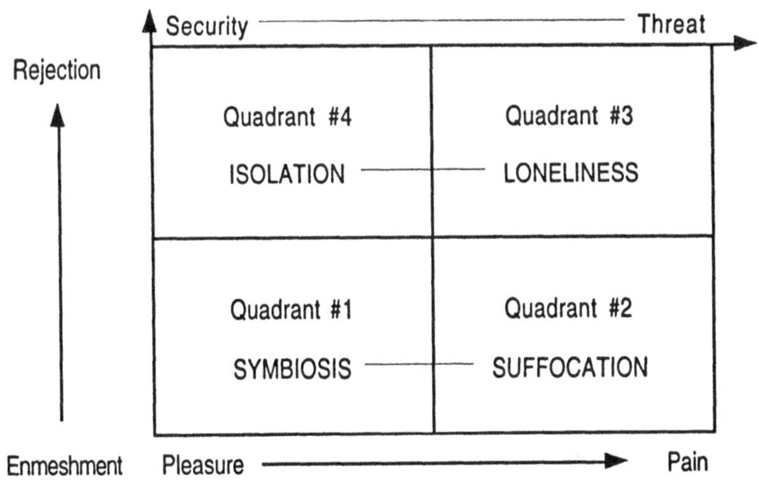

FIGURE 4.4 Unhealthy Response to Threat

may then be sought as a last-ditch effort to save the relationship and to ease the excruciating loneliness and dread.

In such instances the therapy sometimes succeeds in helping the couple renegotiate their union. This means forsaking the symbiotic security and establishing a mutually agreed-upon position between togetherness and separation. More often, however, the dance of pursuit and defensive distancing cannot be significantly altered. The distancer will soon leave and the abandoned pursuer is plunged into depression and isolation (quadrant #4). In that position the person will die emotionally and physically unless one of two other scenarios are played out: in the first, another dependent person appears and a new symbiotic attachment is formed (quadrant #1); in the second, the combination of pain and yearning drives the person to substantial personal change, often through intensive psychotherapy.

Of course, this same pattern may be pursued in reverse. This happened with Jonathan.

Jonathan was bred in a strict Southern Baptist family, the younger son of a minister-father who ruled absolutely. While his brother constantly battled against his father's authoritarian ways, Jonathan assumed the role of the vanishing child. One of his earliest memories, indeed, pictures him alone in his crib, quiet, listening to a heated argument between his parents about the mischievous Jeremy. He learned early on that safety for him meant keeping himself apart and not allowing anyone to ascertain his true feelings.

In the seventh grade Jonathan was failing in art. His parents engaged a tutor for weekly art lessons. These meetings soon became a mixture of artistic and sexual learning as the tutor required embarrassing sexual favors. The young boy tried to signal his distress through his continued failure, but he could not directly break out of the emotional role of the child who never caused anyone any trouble. He suffered through this long year, alone.

He went to the seminary as a young man, yet another attempt to please his father. He met a young woman there, a lonely outsider like himself. They married; he was ordained; he became an assistant minister of a well-established Midwestern church. But his unhappiness deepened. The couple moved back east to be nearer to his family; he took a managerial position in a flourishing corporation. These changes, however, failed to win his family's attention, let alone their concern.

Jonathan turned to his wife and two daughters for solace. Although he had sworn he would never act like his father, he became a demanding disciplinarian of his children and an emotionally abusive husband. He made his family his whole emotional life, controlling it and keeping it to himself as much as possible. He demanded their respect and attention, and he became quite jealous of any outside relationships that his wife and daughters found emotionally satisfying.

In her growing unhappiness his wife finally sought therapy for herself. She grew stronger then, less dependent upon him, more able to challenge his control. Then it happened. She demanded that he change; she was no longer willing to live under his harsh domination. She divorced him emotionally and threatened to do so legally. Panicked at her breaking out of his symbiotic bonds, he was thrown back into the nightmarish isolation and stinging loneliness that had been his lifelong lot before their marriage. In desperation, then, he too entered into psychotherapy, where he learned different coping behaviors and eventually found hope.

Different aspects of Jonathan's defensive maneuvers are generally true of people caught in this web of enmeshment-rejection:

1. Security is maintained through control of oneself or others.
2. Pleasure or a sense of well-being comes from the successful warding off of threat.
3. Validation and self-esteem are looked for outside of oneself.
4. Addiction to these sources of personal worth replaces freedom of choice.
5. The addictive cycle requires the disowning of parts of oneself and the restricting of one's potential for personal and interpersonal growth.
6. Emotional energy is directed toward warding off death rather than being a necessary component of enhanced living.
7. In the search for security, all risk must be eschewed, all calls to freedom rejected, all possibilities of transcendence closed off.

Sadly, all this defensiveness is doomed to ultimate failure. As one client plaintively noted, "You know, on my tombstone you will read these words: 'Here lies Joyce. She wasted her whole life making sure that she would never be here.'" The only real security rests in assuming one's responsibility to risk living.

We don masks; we respond automatically to threat; we also search for stability in a world subject to constant change. The ego furnishes us with the illusion of the permanence we seek through three defensive maneuvers: identification, objectification, and egocentrism.

Ego Identity When we feel overwhelmed by the ongoing flow of daily demands, we may turn inward for security. Instead of making choices and taking stances vis-à-vis our world, we may avoid the task of growth by appealing to "who we are." Actuality thus becomes the enemy of personal creation.

We identify ourselves in a variety of ways. We were born in this time and place in *this* family; we were raised to act in predictable fashions, to hold particular values, to strive for specific goals. We recognize in ourselves enduring needs and drives, likes and dislikes; we emphasize important experiences as those decisive moments that have shaped our lives. We have pursued these interests, developed these skills, made these decisions. No one else may claim this unique ensemble that signifies us.

All well and good. But as we explored in our discussion of time, these facts about us may become bulwarks against the realization of our life's potential growth. Our family *heritage* may be either an inspiring record of our ancestors' struggle to grow within the limitations imposed by their era or a model of behavior we are doomed to reproduce no matter its inappropriateness to our life and times. Our family *destiny* spells out for us the limits of our existence and the realistic possibilities we have of enhanced life. We may, however, turn it rather into a set of fixed demands that yoke ourselves and others into a predetermined position. Within the boundaries of our family's heritage and destiny, we must confront our own *fate.* We may accept this fate as a measure of our particular existence, or we may use it to excuse ourselves from struggling against the given actualities of our present existence.

A threatened ego may latch on to these facts of our personal and familial history as a way of minimizing risk and maximizing protection. A narrowed field of choice relieves us of responsibility, closes avenues of vulnerability, and absolves us of guilt associated with the refusal to live. Like laboratory animals, we can only be expected to move within the conditioned parameters of our predetermined life story, a tale told primarily by others.

Ego Objectification "Who we are," besides being conditioned by our personal and familial experience, may be equated with "what we do." The defensive ego here depends less upon our interior experience than upon the external facts about us. If our identity is determined by the photograph album of our past life, then our ego objectification is contained in our résumé.

Confronted by the myriad possibilities of human choice, we may avoid the responsibility of freedom by calling upon the limits imposed by our social history. We went to specific schools, had this quality of education, majored in these subjects, became friends with this kind of student. During these school years and afterwards, we had these jobs, took these vacations, were members of this church, synagogue, or mosque. We have lived in metropolitan areas or in rural villages; we have owned our own homes or rented from others. As members of this or that economic class, we are accustomed to a certain style of living, a given cycle of acquaintances, a set range of personal possibilities. We can be expected to be attracted to choices congruent with these experiential parameters of our life. In effect we are the names that others call us: white, middle class, American; a "Harvard man" or a "Yalie"; Episcopalian or Baptist; a bank president or a factory foreman; a teetotaler or a drunk; a jetsetter or a family man; a small-town conservative from the Deep South or a big-city liberal from California. How could we, depending upon our specific set of objective truths, ever choose to attend an art opening, ever buy a ticket to a wrestling match, ever sign on for a white-water excursion, ever join the Peace Corps! We can only do those activities proper to "our kind of people." Others may have those experiences, take those risks, make those decisions . . . not us!

Egocentrism In Chapter 2 I briefly described the healthy interaction between the Self and the ego. The Self may be considered to be synonymous with spirit, life, being; the ego is contained within the Self as its reflective ability, one among many human capabilities. In our present material state we need the ego in order to identify ourselves as human beings. Yet the ego only exists in and through the living power of the Self.

In instances of threat the ego may attempt to protect itself from the risk of change by denying the Self's existence and by assuming to itself the Self's central position. The ego chooses this tactic as a desperate means of control. It closes its boundaries to all influences, either from outside forces or from the Self. In doing so, the ego is pretending that in its present actuality it is whole and complete. Further change is neither necessary nor possible. In a prideful assumption of the place of the Old Testament God Who proclaimed Himself to be "I am Who am," the ego declares that "what is, is."

Figure 4.5 gives a graphic illustration of the egocentric ego (cf. Sanford & Lough, 1988, pp. 65–72). The large circle represents that Self. Although it contains the ego, the egocentric ego has imitated the Self by enclosing itself within the Self, taking over its centrality, and by closing itself off from the Self. This happens as outside forces (external arrows) press upon the Self and, therefore, upon the ego. Although the ego's defensive maneuvering is meant to resist these external influences, in reality the ego now finds itself having to handle both them and the living power of the Self (internal arrows). The Self will not suffer the ego pretender to parade as human life any more than other beings will allow the ego to excuse itself from the community of interdependent human beings.

However, when clients have concentrated their defenses at this level of ego, they present an especially difficult challenge in

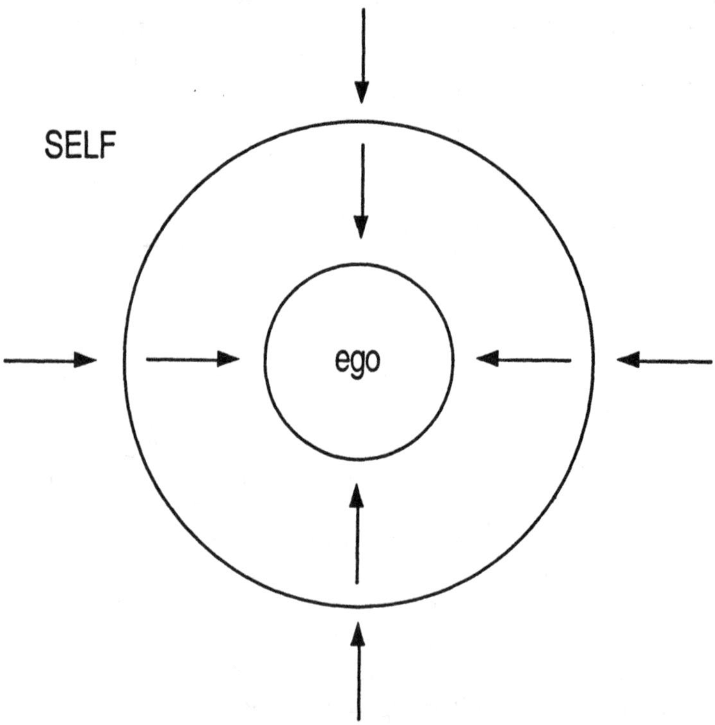

FIGURE 4.5 Unhealthy Interaction Between the Ego and the Self

psychotherapy. They come with the demand that their lives be made better but that this must be accomplished without any simultaneous significant changes in themselves. The ego will fight desperately to keep its central, controlling position; it will ward off any suggestion of personal responsibility and the exercise of freedom as the essential requirements for a happier life. No one taught me more about the stubborn quality of such egocentric defenses than a woman from California.

Margaret was born and raised in Orange County, the only offspring of a doctor and his socialite wife. Given his extended working hours and her plethora of civic obligations, the child saw much more of her nannies than she did of her parents. Because of an extraordinary series of childhood illnesses, culminating in rheumatic fever and juvenile arthritis, Margaret spent much of her school years at home. She did not participate in the ordinary range of socializing experiences shared by others her age.

When she was fifteen, her parents died in an automobile accident. Her mother's older sister, unmarried and living in San Diego, became her guardian. As the aunt worked as a secretary-receptionist in a dentist's office, she could not outfit Margaret with the upper middle class life style that she had previously enjoyed. By the time her parents' will had been settled, Margaret received enough money to support her through her high school years and to ensure her education at the college of her choice, but little more.

Although she had a sharp mind, Margaret had a difficult time reading because of dyslexia. This also negatively affected her ability to write. Still she obtained an undergraduate degree from the University of California in political science. After her graduation she worked for a few years as a legislative assistant to a state representative.

Her budding career halted abruptly when her arthritis worsened to the point where she could no longer maintain a full-time job. Forced to spend some hours in bed each day, following in her mother's footsteps, she took to the path of volunteering. She became active in a group pushing for the civil rights of the handicapped; she also took the position of secretary of her local alumni/alumnae association of the University of California.

I met Margaret when I received a phone call from the psychiatric ward of a local hospital. She had been severely depressed, almost catatonic. As it turned out, she had by age forty-five been in and out of numerous psychiatric facilities and had run through a wide range of social workers, psychologists, and psychiatrists. She had now been referred to me; she could not be released from the hospital unless I consented to see her. As she described her present situation and her plight in general, I felt much compassion and agreed to become her therapist. Thus began a most difficult three-year relationship.

Margaret was a very angry woman. Raised in affluence, she now depended upon social security and disability benefits to supplement her aunt's modest earnings. A doctor's daughter, she railed against the medical professionals who would not furnish her with the medications she desired or who failed to give her special treatment and consideration. She was, moreover, furious at the mental health professionals who had consistently challenged her to stop complaining about the world and to begin to take responsibility for her own unhappiness. A political science major, she disdained the government bureaucracy that discriminated against the handicapped and that failed to supply her with the benefits to which she was entitled. Indeed, Margaret presented a prototypical image of the self-righteous patient.

David Stewart (1991, p. 47) offers this description of the self-righteous person:

> So, what is self-righteousness? It is the confident belief in a person's own rightness or moral just-ness. It is a sense of virtue or ethical purity associated with the person herself or himself. It is expressed outwardly in that person's behavior in his or her smug ("I'm better than you") moralizing and in intolerance of the opinions and behavior of others. This outward expression can be focused on specific individuals or on less specific groups of people. The sense of superiority can be supported by actual, objective data as in the case of someone with a high IQ score feeling "better than" because he or she is smarter than those with lower scores. It can just as easily be focused on less objective differences. The self-righteous person can actually be discernibly (by someone else) right or not. It is the apparent belief in her or his rightness and her or his subsequent attitudes and actions which count.[1]

---

[1] For those desiring a more extensive discussion of the egocentric client, Stewart's *Psychotherapy and the Self-Righteous Patient* (1991) offers abundant theoretical and clinical material written by mental health practitioners.

Given her family background and her college education, her personal and familial tragedies, Margaret claimed the moral high ground against anyone who dared to contest her interpretation of society and her destined position in it.

Her ego defensiveness was manifested most glaringly in her social relationships with men. She wanted desperately to be married. As her aunt approached retirement age, Margaret quite understandably felt a growing urgency to establish some other means of personal and financial security. She spent much money and effort in taking out personal ads and in contacting dating services. In her personal descriptions she invariably emphasized her college education, her civic activities, and her love of the arts. As for the kind of man she hoped to date, she noted her preference for professional men interested in politics and the arts. This fit in with her constantly detailed dream of marrying a lawyer, adopting a child, her days spent supervising a corps of maids and servants, her vacations taken in exotic island paradises.

Margaret seemed oblivious of the need to reckon with other realities in her life: her age (45), her weight (over 200 lbs.), her shuffling gait (she walked supported by two canes), her generally unkempt appearance, her ill-fitting and well-worn clothes, her nonstop talking, her tendency to state her opinions as absolutes even when they were based on very few facts. To her, none of this should matter because, after all, her father had been a successful doctor and she had a degree from Cal Berkeley.

Her infrequent dates turned out predictably. Her irate accounts became an expected litany of male rudeness: being taken home immediately after a movie; dinner at Wendy's instead of a French restaurant; being made to go "dutch treat"; his failure to take her coat, or pull back her chair, or place her order with the waiter; dinners eaten in silence or with only cursory conversation; angry explosions leading to one or the other leaving in a huff. Any attempts on my part to get Margaret to focus on the part she shared in these painful debacles were met with enraged denial and the demand that I confirm her view of the other's responsibility, not hers.

Of course, she played out with me her egocentric way of relating to others and especially to men. In our sessions she delivered extended monologues about her life. I was expected to listen, to agree, and in general to validate her view of the world. Although she spoke fervently and often with much passion, our relationship was distant and without much feeling. It lacked the life that comes with the spirited interchange between two people. Indeed, should I say anything of a vaguely challenging nature, this would lead to instant rebuttal.

Over and over again Margaret's emotional estrangement from others became manifest in our therapeutic relationship: although she paid only $5 a session, she was infuriated that I would not see her twice a week, especially during the summer months when her volunteering activities were at a low ebb; she demanded a special handicapped parking space directly in front of my office on a residential street; she expected me to convince our consulting psychiatrist now to change medications, now to alter dosages; she threatened legal action when a malfunctioning beeper kept her from contacting me one weekend. In no way could she see these demands as unreasonable. And she used crises to draw special attention to herself. Although she had been given a variety of psychiatric diagnoses during her frequent hospitalizations (including paranoid schizophrenia, ambulatory schizophrenia, schizo-affective disorder, and narcissistic personality disorder), she admitted that much of her hospital behavior was simply a ploy. She put it on when she was lonely, bored with her aunt, angry at an unresponsive world. Indeed, our therapy ended when she staged yet another psychotic episode even though I warned her that I would not participate in this deception.

I helped Margaret some, I know. She was hospitalized only twice during our three years together. For a time a mirroring transference seemed to be establishing some sense of inner worth. She even began speaking about going back to school, this time to become a psychotherapist! I was touching her in some small ways, and her own life responded in fits and starts from its prison depths. But in the end I became just another therapist to add to her list of failures. Her ego with its walls of entitlement firmly entrenched ultimately proved impervious to life, mine and her own.

Margaret's identity was firmly knotted into being the angry victim. She disowned any responsibility for her unhappy state by projecting her life outward on to her entitled background. And she desperately kept all living connections—with her own self and with others—from penetrating her egocentric boundaries. This personal defensive structure at the level of ego protected her most certainly—from life.

INTERPERSONAL DEFENSIVE STRUCTURE

Whatever form our personal defenses may assume, we habitually relate to others from an accustomed position, especially during moments of stress. We rely on tested interpersonal patterns to serve us with a minimum of additional effort, like well-worn ruts in a dirt road that easily carry off excessive rainfall. In this way we reserve most of our energy for dealing with the specific requirements of the particular situation.

When the tearful dervish was observed walking through town, his fellow citizens reacted in diverse fashions. Some took in the reported behavior as gospel truth and generalized from it. In the process, however, they lost their ability to judge reasonably and act wisely. Moreover, pontificating out of their ill-based judgment they dismayed others inclined to be followers, not likely to think for themselves. Even the so-called wise man, the one who counseled gathering data directly from the supposedly distressed people, did not take his own reasonable advice. He failed to seek out the dervish to obtain a first-hand account of the rumored tragedy, nor did he strike boldly out for the other street to gauge the danger personally. When his suggestion was dismissed in the spreading dismay, he refused to extend himself for others but rather contented himself with looking out for his own welfare. The first group of people emphasized the allegedly objective facts of the situation; the second found security in being part of the crowd; the counselor relied on himself alone to save himself. None of these townspeople communicated directly with the affected people, none took a proactive stance consistent with their adult status in the community, none risked themselves out of their commitment to others. Instead, they fell back upon their habitual interpersonal defenses for protection. Consider with me in turn the three strategies they employed: extrinsic dependency, mutual dependency, and shared independency.

Extrinsic Dependency "My dad is bigger than your dad"; "I'm going to take my ball and go home"; "they are *all* mine!" From the earliest encounters with a threatening world, children learn to gain strength by identification, control by denial, and importance by possession. They set patterns of behavior by which their sense of worth, meaning, and identity come from living up to culturally rewarded standards of rectitude, ability, and success. As long as they are able to solidify a match between cultural demands and their own behavior, a union forged through control of self and of the environment, they are *somebody.*

Such behavior among children thrust into a new and often overwhelming world run by others seems quite natural. When confronted by hordes of bigger and older and more experienced people who expect given actions from them, they need to call upon extrinsic resources to bolster their generally unformed sense of self. Unfortunately, once these defensive patterns have been established and reinforced by repetitive success, they may become lifetime tactics. Psychological children of all ages measure their worth by extrinsic standards: "My life is truly worthwhile . . . because I graduated from Harvard . . . because I earn in excess of $100,000 annually . . . because I own oceanfront property in Newport Beach . . . because my wife and I regularly vacation in the Swiss Alps." For them a sense of self does not exist in their internal self recognition but rather is determined by how successful he or she is in manipulating the external world to satisfy a broad spectrum of personal needs and desires.

Table 4.1 lists a series of representative statements that extrinsically dependent people may be expected to affirm about themselves. They have been taken from a Relational Preference Inventory that is currently under development.

If a sense of self is sought from without, the person exists only in illusion and as acceptable standards of behavior are maintained. Such extrinsic evaluation works only as long as people are able to perform as "front runners." Shifting circumstances, challenges that become increasingly difficult as one grows, the aging process itself may, however, threaten this successful status. How many students, for example, here and abroad, move from disappointment to depression to suicide because they have been rejected by a preferred college, or have failed to pass a special examination, or have missed obtaining a desired grade? How many employees upon losing their job, how many businesspeople under threat of bankruptcy become abusive, depressed alcoholics, hardly recognizable to family and friends? How many seemingly mature men and women faced with retirement or an empty home, losing roles that once gave meaning, rapidly become old, ill, and soon die? No longer able successfully to run the cultural race, the erstwhile racers themselves vanish into the emptiness of being nobodies with no firm identity to call their own.

TABLE 4.1
Relationship Preference Inventory
Stage 1: Extrinsic Dependency

Item #	Statement
6	I worry a lot about failing.
14	I must succeed.
20	I would be discouraged should I not get the recognition due me.
28	Should I lose my job or position, my life would lose much of its meaning.
32	Getting a low mark on an examination would be difficult for me to accept.
36	It is necessary to do well what is required of me for me to feel good about myself.
43	Having good-looking things is important to me.
47	Having a low prestige job position would seriously threaten my feelings of self worth.
52	I would feel proud should I rarely miss a day of work.

Mutual Dependency As growing children venture out of their home environment and become identified with playmates, dependency may shift from securing parental approval to winning acceptance by "the other kids." Popularity in one's peer group then takes on vast importance. Being chosen for anything by them—to play third base, to come to a party, to serve as class president, to lead the cheerleaders—becomes the measure of personal meaning, worth, and identity. A consistent sense of self, rather than being found in one's self or in standing up for one's self, is sought in the secured acceptance of these personally significant groups. Where previously having something of one's own over against others established one's self, now such difference and separateness are rejected in favor of group membership. Indeed, being excluded from "the gang" can have devastating consequences for one's self-esteem.

Adults tend to smile at the exaggerated expressions of this youthful dependency: "I'll die if he doesn't call tonight"; "Oh,

Mom, *everybody* will be there"; "I don't care what you think because *all* the kids are wearing them"; "It'll ruin my *whole* summer if she can't come on vacation with us!" But for someone whose very identity revolves around dependent relationships, separation from special others may assume life-and-death proportions. Accepted, one seems secure, loved, a "someone"; alone, one wrestles with insecurity, feels unloved, and judges oneself a "nobody." It matters little that in reality this desperate love is need, security dependency, the "someone" a ghostly illusion fading and reviving among the vagaries of others' acceptance.

Some people never grow out of this way of defining themselves. Where "keeping up with the Joneses" may satisfy extrinsically dependent adults, mutually dependent adults cannot rest until they are invited to join the Joneses' circle of select friends. As a lawyer, one's legal degree must be from Columbia, one's mentor a distinguished professor, one's practice as a member of *the* firm. Others may judge that they have "made it" if they have the wherewithal for midwinter vacations to exotic climes; for them such jet-setting must include the legal elite with whom they identify. Being right has nowhere the psychological potency that being with the right crowd does.

Such mutually dependent relationships tend to be exclusive and excluding:

> Identity comes not only from relating to *the* person or group; necessary, too, is being *the* favored one of that person or group. To be included here means to hold a secured place, one which must be protected from all outsiders. Indeed, relationships which fashion high walls and dig formidable moats around "the insiders," which emphasize the difference between them and "the outsiders," clearly signal this stage of interpersonal development.
>
> Many supposedly adult relationships ape the intimacy rituals of juveniles in word ("I'm no one without you"), in feeling (jealousy), in manipulation and control ("you may think of, look at, relate to, go out with, share with me alone"), and in identification ("I love you because I *need* you for me to be a person"). (Willis, Spring 1984, p. 21)

Table 4.2 gives a representative sample of the kind of statements a mutually dependent person might make in speaking about an intimate relationship or group membership. Note how two themes predominate: giving up (of one's happiness, freedom,

TABLE 4.2
Relationship Preference Inventory
Stage 2: Mutual Dependency

Item #	Statement
1	My security depends on your love.
7	I would become depressed should I not be invited when others of my group are invited.
11	I'll do most anything to have important people in my life accept me.
19	I am willing to give up some of my freedom in order to belong.
22	Just tell me what to do and I'll do it.
34	On the chance I might offend somebody, I rarely bring up controversial subjects.
39	I lose my self confidence when I'm not in a "special relationship."
42	I feel more comfortable when I'm wearing what my peers do.
50	I generally "go along with the crowd."
56	If you die, I'll have little to live for.

independence, separate life) in order to obtain (security, acceptance, self-confidence, comfort) through relating to others. Although these statements may have more of a rhetorical than literal flavor to them, depending upon the depth of one's personal insecurity, they may feel literally quite true. In a threatening world this way of protecting oneself may for some be just as automatic and pervasive as meeting external standards of excellence is for others.

One may reasonably question whether these two kinds of dependency constitute separate interpersonal growth stages.

Shared Independency Young people moving through their adolescence face increasingly personal decisions as parental restrictions loosen and societal expectations allow a diversity of life choices. They take jobs according to their specific abilities; they select schools that match their needs, capabilities, and available resources; they seek out living partners to replace family and to assist them in building a desired future. Individual differences in background, capabilities, and wishes demand breaking with group uniformity and family security; they also require personal differentiation and self-reliance.

As choices are made and individual life paths are pursued, the consistent sense of one's worth, meaning, and identity may shift from external measures to one's sense of self. Should such happen, it does so gradually. Strong forces, both psychological and social, tend to draw the young person back into group conformity as the safest yardstick of one's being. Feeling the seductive pull of security and certainty struggling against the urge to take responsibility for one's own life, the individual self may seem torn and fragile. If so, safeguards must be erected and vigilance maintained lest the newly independent person fall back into the dependent way of being only recently abandoned.

Interpersonally, this independence manifests itself in a search for respect and equality. Any expectation of subordination other than the one freely chosen is immediately rejected. To others such unwillingness to follow another's lead may appear narcissistic; to the one striving for personal security in the self it seems a necessary and just self-absorption. Because of the dread possibility of losing one's self through another's power and control, trust does not come easily and commitment remains tentative at best. The call to *give* of oneself feels dangerously close to *giving up* or *giving away* one's hard-won independence. And the request to share oneself with another echoes past demands to lose oneself through compliance with the other's wishes.

Anyone counseling young people attempting to develop intimate relationships while protecting their autonomy and self-respect hears a repetitive chorus of pronouncements like the following:

> "I think our relationship is over: I've written him twice in the past month and he hasn't replied yet";
>
> "I don't consider it fair that I must pay simply because she's a woman; why can't we go 'dutch treat'?"
>
> "But it's *his* turn to call *me*!";
>
> "We like living together without the pressures and obligations of marriage";
>
> "I value my freedom too much ever to get married";

"I would never marry without a written contract spelling out our separate obligations and responsibilities";

"I'm buying *him* a birthday present, so he better remember *mine*!";

"I may be lonely but I'm my own person";

"I can't imagine being tied down to one woman!"

These and similar statements show little recognition that one may in fact *find* oneself in and through a relationship based on love and trust. Rather, one entertains the risk of relating only as a kind of necessary evil, as a way of overcoming loneliness, enhancing social possibilities, and making life easier through a division of responsibilities and pooling of resources.

Some people live forever in the tension between the desire to share and the requirements of independence. Think of a friend who moves restlessly from job to job "because they don't value me," or one who constantly uproots his family as he searches for new growth opportunities. Recall stories you have read about brides being left at the altar or of wives suddenly bereft because of the husband's whirlwind affair with his secretary. Consider the undernourished marriages of corporate America where the employee pursues jobs that demand extensive time away from home and spouse while the partner looks after the house and sheds loneliness through involvement in civic activities. How many households do you personally know about where division into her territory and his reveals lives of shared independency at best: for example, she controls the kitchen and raises the kids, he oversees the finances and makes major decisions; she invites friends and family to *her* home while he invites her to *his* bed; she takes responsibility for religion in the home while he looks to their position in the community; she initiates trips to local museums or suggests weekend trips to visit family, and he sets aside his time for summer vacations and makes the family decisions as to when, where, how long, and how expensive it will be. In such homes these domains are often inviolable; even a suggestion from "the other" is deemed intrusive and may generate arguments laced with demands for equality and smeared with accusations of disrespect.

The flavor of such relating comes through the typical statements listed in Table 4.3. On the one hand, these people must look out for themselves; on the other, they enter relationships slowly, structure them carefully, and stay in them tentatively.

TABLE 4.3
Relationship Preference Inventory
Stage 3: Shared Independency

Item #	Statement
3	I'll give as much as you do.
9	I demand equal rights.
17	I'm quite hesitant about getting involved.
25	I feel better when close relationships are spelled out in a firm verbal agreement.
29	My life comes before the needs of others.
33	I'm my own boss.
40	If I don't look out for myself, who will?
48	If you write, I will.
54	Justice demands that we share the chores equally.
58	I'm very careful when it comes to getting close to people.

5

THE THERAPEUTIC ENCOUNTER

A woman came to Rabbi Israel, the maggid of Koznitz, and told him, with many tears, that she had been married a dozen years and still had not borne a son.

"What are you willing to do about it?" he asked her. She did not know what to say.

"My mother," so the maggid told her, "was aging and still had not had a child. Then she heard that the holy Baal Shem was stopping over in Apt in the course of a journey. She hurried to his inn and begged him to pray she might bear a son. 'What are you willing to do about it?' he asked. 'My husband is a poor book-binder,' she replied, 'but I do have one fine thing that I shall give the rabbi.' She went home as fast as she could and fetched a good cape, her 'Katinka,' which was carefully stowed away in a chest. But when she returned to the inn with it, she heard that the Baal Shem had already left for Mezbizh. She immediately set off after him and since she had no money to ride, she walked from town to town with her 'Katinka' until she came to Mezbizh. The Baal Shem took the cape and hung it on the wall. 'It is well,' he said. My mother walked all the way back, from town to town, until she reached Apt. A year later, I was born."

"I, too," cried the woman, "will bring you a good cape of mine so that I may get a son."

"That won't work," said the maggid. "You've heard the story. My mother had no story to go by." (Buber, 1947, p. 286)

In a quest for new life, two different women sought out expert assistance. Each in her own way interpreted the demands of the situation. Depending upon how they engaged their teacher and participated with him in a mutual endeavor, they achieved their desired goal.

CENTRALITY OF RELATIONSHIP

In these modern times, other life searchers often use psychotherapeutic expertise as a way to grow. With the development of the professional understanding of how psychotherapy works, more and more practitioners across the psychological spectrum recognize that the developing relationship between therapist and client impacts dramatically upon the client's possibilities for growth through therapy. Listen to a sampling of their judgments in this regard.

Speaking from the vantage point of psychoanalytic psychotherapy, Paolino (1982) notes that

> the relationship between analyst and patient operates in four dimensions: 1) transference neurosis, 2) therapeutic alliance, 3) narcissistic alliance, and 4) real relationship. All four qualities of the patient/analyst relationship must be fully recognized and actively utilized by analyst and patient for the psychoanalysis to be successful. (p. 218)

The emphasis on transference neurosis goes back to Freud and surely surprises no one, while the therapeutic alliance has received a great deal of attention since the pioneering writings of Sterba (1934) and Bibring (1937).

Concern with the narcissistic alliance and the real relationship appear to be more recent. According to Paolino,

> the narcissistic alliance can be defined as that aspect of the relationship between patient and analyst whereby the bodily presence of the analyst serves as a substitute for some of the patient's previously used major coping and defensive psychic devices. (p. 226)

This alliance differs from the transference relationship in being the patient's present response to the therapist as the perceived source of emotional solace.

For analysts schooled to remain philosophically neutral as the necessary stimulus for transference, attention to the real relationship between analyst and patient constitutes a genuine departure. This relationship develops naturally as the therapy progresses. It must be recognized for two reasons. In the first instance because

> in both analyst and patient, the real relationship is genuine, that is, it is a psychic reality since it reflects what the inner experience is; and it is realistic, that is, it is an external reality, not imaginary, really existing outside of the mind and the treatment situation. (Paolino, p. 232)

And secondly because

> the real relationship is just as important to the psychoanalytic process as the other aspects of the therapeutic relationship. If the real relationship is not actively recognized and utilized in the therapy sessions then the patient is exposed to a relationship with the analyst that is interpersonally sterile and lacking the opportunity for the patient to develop a meaningful and therapeutic object relationship. (Paolino, p. 232)

If psychoanalysis traditionally stressed relationship neutrality, behavioral therapy emphasized technical expertise and downplayed relationship. Therapist and client related solely around the tasks of extinguishing symptoms and reinforcing desired behaviors. Function determined the relationship; efficiency and effectiveness alone justified its being.

Margolin and Goldman (1974), however, argue for the importance of a warm, human relationship in behavioral therapy. Looking at the reinforcement process itself, one central to their mode of therapy, they accept Franks' assertion that the therapist "must first establish himself 'as a source of reinforcing stimuli'" (p. 98). And they expect that clients will follow more readily, precisely, and expeditiously the directions of someone with whom they relate positively. Such a good relationship

> consists of behavior which constitutes social reinforcement for the client from the therapist, which enhances therapy in several ways: verbal interaction in the interview is maintained; clients will attend to the therapist's instructions and

> execute them with greater accuracy, speed, and frequency. On an even more basic level, the client will return again for his next session of therapy. (p. 99)

In discussing an article by Truax they point to the relationship itself as reinforcing to the client:

> He states that therapists who convey, in high frequency, qualities of relationship are more effective therapists because they are more potent positive reinforcers and because they elicit positive affect from the client. This increases the client's level of positive affect communicated to others. In turn, others in the environment respond with positive affect and reinforcers. Conversely, therapists lacking relationship qualities become noxious stimuli to their clients, are negative reinforcers, and elicit negative affect in the client. (Margolin & Goldman, pp. 100–101)

They conclude "that relationship does play a facilitative role in therapeutic change" (p. 101) for it helps to "create a situation in which learning can take place" (p. 102). For them, a positive relationship becomes facilitative of the client's acceptance of the therapist's reinforcements and directions.

Jacobson (1989), a cognitive behavioral therapist, regards the interpersonal relationship between the therapist and a depressed client to be much more than a means of acceptance and successful reinforcement. In his work with such clients, people regularly entering "therapy with interpersonal problems predominating" (p. 89), he uses the therapeutic relationship itself as a source of new learning:

> In addition to the healing potential of an interpersonal relationship which is not plagued by discord and disruption, the therapeutic relationship often provides depressed clients with an opportunity to explore new modes of interpersonal behavior in a safe interpersonal environment. To the extent that the relationship fails to replicate previous dysfunctional patterns, and when new more adaptive modes of behaving are met with success, the client may be ready for the first time to promote response generalization through venturing forth with these new behaviors into the natural environment. (p. 89)

Although clients may be helped to work through acute depressive episodes without explicitly using the therapeutic relationship, their underlying assumptions and core beliefs about themselves and themselves in relationship will not be changed until they can risk themselves in a healthy interpersonal relationship. This may happen most readily in the relative safety of the therapeutic situation. Jacobson, therefore, concludes that

> in order for it [cognitive behavioral therapy] to be a comprehensive approach which achieves long-term and even permanent changes in the majority of its clients, it will have to incorporate some of the concepts of interpersonal formulations. . . . (p. 94)

Although the therapeutic relationship ordinarily refers to individual therapy, family therapists do speak about "engagement" as an integral aspect of their work. Jackson and Chable (1985) define engagement as

> a complex, reciprocal process concerning the relationship between the therapist and the family. It refers to the specific adjustments which the therapist makes to him/herself over time to accommodate to the particular family. (p. 65)

They distinguish engagement from Minuchin's notion of "joining" the family, the accepting of its organization and style so as to be able to blend with it. Joining may happen almost immediately while engagement continues to the very end of therapy as the therapist continually modifies

> behavior and responses to ensure that family members feel sufficiently acknowledged and involved to continue to attend for the duration of therapy. (Jackson & Chable, p. 65)

In discussing the facilitation of this engagement process these therapists point to a number of specific strategies. Among these are clarifying the problem, linking affect and behavior, and expressing warmth and empathy.

As regards the first of these, they note that

> the simple process of trying to develop a clear understanding of the specific problem seems to enhance the therapist's

> relationship with families. Perhaps this is because the families feel that the therapist is genuinely interested in them or aligned with them. . . . Perhaps the family's belief that the therapist is attempting to be "of service" is helpful in developing the therapeutic relationship. (Jackson & Chable, p. 68)

When family members express strong reactions to particular behaviors, the explicit noting of this both helps them "to develop a clear understanding of their difficulties" and enhances the therapist's relationship to the family. This probably "is due to the therapist's appearing to have 'increased understanding and sensitivity to what's really happening'" (p. 68).

Finally, empathy, which

> has been described as the therapist's "ability to perceive and recognize the private, inner feelings and experiences of the client as the client experiences them" . . . does seem to facilitate the therapy process. (Jackson & Chable, p. 68)

The authors conclude that the process of engagement is a

> key component of the therapeutic relationship . . . particularly as mastery of this area is a crucial skill for therapists to acquire, underpinning as it does all successful therapy. (Jackson & Chable, p. 69)

For therapists espousing the humanistic tradition, the relationship has always been portrayed as the critical core of psychotherapy. Carl Rogers (1957) maintains that in a relationship characterized by empathic understanding, congruence, and unconditional positive regard, it functions as both the necessary and the sufficient means of positive therapeutic change. In his book on *Relationship Counseling and Psychotherapy* (1974), Patterson emphasizes that this relationship works for all psychological disorders:

> A loving relationship is the therapy for all disorders of the human spirit and of disturbed interpersonal relationships. . . . If the therapist is to help the client he must feel for him, love him in the sense of agape. It is perhaps a basic fact of human relationships that you can't really help a person

> without becoming involved with him, without caring for him or liking him. (p. 90)

Even a cursory glance at the writings of this school of psychotherapy makes abundantly clear that the therapeutic relationship is *the* essential factor in therapy.

Given this brief review of how other orientations explain the therapeutic relationship, in comparison we may now situate it in existential psychotherapy. This may be accomplished by describing, first, the transference relationship, since it has traditionally been the core of psychodynamic psychotherapy. How do existential psychotherapists understand it? Then, we will examine somewhat extensively the real relationship between therapist and client, a relationship only recently given special notice by psychodynamic and behavioral therapists. Interpersonal, humanistic therapists have unfailingly accorded this relationship a central importance in the psychotherapeutic endeavor. Do existential psychotherapists differ from these precursors in their understanding of the shape and effect of the real relationship?

TRANSFERENCE RELATIONSHIP

When the tearful woman heard that Rabbi Israel's mother became pregnant through the gift of her Katinka, she immediately concluded that her own cape could produce a similar result. She put into the rabbi's mouth a request for this gift as the price of a child. You can almost hear her musing, "If I do what he wishes, I shall be rewarded. He told me the story to see if I could be as generous as his mother had been. Well, I can!" We may further speculate that her certainty in this regard came from a lifetime of doing what significant people desired as her way of obtaining what she required from them. This authoritative rabbi may well have represented for her a host of other authorities upon whom she had long been overly dependent. In that case she would be transferring on to him and on to this particular problem her life's experiences with those more powerful than she. Moreover, what worked with other authorities stood a good chance of being successful with him.

If she had been the rabbi's "patient," we could speak about her being in a "transference relationship" and about the rabbi needing to assist her in working through her "transference neurosis."

Indeed, in the psychoanalytic tradition, "Many Freudians consider the explanation of transference neurosis to be the most effective procedure by which the patient surmounts the resistance to the repressed and painful unconscious" (Paolino, 1982, p. 219). Imagine the woman's dismay when the rabbi dismissed her facile solution, her anger at his supposed rejection, her protestations that he reconsider or her sullen dejection over her defeat. These feelings and others could easily be projected on to this situation as learned responses to innumerable past encounters with other authorities.

An existential psychotherapist recognizes

> that feelings and emotions directed toward the therapist fall primarily into two groups. First are the feelings that are an understandable response to some of the attitudes and behaviors of the therapist. (Rogers, May 1987, p. 182)

If, for example, the rabbi had responded coldly and in a superior tone, dismay could be generated by behavior unbecoming a holy man and anger could be a normal response to ecclesiastical chauvinism. However,

> the second category of client reactions are the emotions that have little or no relationship to the therapist's behavior. These are truly "transferred" from their real origin to the therapist. (Rogers, May 1987, p. 183)

Confronted with this latter category of transferred emotions, the therapist faces two questions: whence do they arise, and how should they be handled? The first of these will be considered here; the second will be addressed in the next chapter.

Therapists following Freud's metapsychological division of the human psyche into id, ego, and superego would respond that truly transferred emotions, the kind that make up the transference neurosis, emerge from the unconscious id. They constitute repressed reactions to others that are not supposed to be, or are not permitted to be, remembered. These nonconforming reactions must be hidden from oneself and one's contemporaries, for they do not fit the contemporary view of what constitutes acceptable behavior. The therapist attempts through interpretations to bridge the gap between known behavior and unconscious motivation in order to make the unconscious conscious. How are we to understand that process?

Although Freud initially considered the unconscious "to be simply the enigmatic quality of a certain process," he later declared that the

> value of the unconscious as an index has left its significance as a quality far behind. . . . We use the name "the unconscious" for a system that makes itself known to us via the characteristic that the individual events of which it is composed are unconscious. This is the most important meaning that the expression "unconscious" has acquired in psychoanalysis. (1925, p. 29)

Freud considered the unconscious to be the place of repression; indeed, "for us, the repressed is the prototype of the unconscious" (1961, p. 14). Commenting on this, Boss (1990) says that unconscious material may be

> defined as that which a person by *himself* has concealed, and that the concealed is concealed *from himself* because of a nonconformity. To conceal something from oneself amounts to self-deception. (p. 241)

Why did Freud consider it necessary to posit the existence of a non-verifiable unconscious? Boss (1990) summarizes it well:

> 1. One can be completely absorbed by something either in beholding it or simply "in thought." In the next moment, however, something entirely different may completely engross one. Then immediately afterwards one devotes one's attention to the first thing again. Freud could not think of the time in-between except as a span in which "the representation" of the first thing had disappeared by being thrust into "the unconscious" of a psyche, or more precisely into its "preconsciousness." Otherwise, how would it have been able to resurface forthwith in "consciousness"?
> 2. There are doubtless a great number of parapraxes in everyday life, in which one does or says something which one did not at all knowingly want to do or say. Must there not be a corresponding slip of thought (*Fehlgedanke*) present in the "unconscious"?
> 3. Most dreams consist of "images" (*Bilder*); if they are to be understood, they must be reinterpreted in terms of something which heretofore lay in the "unconscious."
> 4. According to Freud, it is possible to make sense of psychoneurotic symptoms as well only if one explains them by representational or affective contents enclosed in an "unconscious" in the narrower and genuine sense. (p. 243)

For an existentialist none of these experiences require some unconscious psychic depository. Consider each of the above explanations more closely.

When you direct your attention now here, now there, and then back to the original attractive object, in the interim it did not exist in you solely as a representation or a thought that had to find a temporary home somewhere else. It rather stayed on in you as a participant in your world but now as part of an unattended-to background out of which your present focus has caused a new figure to emerge. For example, as you are reading these words, you are most likely not attending to your hometown, to your family, to the grade school in which you developed your reading ability. As you now pause to remember them, you may recognize that they are an ongoing part of your conscious, if at any given moment unattended-to, experiential world. They exist in your feelings about reading, in the value you put upon continued learning, in your sense of yourself as an educated person, in your ability to read and comprehend, absorb and criticize this existentialist critique of the unconscious. You do not need a "preconscious" locale to explain this sudden prominence in your attention any more than you require some geographical "holding pen" for Mongolia and Madagascar when you are busy exploring Helena, Montana! Yes, indeed, when that philosophically prominent tree again falls in the forest, it *does* make a sound whether or not you or I have the misfortune to hear it!

How might we explain the "Freudian slip" other than as a kind of psychic leakage from some unacceptable, uncivilized pool?

When you, for example, open a meeting by declaring it closed or say "goodbye" when you intend to say "hello," careful attention to your experience prior to these slips would probably reveal that you had mixed feelings about being out yet another night this week or about entering into yet another conversation after a day filled with people. "Open" and "closed," "hello" and "goodbye" are simply verbal representations of the actual divided state in which you were existing at the time. For personal reasons you may have chosen to give prominence to "open" and "hello," but their negative opposites belonged just as surely to your inner voices as the positive ones did to your expressed voice. And the force of your need for rest or your desire for quiet simply won out in the moment as you made the "un-nice" slip. Previously you may not have been giving sufficient weight to these physical and psychological requests for a healthy decision; now they *will* catch your attention.

In Chapter 7 I will present abundant case material demonstrating how imagery, including dreams, may be worked with in therapy. Let it suffice here to note that Freud required an unconscious dream repository because he understood dream images to be some kind of arcane code that must be broken by the conscious analytical mind. For him, in the "unconscious" bald truths dwell. Because they would not enjoy ready approval in the society of our friends or in our own inner community of self-identified voices, they must adorn themselves with masks that we may choose to hide behind or peek out from as we are prepared to accept yet another truth about ourselves. We make an "unconscious" choice as to appropriate raiment; we make yet another as to the moment of acceptable release into the conscious world.

An existential psychotherapist does not make the imagination subservient to the intellect. Dream images do not find their personal worth in intellectual understanding any more than breathing does, or intuitive hunches do, or love does. They all express in their own way the reality of the given person's world. That expression may come easily or only with immense labor depending upon the divided or undivided state of our physical, psychological, and spiritual organism. The asthmatic struggles to breathe, the dependent battles with the call to responsibility, the controller flinches at a lover's call to vulnerability, the dreamer pictures the conflict and enlists the imagination's assistance in striving for wholeness. Just as our lives depend on breathing, not simply on this breath, and matures through choosing, not simply through this choice, and expands through committing, not simply by this loving feeling, so it moves toward oneness through imagining, not simply by recalling and decoding this image.

Turning, finally, to Freud's most important reason for hypothesizing an existing unconscious, how may we explain psychoneurotic symptoms without it?

In his masterful existential treatise *Being and Nothingness* (1956), Sartre finds an answer in *mauvaise foi.* Hazel Barnes translates this as "bad faith," while Walter Kaufmann (1966) calls it, preferably, "self-deception." Sartre devotes a whole chapter (Chapter 2, pp. 47–70) to his criticism of Freud's theory of the unconscious and to his understanding of self-deception. What follows is simply my summary of Sartre's argument.[1]

Sartre distinguishes a lie from self-deception in that the former requires a difference between the deceiver and the deceived, while the latter depends upon the unity of the two. Freud seeks to explain self-deception by splitting the psyche in two: in this way the unconscious id becomes the deceiver of the conscious, deceived ego.

> Thus psychoanalysis substitutes for the notion of self-deception, the idea of a lie without a liar; it allows me to understand how it is possible for me to be lied to without lying to myself since it places me in the same relation to myself that the other has in respect to me; it replaces the duality of the deceiver and the deceived, the essential condition of the lie, by that of the "id" and the "ego." (Sartre, 1966a, p. 246)

In psychotherapy the task of the Freudian analyst consists in elucidating the deceptions of the unconscious id. But as the therapist approaches the truth, strong resistance is regularly encountered. Sartre asks, quite reasonably, *who* is resisting?

It cannot be the ego, taken as the totality of consciousness, for it does not know the truth and thus would not know when to resist. Indeed, *if* it knows the truth, then the therapeutic endeavor to find the truth becomes nothing more than an elaborate, time-consuming, and costly sham.

Nor can resistance be the activity of "the complex which the psychoanalyst wishes to bring to light" because it is "rather the collaborator of the psychoanalyst since it aims at expressing itself in clear consciousness, since it plays tricks on the censor [through dreams and parapraxes] and seeks to elude it" (Sartre, 1966a, p. 247). And, moreover, these unconscious complexes know nothing of external reality so they could have no sense of any threatening detective maneuvers on the therapist's part.

---

[1] The reader is referred to Mark Conkling's (1990) lucid explanation of this challenging and tightly reasoned material in his article "Sartre's Refutation of the Freudian Unconscious." Moreover, in *Psychoanalysis and Daseinanalysis* (1962), Medard Boss reevaluates the basic conceptions of psychoanalytic philosophy. He devotes a whole section to "The 'Unconscious' and 'Psychic Topography'" (pp. 85–101). From a Daseinanalytic perspective he shows how the phenomena that forced Freud to hypothesize an unconscious may be otherwise explained.

The repressive force, therefore, must be exercised by "a censor, conceived as a line of demarcation with customs, passport division, currency control, etc. to reestablish the duality of the deceiver and the deceived" (Sartre, 1966a, p. 244). For the censor "alone can comprehend the questions or the revelations of the psychoanalyst as approaching more or less near to the real drives which it strives to repress—it alone because it alone *knows* what it is repressing" (Sartre, 1966a, p. 247).

But this censor allows some drives, such as lawful sexual impulses, and some needs, including hunger and thirst, to pass through from the id into consciousness. And it relaxes its surveillance at times enough to allow tantalizing clues from the unconscious to emerge. This psychic watchman not only serves the role of repressor; it also knows what must be repressed and what may be released, and chooses to do both.

The censor, therefore, must understand the following: 1) what is being repressed; 2) that it functions as the repressor; 3) where the observations of the therapist are leading; 4) the comparative truth between the therapist's interpretations and the repressed material; 5) that it is consciously repressing certain material "*in order not to be conscious of it.* What does this mean if not that the censor is in self-deception" (Sartre, 1960, p. 248)?

Conkling (1990) summarizes well this state of self-deception:

> Bad faith or self-deception is the act of lying to oneself. A person is aware of the truth but tries to hide it from himself. He is the deceiver and the deceived simultaneously and knows that he has deceived himself. He believes the lie he has created and hides from himself the fact that he is the creator of the falsehood. He is fleeing from the truth, but he is not totally unaware that he is fleeing.
>
> For Sartre, then, Freud has substituted for self-deception a lie without a liar, namely, the unconscious. The liar, which I myself am, is replaced by the concepts of repression, suppression, and the unconscious. This is tantamount to saying, "I *am* my ego, but I *am not* my id. I am not that unconscious instinct or impulse which compels my act" (pp. 258–259).

If we do not explain self-deception through such a reliance on an unconscious deceiver, how may we otherwise understand it? How may we believe and not believe something at the same time?

We could, perhaps, say that the believing and disbelieving occur sequentially, at different moments, but that would simply be a change in belief and not self-deception. More true to our experience we may recognize that

> there are two levels of awareness: one is simple (like the prereflective consciousness), the other includes attending or noticing (like the reflective consciousness). In this way I can be aware of something without at the same time attending to it. For example, I am aware of sitting before my desk, but I am not attending to it. . . . Self-deception is possible because a person may yield to one belief by lying to himself and by failing to notice or by ignoring the truth of the matter. (Conkling, p. 259)

We thus return to our previous comments about Freud's hypothetical unconscious: clients in therapy are not dealing with unconscious facts about themselves; rather they have not been attending to some aspects of their personal experience because of the momentary centrality of other aspects. At this time and place their worth and meaning, needs and desires, their very identity are tied up with certain facts and not others. They therefore attend to these; they give scant notice to those. Existential psychotherapy, rather than being a process of unlocking the unconscious, functions as an arena for expanding their attention to include other aspects of themselves, truths about their lives that were always available but for a multitude of personal reasons have gone unnoticed.[2]

---

[2] The reader is referred to Needleman's (1963) discussion of Ludwig Binswanger's idea of "horizon" as an alternative explanation of the unconscious when it is presumed to be more than just a quality. As Needleman rightly notes:

> It is clear that the concept of horizon as delineated above does not preclude a usage of the term "unconscious" as adjectival, as *descriptive* of an aspect of experience. . . .
>
> Our concern here, however, is with what is called the "specific psychoanalytic meaning" of unconsciousness. In cases where Freud describes his work as "the scientific method by which the unconscious can be studied," he is implying a concept of the unconscious that goes beyond the merely adjectival; when he speaks of that unconscious as discriminating and censoring, he is implying a concept that goes beyond the function of a theoretical explanatory concept. It is this strict meaning of the concept of the unconscious that Binswanger opposes to his own views. . . . (pp. 94–95)

Return also to the original question about the transference relationship: whence do the transferred emotions and feelings arise, especially if we reject the Freudian explanation?

One way of explaining this phenomenon simply denies the reality of any so-called transference of emotions. As Boss (1963) remarks: "Transference is always a genuine relationship between the analysand and the analyst" (p. 123). In this view clients encounter their therapists according to their ability to relate more or less maturely to another adult. They may, indeed, function intellectually in an adult fashion, but often they have only a limited capacity for disclosing themselves emotionally or for receiving without distortion genuine, self-disclosing, emotional responses from another. Rather, like children they perceive all adults in a dependent or aversive way. They have not developed the capacity to relate as an emotional equal. They react to the therapist, therefore, much as they related as children to the adults in their world.

Boss (1963) illustrates this viewpoint about transference with a pointed example:

> A child plays with a burning candle. It closes its eyelids almost completely and it sees a star-like arrangement of narrow rays instead of a full-sized flame. Suppose that the child were to burn his eyelids while playing with the candle and that they became permanently sealed together. The child would then continue to perceive all candles in the same fashion for the rest of his life. But nobody would claim that his manner of perceiving the flame is due to a "transfer" of the experience he had as a child to a similar situation happening in the present. The reason for the distortion of perception is the same in both childhood and adulthood: the closing of the eyelids. The situation of the adult neurotic is similar. (p. 124)

When a client reacts emotionally to the therapist, these emotions are not transferred from past experiences. Although they may be immature and distorted reactions because of the distorting effect that past harmful experiences with others had on the ability to relate, they do represent a child-adult's relationship at this moment with the adult person sitting in the same room with him or her. Therapy, therefore, becomes a process of emotional growth in relationship, a process aimed at realizing a developed capacity to interact emotionally and openly with others as a mature adult.

Another viable explanation accepts that in the transference relationship undeserved or excessive reactions are projected onto the therapist. An existential psychotherapist may understand these reactions to be unresolved emotional clusters that have attached themselves to remembrances, both images and words, that over time have been relegated to the fringes of awareness. When the therapist acts in some manner resembling those remembrances, an association between them and the present situation may occur. This allows some of the calcified emotions to break loose from their attachment to the past and to release a measure of their pent-up energy. As the therapist draws attention to the emotional reaction and its current behavioral incarnation, the client may follow these expressions out to the limits of awareness where the unresolved memories dwell. In this fashion they now assume center stage, where they may be attended to with the combined skills of therapist and client, and within the framework of the client's present capabilities.

For this transferential journey to reach its hoped-for growth destination, the client must do the following: 1) make an association between the present situation and the past memory; 2) be willing to focus on the transference reaction; 3) be willing to expand awareness out of the present situation; 4) be capable of using imagination, intuition, and memory to do so; 5) be open to integrate disowned parts of the self; 6) be prepared to alter significantly the ego's self-image; 7) take the risk to overcome inner divisions; 8) give up ego control over how life should be and accept instead the reality of how life is; 9) assume responsibility for his or her present life instead of focusing on the irresponsibility of others. This will happen only in the context of a positive real relationship and a working therapeutic alliance. The remaining chapters of the book will focus specifically on the kind of interventions an existential psychotherapist might make that may facilitate this trip to wholeness, one aspect of which is this so-called transference relationship.

Real Relationship

In his discussion of existential "Isolation and the Patient-Therapist Encounter," Yalom (1980, pp. 401–415) emphatically stresses the need for a real relationship in psychotherapy. For him, indeed,

> "it is the relationship that heals"—[and that] is the single most important lesson the psychotherapist must learn. There is no more self-evident truth in psychotherapy; every therapist observes over and over in clinical work that the encounter itself is healing for the patient in a way that transcends the therapist's theoretical orientation. (p. 401)

How does this relationship contribute to healing?—through the experience of intimacy. Most patients enter therapy because of isolation, a separateness from others and an internal division within their own life. But

> once a patient is able to relate deeply to a therapist . . . then he or she has already changed. The patient learns that the potential for love exists within oneself and experiences feelings that have lain dormant in dissociated realms for years or decades. . . . No matter that the patient's relationship to the therapist is "temporary," the *experience* of intimacy is permanent. It can never be taken away. It exists in one's inner world as a permanent reference point: a reminder of one's potential for intimacy. The discovery of self that ensues as a result of intimacy is also permanent. (Yalom, 1980, p. 406)

Yalom describes this relationship as "psychotherapeutic love," a term he takes from Carlos Sequin's *Love and Psychotherapy* (1965). He summarizes this special kind of love this way:

> . . . the therapist relates to the patient in a genuine caring fashion and strives to achieve moments of authentic encounter. The therapist should be selfless in this endeavor—that is, concerned with the patient's growth and not with his or her personal needs. The therapist's caring should be indestructible and not dependent upon reciprocal caring by the patient. The therapist should be able to be both with himself or herself and with the patient and should thus be able, in caring, to enter the patient's world and to experience it as the patient experiences it. This requires the therapist to

> approach the patient without presuppositions, to focus on the project of sharing the patient's experience without rushing in to judge or stereotype the patient. (Yalom, 1980, p. 409)

Yalom's emphasis on the centrality of the real relationship in existential psychotherapy is clearly consistent with the existential focus on being as "being-with" described in Chapter 2. Moreover, his position stands firmly among those taken by other existentialist writers concerned with psychotherapy.

In his dissertation on healing in psychotherapy, Heckler (1981) summarized the reported experience of therapists using an existential orientation:

> In existential therapy it is felt, especially in relation to feelings of isolation, that it is the therapeutic relationship, the repeated genuine encounter between therapist and client, which enables the client to move into direct confrontation with the fundamental truth and transcend the experience through deepening one's relations with one's world. (p. 36)

Friedman (1986), in his comments upon the historic dialogue between Carl Rogers and Martin Buber, asserts that

> the real essence of therapy, correspondingly, is not so much the client's memory of the past, explorations of problems, or admissions of experience into awareness as it is the client's direct experiencing in the therapeutic relationship. (p. 413)

Moreover, he positively associates himself with Sidney Jourard's (1968) demand for authenticity on the part of both people in this encounter:

> As the therapist grows in the capacity for dialogue, he or she becomes more whole-hearted in the "invitation to terrified, self-concealing people to disclose themselves as they are. . . . A therapist, himself a rehabilitated phony, invites the patient to try the frightening rigors of the authentic way, first with the therapist and then with others." Jourard not only makes the I–Thou relationship the center of healing, he sees it as the sine qua non for any good interpersonal relationship between therapist and client, "where the influencer is as vulnerable and open as the one to be influenced.

> . . . Only within such a mutually open relationship can the therapist maximally present his therapeutic influence, at the risk, incidentally, of being demoralized or sickened by the patient. . . . No technique will work when I and thou are not thus open. (Friedman, 1985, p. 11)

And finally, Rollo May (1979) insists that this relationship should be called an encounter because of the stress that it places upon the therapist as well as the client:

> To be able to sit in a real relationship with another human being who is going through profound anxiety or guilt or the experience of imminent tragedy tries the best of the humanity in all of us. That is why I emphasize the importance of the "encounter" and use that word rather than "relationship." . . . In this encounter I have to be able, to some extent, to experience what the patient is experiencing. My job as a therapist is to open to his world. He brings his world with him and therein we live for fifty minutes. Learning to do so may be highly taxing; to experience somebody else's anxiety can be extremely painful. It is painful enough to experience one's own, when one has no choice but to bear one's own world. (p. 108)

"A healing relationship," "intimacy," "psychotherapeutic love," "genuine caring," "authenticity," "encounter": all words used to describe the real relationship. Because these words mean such diverse things, meaning coming as it does unavoidably from our own experience, it seems necessary to attempt to describe it behaviorally. How, indeed, would a therapist act in a "real relationship"?

Rabbi Israel's mother came seeking a wise man's assistance. How could she grow as a human being? The Baal Shem knew the answer: by taking responsibility for her own life. He, therefore, urged her to consider her own resources and to take actions that could bring fresh hope to her stagnant life situation. In so doing he refused to assume the kind of expert role calculated to keep her dependent upon *his* efforts. *Her* creativity, willingness to give of herself, openness to new experiences, *her* dogged efforts to meet whatever requirements: these human capabilities *will* eventually produce new life. She needed to learn this; only in a supportive yet challenging relationship could she take the necessary risks.

So she mobilized herself, made decisions, and set out on the road to growth. In doing so she trusted the holy man and more importantly she trusted herself. By the time she reached Mezbizh we can well imagine that she had left her dependency and copious tears far behind. The woman who finally faced him in trust and determination, openness and courage, stood ready for healing and growth.

They met . . . and something happened. Few words were spoken; only an enlivening contact was required. In it life quickened within her. All obstructing internal divisions suddenly disappeared as their spirits touched and as they became joined in and through the power of Life.

The Baal Shem in modern terms had developed a real relationship with his client. He established a relational context of interdependency that helped her to mobilize and to take charge of herself. Because that happened she could risk meeting him in a unitive moment that resulted in healing and growth. This eighteenth-century rabbi well illustrates for us two aspects of a real relationship. Consider with me each in turn.

Shared Interdependency In Chapter 4 we considered how clients ordinarily enter therapy long practiced in relating interpersonally from dependent and independent stances. For the therapeutic interaction to be transforming, it must facilitate an essentially different relational experience. Clients know well how to use others to manufacture an identity or to protect a fragile sense of self; they need to test themselves in a relationship flowing from the self and fittingly expressing that self.

Such a relationship depends upon three basic shifts in relational perspective. Previously, extrinsic possession fostered the illusion of individual identity; only internal presence to the self builds a firm basis for personal identity. Employing an external focus, people scurry about hunting for certain signs of personal worth; turning within, they come to appreciate the basic, intrinsic goodness of their own lives. The drive for security motivates the insecure to pursue extrinsic guarantees of acceptability; the desire for continued growth moves the self-identified to risk an unfolding self-expression. Shared interdependency may occur only as the byproduct of these changes in relational capacity. Therapists must possess the requisite self-identity and self-worth, and they must find within themselves the willingness to summon their clients to participate in an interdependent relationship.

What kinds of behavior attest to the presence of this mode of relating in either or both persons?

In the first place, each relationship is unique. The therapist engages *this* client as an individual, not mechanically or according to some previously determined pattern. The relationship grows as the people involved strive to meet each other and as a function of their relational ability. No two relationships will shape themselves identically or assume identical expressions. Through openness, vulnerability, and trust, the therapist invites the client to create with him or her a new being, *this* relationship, the free expression of their encounter.

Unlike dependent relationships, which exclude others in order to secure personal possession of *the* other, an interdependent one beckons others to participate in the fruit of its expanding life. It flows naturally out to others like the sun sharing its life-giving warmth or water its nourishing moisture. The energy pulsating in one relationship may vivify every other one; the therapist desires nothing more than that the client enter into intimate, healthy relationships outside of therapy because of an expanding capacity for intimacy realized through therapy.

This intimacy grows as the fitting expression of each person's life. The therapist does not relate to a client out of some necessity, either the therapist's or the client's. Nor does the offer of intimacy depend upon the client's reciprocal sharing of self. Rather, the therapist decides to become open with and vulnerable to this person because to be this way suitably expresses his or her own life and values. The lovableness of the client notwithstanding, the therapist shares of herself or himself because, in a phrase, "I love myself loving you." Granted, to love the immediately lovable comes more easily, but interdependent loving depends not on the other's constant lovableness, but on the recognition of a healthy life energy flowing between the two people.

Indeed, in interdependent relating the therapist is committed not to the client but to the relationship. The relationship expresses at this time the therapist's life; it energizes and expands it. Self-worth deepens through it; the sense of self grows stronger through the repeated choice to risk being oneself transparently to another in it. The client's actions and responses, whether pleasant or not, do not determine the stability of the relationship or the extent of the therapist's commitment. As long as the therapist finds a worthy self-expression in this relationship and receives increased life energy through that expression, the commitment may last.

TABLE 5.1
Relationship Preference Inventory
Stage 4: Shared Interdependency

Item #	Statement
5	Through our love I grow.
12	Loving others flows naturally from loving you.
16	Sharing our life with others, rather than diminishing my love for you, fills it with increased life.
23	Because of my relationship to you, I am more open to relate to others.
26	Our relationship gives me increased energy and motivation for living.
37	Through our relationship we grow both as separate persons and as a couple.
41	Although I relate more or less deeply with others, I always bring your life with me to them.
46	Our life together frees me to be myself.
51	My gift of myself to you is more important to me than what you give me in return.
60	I love myself when I choose to love you.

Table 5.1 illustrates shared interdependency through a list of representative statements about one's experience in it. Note especially how the opening up of one's life, love, and self to the other expresses and enhances personal life in and through that very decision. Life grows not as an accumulation of others' positive responses, but as an unconditional gift to itself.

One may legitimately question how "real" a relationship may be if in that relationship one person, the client, comes as a suppliant, while the other, the therapist, accepts the engagement as the acknowledged expert. Moreover, equality and mutuality demand vulnerability on both sides, but the course of therapy focuses upon the tensions and divisions within the client's world, not that of the therapist.

In their 1957 dialogue Buber and Rogers disagreed precisely on this point of mutuality in therapy. Buber maintained that since therapy necessarily revolved around understanding the client's issues and not the therapist's that, at least potentially, the therapist could experience more deeply and completely the client's world than *vice versa.*

Friedman (1985) reports that

> Rogers suggested, in response, that what Buber said applied to the situation looked at from the outside. This has nothing to do with the relationship that produces therapy that is "something immediate, equal, a meeting of two persons on an equal basis—even though, in the world of I–It, it could be seen as a very unequal relationship." (p. 15)

Near the end of his life, Rogers published some "Comments on the Issue of Equality in Psychotherapy" (1987) in which he steadfastly clung to the position he had espoused thirty years earlier with Buber. He amplified his response this way:

> The reason I love to carry on psychotherapy is that at times I too look with awe on the incredible strength and wisdom of this vulnerable client. I participate in a miracle. At such moments I feel an almost ectoplasmic bond between the client and myself. It is truly an "I–Thou" relationship. At such important moments of change in therapy, the question of equality or inequality is *totally* irrelevant. The important thing is that two unique persons are in tune with each other in an astonishing moment of growth and change. Both of us are changed, although the growth may be greater in the client. Since I, as therapist, hope that I have helped this moment to come about, the relationship can be looked upon as an unequal one. But in the moment itself, all such issues disappear. (p. 39)

Both men speak correctly about the psychotherapeutic experience; they comment, however, from quite different vantage points.

If one draws attention to the *content* of therapy sessions, undoubtedly the two people come to know vastly more about the client's world, both internal and external, than that of the therapist. Moreover, if one focuses upon the number of occasions of empathic understanding of the client's ongoing experience during the therapy session, they far outnumber a similar understanding of the therapist's experience. If psychotherapy were essentially about facts, both public and private, and about the sensitive entry into the other's world, then Buber clearly wins this academic dispute.

For an existential therapist these conditions merely form the necessary context for healing to take place through psychotherapy. Yalom (1980) says as much when he comments on the growth of the therapeutic relationship:

> No, a therapist helps a patient not by sifting through the past but by being lovingly present with that person; by being trustworthy, interested; and by believing that their joint activity will ultimately be redemptive and healing. The drama of age regression and incest recapitulation (or, for that matter, any therapeutic cathartic or intellectual project) is healing only because it provides therapist and patient with some interesting shared activity while the real therapeutic force—the relationship—is ripening on the tree. (p. 227)

For an existential psychotherapist, one who recognizes that "being" equals "being-with" and that human beings exist as a process of becoming (cf. Chapter 1), psychotherapy does indeed happen through the act of *meeting.* This occurs in those instances of personal time when separateness dissolves, when out of nothingness "we" spring into existence as a new "creature of the between" (Buber, 1965, p. xx). "I" and "you" recede back into the ground of nothingness as "we" becomes the energized center of awareness. In such transcendent moments the connectedness, the flow of living energy, *does* feel like "an ectoplasmic bond" that overcomes the barriers of material existence. Thus does shared interdependency prepare the way for this experience of contemplative incorporation.

Contemplative Incorporation In Chapter 3 we explored the human possibility of transcendence. It occurs as passing time collapses into personal time or as location (as in *this place*) is subsumed by situation (as in *taking this position*). Neither can be forced to happen but both may be prepared for by a discipline analogous to hospitality.

As a young lad, I went downtown one Saturday afternoon with a buddy to see "The Jolson Story." As I drank in the lively music and became absorbed in the emotions of his life, I left my small Northwest town for the exciting world of vaudeville. In fact I remember thinking at one point, "This is heaven!" And I fervently wished that this moment could stretch on and on, forever. Alas, movie over, I was startled to see that the sun had set ("where did the afternoon go!") and that I was again walking down a familiar, yet somehow changed, hometown avenue ("where have I been!").

On occasion we all experience this altering of our experience of time or place as we get lost in a good book, or swept up in a symphony, or mesmerized by a dazzling sunset. All ordinary sense of time and place shut down, and the separateness they manifest disappears. We take on the character's life as our own; we become the musical energy; we bask in our new coat of brilliant, living colors. Should others attempt to downplay our experience as being "just in your imagination," we know that in the fullness of that time we became one with the object of our enrapt attention.

In the intense playfulness of sexuality we may both find time dissolving and discover how difficult it is becoming to distinguish clearly any sensual difference between our energized bodies. The combination of emotional tension, imaginative interaction, and physical excitement narrow our focus until nothing exists but *us . . . now*!

Table 5.2 illustrates further the experience of contemplative incorporation. These statements reflect the experience of an intimate relationship. Note how time and space are in given instances overcome through an altering of consciousness that gives an experience of unity. In various degrees this may happen during and outside of therapy sessions, or because of the therapeutic relationship.

Shared interdependency as previously described serves as the context out of which contemplative incorporation springs and as the loving discipline that leads up to the moment when healing happens through *meeting*. Just as no one can coerce this movie or book, this symphony or sunset, this act of sexual relating into an ecstatic moment of unity that overcomes isolation and division, so no therapist can program a moment of healing encounter. As Yalom wisely notes, we must simply wait in joyous and earnest expectation "while the real therapeutic force—the relationship—is ripening on the tree."

TABLE 5.2
Relationship Preference Inventory
Stage 5: Contemplative Incorporation

Item #	Statement
4	Even in your absence I feel your presence.
10	When I'm quiet and reflective, I discover you within me.
15	We are growing into a life that's greater than our individual lives.
21	Past moments of overwhelming illumination are strongly present to me.
30	In special moments I forget that I am existing separate from us.
35	In relating to you I sometimes lose all sense of passing time.
44	Where once I actively chose to share myself with others, now I often find their presence already within me.
49	Now and then I feel us being drawn into a reality quite different from our ordinary life experiences.
55	Occasionally I know how you are at the moment even when you are physically absent.
59	We may communicate in ways that differ substantially from ordinary communication processes.

In 1980 Rogers published *A Way of Being*. In a section on altered states of consciousness, he describes his experience in psychotherapy of what I call "contemplative incorporation":

> When I am at my best, as a group facilitator or as a therapist, I discover another characteristic. I find that when I am closest to my inner, intuitive self, when I am somehow in touch with the unknown in me, when perhaps I am in a slightly altered state of consciousness, then whatever I do seems to be full of healing. Then, simply my *presence* is

> releasing and helpful to the other. There is nothing I can do to force this experience, but when I can relax and be close to the transcendental core of me, then I may behave in strange and impulsive ways in the relationship, ways which I cannot justify rationally, which have nothing to do with my thought processes. But these strange behaviors turn out to be *right*, in some odd way: it seems that my inner spirit has reached out and touched the inner spirit of the other. Our relationship transcends itself and becomes a part of something bigger. Profound growth and healing and energy are present. . . . I am compelled to believe that I, like many others, have underestimated the importance of this mystical, spiritual dimension. (pp. 129, 130)

Some commentators on existential psychotherapy consider it to be more of a learning process than a healing one. Corey (1991) introduces his treatment of the subject by pointing out that

> existential therapy can best be described as an *intellectual* approach to therapeutic practice, or a *philosophy* that a therapist follows. As such it is not a separate school of therapy or a neatly defined model with specific techniques. (p. 174)

This echoes Van Deurzen-Smith's explanation that

> the aim of existential counseling is to clarify, reflect upon and understand life. . . . The assistance provided is aimed at finding direction in life by gaining insight into its workings. The process is one of reflection on one's goals and intentions and on one's general attitude toward living. (pp. 20, 21)

And Bugental (1965) maintains that

> psychotherapy is not a healing process. It is a philosophic venture. It is not a treatment of an illness. It is daring to confront self-and-world. (p. 42)

In these comments I find three basic confusions:

1. *Between counseling as guidance and as psychotherapy.* Granted, existentialism does furnish a perspective from which

our existence as material beings faced with the anxiety-creating realities of isolation and death, freedom and meaninglessness may be examined. Granted also that such topics may be explored in the course of existential psychotherapy. I would, however, take Patterson's (1974) position concerning such discussions:

> When conditions other than the therapeutic relationship are necessary for solving a person's problems, the relationship is not counseling or psychotherapy, but something else—reeducation, retraining, teaching, advising and so on. However, the incidental inclusion of other elements, such as information-giving, does not justify calling the process other than counseling or psychotherapy. (p. 12)

2. *Between psychotherapy as problem-solving and as healing.* In the course of psychotherapy clients present a diversity of problems and do solve many of them. This happens in the context of a therapeutic relationship marked by shared interdependency. But personal and interpersonal healing and growth occur also during those times of meeting that I have characterized as moments of contemplative incorporation. This experience of intimacy overcomes lifelong internal divisions and opens up the ongoing possibility of breaking out of existential isolation.

3. *Between existential psychotherapy as a set of techniques and as a systematic method.* Since learning and problem-solving, both processes amenable to strategic maneuvers, do not constitute the essential core of this kind of therapy, techniques have only an accidental (that is, a nonessential) place in it. They are appropriate only as they fit the needs of the particular client and as long as they do not substitute the therapist's activity for the client's responsibility to take charge of his or her own life. Moreover, therapists certainly may bring an "existential attitude" to whatever kind of psychotherapy they espouse. However, in itself this does not preclude the possibility that a systematic process of psychotherapy may be developed based on existential principles. Indeed, this book is attempting to put forth just such as process. And therapists may use particular kinds of interventions, ones always shaped to suit this client in this unique therapeutic relationship, to open up the possibility for healing. This means on the therapist's part refusing to relate to the client from a dependent or independent stance, and choosing instead to foster a context of interdependency. It further calls for the therapist's capability to transcend personal boundaries and his or her willingness to join the client in the healing encounter of contemplative incorporation.

6

THE PROCESS OF THERAPY

Once upon a time, there was a man who strayed from his own country into the world known as the Land of Fools. He soon saw a number of people flying in terror from a field where they had been trying to reap wheat. "There is a monster in that field," they told him. He looked, and saw that it was a watermelon.

He offered to kill the "monster" for them. When he had cut the melon from its stalk, he took a slice and began to eat it. The people became even more terrified of him than they had been of the melon. They drove him away with pitchforks, crying, "He will kill us next, unless we get rid of him."

It so happened at another time another man also strayed into the Land of Fools, and the same thing started to happen to him. But, instead of offering to help them with the "monster, he agreed with them that it must be dangerous, and by tiptoeing away from it with them he gained their confidence. He spent a long time with them in their houses until he could teach them, little by little, the basic facts which would enable them not only to lose their fear of melons, but even to cultivate them themselves. (Shah, 1968, p. 207ff)

Oftentimes, clients entering therapy feel like fools. "I *should* be able to handle it myself," one man complains. Yet "it" seemed simply too huge to move alone. "It" had assumed monstrous proportions.

Sometimes, to outsiders the solution appears obvious. "Do this" or "don't do that"; but, then, the monster does not belong to them. And clients usually need their demons anyway. Only kindness and patience may wean them away from these frightful excuses for not living. Roads leading toward exuberant existence wind through dark forests, plunge precipitously into narrow ravines, twist tortuously up imposing granite mountains. Everywhere one sees signs counseling caution: "slow down," "dangerous curve ahead," "one way bridge," "slippery when wet." Both driver and companion must heed these warnings and proceed carefully lest the trip be aborted.

The initial watermelon hunter recklessly thought that he could save the townspeople from their monster by performing a miracle for them. He slew it himself and even made it into a delicious snack! He did not realize that folks must confront their own darkness, sink into it slowly, and finally incorporate it into themselves in their own time. As Van Deurzen-Smith (1991) wisely notes, "Existential counselors decline to do the work for the clients" (p. 113).

The second wayfarer knew a lot about monsters and about people. He recognized that the villagers needed something to fear, for without it they would have to deal with the anxiety of human existence. (Anxiety *always* tries desperately to fear something *out there*; then we only have to face it, not ourselves.) Moreover, he realized that he would assist them only if he were willing to dwell with them, to enter into their sometimes exciting, often boring, daily experience. By his very presence, as long as he kept true to his own life, he could occasion for them new opportunities for self-expression and personal courage. As they dared self-revelation, as they took the risk of changing in and through their meeting, they would grow in their capacity to live within the existential limitations of their existence. Someday, they might accept their limits, embrace their monster, and settle down responsibly into the business of human living.

In a century and in a country where psychotherapy has become for many a way of being, we have learned quite a bit about helping people confront their fears and live with their anxieties. We may describe, at least in general, the therapeutic journey; we may also indicate what facilitates this trip. It has three phases: a beginning one in which commitment to the endeavor solidifies; a middle one in which fears are overcome; a concluding one in which healing and enhanced life occur. The existential therapist brings to each phase three general methods of assistance: the real relationship, the therapeutic alliance, and specific kinds of interventions. All of these change in some fashion as the therapy moves from phase to phase. Let us in this chapter now chart this course.

ENGAGEMENT

The Real Relationship In Chapter 5 we dealt at some length with the existential therapist's conception of this relationship. We did not at that point discuss how it is established, however.

Rogers (1980) has offered three conditions that have been widely accepted as facilitative in establishing a healthy and potentially healing relationship: congruence, unconditional positive regard, and empathic understanding.

He states that

> the first element could be called genuineness, realness, or congruence. The more the therapist is himself or herself in the relationship, putting up no professional front or personal facade, the greater is the likelihood that the client will change and grow in a constructive manner. This means that the therapist is openly being the feelings and attitudes that are flowing within the moment. . . . As for the therapist, what he or she is experiencing is available to awareness, can be lived in the relationship, and can be communicated, if appropriate. (p. 115)

Note especially the phrases "the first element" and "if appropriate."

As Snyder (1982) correctly notes, earlier in his career Rogers placed empathy in the initial position within the relational triad, probably as a way of emphasizing that the therapist's genuineness in relationship may be a bit much for a new client used to social nonconfrontation. Congruence certainly functions

> as a central aspect of the therapeutic situation. Indeed, the full acknowledgment of the intrinsic engagement in counseling and psychotherapy occurs with the participation of a genuine therapist. (p. 99)

True, but recall the fate of the eager watermelon hunter! He told the truth, but "The truth does *not* make people free. Facts do *not* change attitudes" (Kopp, 1972, p. 13). The beginning relationship calls for an emphasis on empathic listening and responding, and on unconditional acceptance; genuine sharing of one's reactions to the client's world must be tempered with appropriateness. It makes little therapeutic sense to communicate what cannot be accepted at that moment as helpful.

That said, we must recognize that as therapists we *are* reacting constantly to our perception of the client. An experienced therapist

> acknowledges that this engagement is not mediated through verbal contact alone. It is based on experiential contact involving the manner in which each person develops his/her world. Each participant's perspective may be conveyed bodily, intellectually, or emotionally. But the foundation for this conveyance remains an experiential meeting of the participants. The therapist interprets to the client in the very act of his/her being, not just in verbal statements. The manner in which the therapist's office is set up; the therapist's greeting at the beginning of the session; the therapist's seating in relation to the client; whether or not the therapist is the first to speak, how often the therapist speaks and in relation to what kinds of actions and statements by the client; the degree of emotionality and intellectual formulation present in his expression to the client; the limits set by the therapist for behavior in the session; the degree of self-revelation by the therapist to the client; the manner in which the therapist participates in ending the session are examples of interpretation by the therapist towards the client. Interpretation is the revelation to the client of what the therapist perceives from his/her perspective. The therapist's communication with the client is an expression of the particular way that the client affects the therapist. The perspective of the therapist is the way in which he/she develops and acts in his/her world. (Snyder, 1982, pp. 99–100)

Thus therapists must be sensitively aware that everything about the therapeutic situation is confronting their clients with their perception of them. Congruence calls for both appropriateness of messages and consistency among them if a healthy relationship is to be forthcoming.

Rogers (1980) describes the next necessary relational quality in this fashion:

> The second attitude of importance in creating a climate for change is acceptance, or caring, or prizing—what I have called "unconditional positive regard." When the therapist is experiencing a positive, acceptant attitude toward whatever the client *is* at that moment, therapeutic movement or change is more likely to occur. The therapist is willing for the client to be whatever immediate feeling is going on—confusion, resentment, fear, anger, courage, love, or pride. Such caring on the part of the therapist is non-possessive. The therapist prizes the client in a total rather than a conditional way. (p. 116)

In this echo of the religious admonition to "hate the sin but love the sinner," Rogers posits a deceptively difficult condition. To prize the beautiful, to care for the loving, to accept the accepting: how easy! But how about doing so with the nasty! In an article on evil in psychotherapy (1991) I recorded this opening gambit in my first session with a "toxic patient":

> He threw himself heavily down on my couch. Only after he had attained some measure of comfort in and ownership over it, did he look at me. With a surveying glare over me and the office, he opened with this salvo:
> "Well, I'm here."
> "So you are."
> "We'd better get one thing straight right off. I've been to three other shrinks. They were phonies! That's why I don't respect you guys."
> "Oh."
> "And another thing: the last guy wouldn't let me get mad at him. (Voice rising in strength and volume.) Can you imagine! Who the Hell do you guys think you are telling me how I may or may not be?"
> With that he stopped and glared daggers at me. The gage had been thrown. My turn. . . .
> "I see. Guess you've found a different guy this time. You've been here only five minutes and you're already fuming at me!"
> So began a ten-month tussle with Joe. (p. 61)

In this instance accepting Joe did not require that I enjoy his behavior or feel positively stroked by his bitterness. Nor did I have to like him as he was currently presenting himself to me. I did, however, have to respect his right to be who he was, even if that seemed unpleasant to me. Our clients do not assume the task of making us happy! Indeed, over the course of therapy they will present themselves with some regularity in places that we will both experience as quite painful. The relationship demands that we stick with them and accept the fact of their present position, no mater how we might wish them to be different.

Finally, Rogers (1980) gives us this description of therapeutic empathy:

> The third facilitative aspect of the relationship is empathic understanding. This means that the therapist senses accurately the feelings and personal meanings that the client is experiencing and communicates this understanding to the client. When functioning best, the therapist is so much inside the private world of the other that he or she can clarify not only the meanings of which the client is aware but even those just below the level of awareness. (p. 116)

Later on in the same book he expands this by pointing out that

> it involves being sensitive, moment to moment, to the changing felt meanings which flow in this other person, to the fear or rage or tenderness or confusion or whatever else that he or she is experiencing. It means temporarily living in the other's life, moving about in it delicately without making judgments; it means sensing meanings of which he or she is scarcely aware, but not trying to uncover totally unconscious feelings, since this would be too threatening. It includes communicating your sensings of the person's world as you look with fresh and unfrightened eyes at elements of which he or she is fearful. It means frequently checking with the person as to the accuracy of your sensings, and being guided by the responses you receive. (p. 142)

Note how in this explanation Rogers moves from "felt meanings" to "meanings" to "unconscious feelings" to "elements." They all appear to be synonymous to him.

In the 1960s "sensitive" counselors spoke about "getting to the feeling level" as if it were the psychotherapeutic mother lode! It often proved to be more like a cache of fool's gold, however, as responses rivaled each other for obviousness and banality. For example, "I'm very upset with him"; response: "I can see you're angry."

Rogers (1987) bemoaned the distortion of what he was sharing with therapists about empathy and the sterility of such canned responses:

> I even wince at the phrase *reflection of feeling.* It does not describe what I am trying to do when I work with a client. My responses are attempts to check my understanding with the client's internal world. I wish to keep an accurate, up-to-the-minute sensitivity to his or her inner searchings, and the response is an endeavor to find out if I am on course with my client. I regret that the phrase *reflection of feeling* has come to be used to describe this complex type of interaction. (p. 39)

From these comments on empathy we may understand that for Rogers a "feeling" is not the equivalent of an "emotion." He is stressing the accurate reflection of that significant aspect of the client's present experience where something is struggling for expression. This "feeling" may be a thought, a bodily experience, an intuition, an image, and yes, sometimes an emotion. I like to think of empathic communication as a form of midwifery: it helps bring into the light some new life; in the mutual delight in its presence, the client grows.

These qualities of healthy interaction contribute to therapeutic change as long as the therapist relates from a stance of shared interdependency. Snyder (1982) makes an interesting observation when he remarks that Rogers somewhat unwittingly joins Freud when he focuses "on leaving the client to develop his/her emotional life while being seen in the thoroughly accepting attitudes of the therapist" (p. 98). He further notes that

> Rogers' concern with congruence as an important therapeutic phenomenon led part way to a position emphasizing the intrinsic relatedness of one person to another. But he stopped short and undervalued this concern. (p. 99)

Whatever the validity of Snyder's critique of Rogers' position, existential psychotherapists do not see their clients as objects to be observed and valued, but rather as participants in an intersubjective world. Therapists present themselves openly, vulnerably, with a willingness to be involved and influenced, with commitment, and with a desire to share life in a mutual world. Any sort of independent self-presentation as described in Chapter 5 would not issue in the kind of presence and meeting that contributes to healing and growth.

The Therapeutic Alliance Upon entering the therapist's presence, the client as "being-with" and a "being-in-the-world" changes. So does the therapist. As Boss (1963) rightly observes

> the fact that human existence is in every case "my" existence does not *exclude* "being-with" others of my own kind. On the contrary, it is the essence of *Dasein* to "be with." The "world" of man's being-in-the-world is ever and primordially one which I share with others. The world of *Dasein* is essentially *Mitwelt.* For we never exist primarily as different subjects who only secondarily enter into interpersonal relations with one another and exchange ideas about the objects all of us perceive. Instead, as any direct observation shows, we are all out there in the world together, primarily and from the beginning, with the same things shining forth in the common light of all our existences. (p. 55)

The therapeutic alliance is all about "the *Mitwelt,* literally the 'with-world,' the world of beings of one's own kind, the world of one's fellow man" (May, 1967, p. 61).

Two strangers, each for his or her own reasons, decide to share an interpersonal world. For some, such an entrance may feel like an invasion; for others, it may call forth patterned responses of domination or submission. For the therapeutic enterprise to succeed, structures must be erected that will minimize intrusion, introduce equality, and forestall separation. Both parties need such structural protections.

At the very least this means that two people have decided to be "engaged in a mutual endeavor to help one become more effective and fulfilled in his life experience" (Bugental, 1965, p. 85). In addition they will "need to agree explicitly or implicitly on the goals and tasks of therapy as well as to develop a bond appropriate to the tasks in which they would engage" (Greenberg, 1985, p. 252). They must also negotiate satisfactorily requisite boundaries of time and space: when, where, how often they will meet; how they will be physically present to one another during these meetings; the ordinary length of sessions and the probable duration of treatment. Finally, they must have fair expectations, each of the other. As regards the client's behavior, these include the amount, mode, and time of payment; necessary notice about cancellations; contact with the therapist outside of sessions; compliance with requisite "homework"; appropriate behavior during therapy sessions. On the therapist's side, the client may reasonably demand professional judgment in using his or her abilities; reasonable protection during sessions and appropriate avenues for necessary assistance between sessions; attention to and maintenance of therapeutic boundaries; and the establishing of a context in which a healthy relationship may flourish.

Lurking behind this world of relationships lies the *Umwelt*, "the world of objects about us, the natural world" (May, 1967, p. 61). Both people relate to the physical environment in their own idiosyncratic ways. "Subjective reality can thus be extremely diverse, even at this most basic and apparently concrete level of experience." That relationship includes reactions to summer humidity and winter chill, to intrusive noise and uncomfortable quiet. It also embraces such personal factors as "body image, ability to stave off illness, fitness or weakness, attitudes toward food, sex and procreation [for these] are all part of the particular natural world of the client" (Van Deurzen-Smith, 1991, p. 70) and of the therapist.

When a client enlists *this* therapist's assistance, the external environment becomes part of the therapeutic contract. Any changes may have an impact, positive or negative, upon the relationship. Two brief examples may illustrate this.

At one point in my career I saw a few clients at my home. One man, a rather rigid and uptight fellow, especially appreciated our cat, who had taken a fancy to him. She rarely approached strangers; him, however, she immediately warmed up to. She usually spent the hour on his lap or next to him on the couch. Somehow she knew he needed her physical presence, warmth, and affection. And he did. When circumstances changed so that I no longer saw anyone at home, Stan complained not about the shift in venue, but at the loss of his feline companion. "It's not fair!"

As clinical director of an agency in New England, I always wear a suit to work. One late afternoon, having just given a rather informal workshop, I showed up for my sessions dressed in slacks, a sport coat, and an open-necked shirt. No one seemed even to notice. The next week, however, one woman told me that since that session she had been obsessed with sexual images and reactions to me. "Don't you ever," she demanded, "come to our sessions again without your tie. You're just too available without it."

In this beginning phase of therapy, moreover, the content of the sessions, what the client inevitably experiences as problematic and in need of adjustment, ordinarily centers upon the *Umwelt* and *Mitwelt* of the client's life. As indicated in Chapter 4, clients generally recount their problems so that the "doctor" may fix them. These recitations may describe relational problems at home or work, in the city, with one's family or friends. Enmeshment or abandonment and shifting power balances are causing psychological pain. The necessary structures in the *Mitwelt* for mutually acceptable relationships have failed. Or they may detail a variety of distressing physical symptoms that feel out of their control. All, moreover, cause stress. They expect the therapist either to help them cure these ailments or, that failing, to teach them how to live with them less unhappily. Any attempt during the engagement phase of therapy to shift the conversation away from this focus on physical and relational problems will be sabotaged. Clients feel that they have both the duty and the right to lay this particular litany of pain before a concerned therapist. After all, "that is what I'm paying you for!"

Therapeutic Interventions Besides working to establish both a real relationship and a therapeutic alliance as has been described, some specific interventions seem particularly suited to this engagement phase. They serve either to meet legitimate client needs or to counter the personal and interpersonal defensive patterns discussed in Chapter 4.

Most clients initially wish desperately to tell their story. They yearn for a respectful forum with a good listener. In the telling they also seek some immediate cathartic release: so many emotions have been held in because of the facts themselves and the fear of sharing them. Sometimes they require some facilitative structure to assist them; otherwise; they need most an accepting ear and a quiet but attentive presence.

Bruce, a grade-school teacher in his early thirties, began our first session this way:

Client: I'm so glad I'm finally doing this. I've known for a long time I just have to talk with somebody. There's so much . . . I don't know where to begin.

Therapist: Feel free to jump in anywhere. Most people find it helpful sooner or later to get to painful happenings in their life, especially ones they just can't tell *anybody*.

Client: (quietly) Well, I know where that is. I see so many kids that have been physically and sexually abused in their families. That always hurt me a lot . . . because I was too, I think. I *really* need to check that out with somebody. I might as well begin there.

He then recounted in exhaustive detail his early life with an older brother whom he worshipped but who answered the idolatry with cruelty. This included pushing him down the basement stairs so that he crashed into a wall, or luring him down the stairs and then locking him in the pitch blackness. After some minutes of spilling out similar incidents, Bruce also managed to describe a lifelong secret: one time his eleven-year-old brother persuaded this six-year-old to engage in a round of oral sex with him. As a Catholic child he knew vaguely that he should not, but as the "nice guy" who wanted his brother's acceptance he felt compelled to join in. As this story unfolded anger and sadness and guilt vied for dominance within him. For the most part I simply remained silent but nonverbally present and supportive. He left the session with some of his burden shared and somewhat lighter.

Bugental (1965) gives this overview of his therapy sessions:

> With many individual variations, then, the usual pattern of the therapeutic hour is the brief greeting as we meet, perhaps a quick comment on the weather or some other superficiality, and then the patient takes the couch and begins talking where he deems appropriate and without my intervention. From time to time I may comment or question, but for the most part I am silent. (p. 116)

Although I don't use the couch as the structure, I too encourage my clients, especially in the early sessions, to speak freely about their lives while I, too, am mostly silent.

In this early recitation clients often need to examine their family relationships in depth. This can be quite a complicated task, especially in larger families, or where the tale crosses many generations. In such instances a genogram may furnish a useful structure as a way of picturing family relationships. Such an analysis may also flush out individual family roles, reveal covert family rules, and illuminate the patterned ways of relating that have made this most intimate *Mitwelt* a source of psychological disturbance. Notice that it is best not to employ it simply as a way of obtaining information about the client. Patterson (1974) correctly assesses the danger in such fact-finding interventions introduced to meet the therapist's need for knowledge:

> There are those who feel that if the counselor is to understand the client, he needs certain kinds of information about him, which should be obtained in the initial interview. But such an approach does two things: (a) it sets the structure of counseling as one in which the counselor leads and the client follows; and (b) it may lead to knowledge *about* or understanding *about* the client but not to an empathic understanding from the client's frame of reference. Such an approach meets the counselor's needs, such as the inability to tolerate ambiguity and the fear of an unstructured encounter, rather than being helpful to the client or to the progress of therapy. (p. 101)

In Chapter 3 we considered time from an existential perspective. Depending upon an emphasis on passing time or personal time, it becomes a reason for resignation or a call to resoluteness. In the former, family heritage becomes a demand to replicate the past even if it is unhealthy or at this moment inappropriate. Moreover, viewing family destiny as passing time places expectations upon the world to give to the destined his or her due.

Quite often clients have internalized their family heritage and destiny as personal fate. They must live according to an ancient script written by others, one to which they must faithfully adhere. Morality and values as expressed in education and religion, in choice of friends and selection of a life partner, in pursuit of a vocation and following of avocations seem predetermined. "We" can only act in certain ways; the world, moreover, should respond to us as programmed.

In such a scenario clients assume a reactive stance toward both family and world. Whether they rail against rigidity or complain about narrowness, they are caught within a relational system they had no part in fashioning. They carry within them ancestral voices outlining particular choices, criticizing performance, demanding compliance, and sternly judging disobedience. When their directions are dutifully followed they bestow only cautious praise, lest these descendants of theirs become self-sufficient and no longer pay them requisite obeisance.

As clients unfold the family *Mitwelt*, two interventions may prove helpful. By calling attention to these overidentified voices, those issuing a continual stream of directives and accusations, the therapist makes starkly evident the split between the self-directing adult and the trapped descendant. The litany of "shoulds" and "can'ts," the barrage of self-defeating statements, the dark flow of guilt-inducing judgments come from "the family." These internalized guardians of right order, whether recognizable individuals or behavioral composites, keep one's inner world divided and one's external relational world unsatisfying. At some point these voices must change in the name of happiness and health.

The second intervention begins this process by expanding those inner voices to include family voices not so easily heard. These call for personal responsibility within one's limited potentialities and urge their realization. They preach the integrity of living out of deeply held values in accordance with one's personal life vision. They speak up as the roles and rules, patterns of communication and critical decisions of one's family history are reviewed and reframed.

A personal example may be illustrative.

I grew up in a family loudly proclaiming respect for and obedience to all authority. My father, a superior court judge, embodied this voice in his personal, familial, and civic life. As the eldest, I strove to emulate him through taking on the role of "the perfect one": successful at school, well liked by classmates and teachers, either participating in sports or holding down a part-time job after school, active in the Boy Scouts and in my church. As the "Judge's Son" my behavior was expected to be above reproach: I was questioned about any conduct grade below an "A"; I remember only one youthful fist fight, which troubled me especially lest I be found out; "talking back" to one's parents merited immediate punishment. Be successful, compliant, obedient; respect authority and seek others' approval: this voice spoke constantly and strongly within me.

After graduation, I followed this voice's direction by entering the Society of Jesus. I exchanged my earthly father for a Heavenly one as I became one of the "Jesuit Fathers." In joining an order renowned for its unquestioning obedience, I was fulfilling my family destiny.

All went reasonably according to plan until we got embroiled in Vietnam. As our civic representatives demanded patriotic compliance with their martial wishes and our church leaders preached civic responsibility in God's name and our judges treated protesters as felons, I became increasingly troubled.

And I began to hear other, less familiar, family voices inside my head. Besides obedience, my father, a Democrat in a Republican town and a Catholic in the predominantly Protestant Pacific Northwest, lived independence. As a judge not swayed by public sentiment but rather guided by his own assessment of rectitude, he modeled integrity. In his prohibition against violence, his stern reaction to "talking back," and his settling of disputes generally without any display of anger, he stood for nonviolence. My mother's voice, too, started to move more centrally into my consciousness. It had all but disappeared due to her long illness and early death. Moreover, during my growing years her voice always sounded weak because of her submission to my father's rationality. But now I came to recognize new rules inside me, ones she hoped I'd live by: "whatever else, always be a *gentle man*"; "don't let pain override life"; "enjoy life" and "be creative."

Under the influence of my father's voices reframed and expanded, and the attention paid now to those of my mother, I too became a protester, to the dismay of *all* of my earthly fathers. Then one day I realized that all their controlling voices had left me. I could now only take responsibility for my own life.

So now I am married. I am also a pacifist. I remain grateful to this day for my family heritage. I no longer feel trapped by its rigidity or angry at its repression because in its complete chorus I hear one harmonious voice over all: "Stand for what you believe."

Clients act out their family roles in the therapist's office. "Nice boys" strive to please while "rebels" challenge everything, "vanishing ones" wait passively for direction, "cheerleaders" put up a good front no matter what while "martyrs" nicely complain and "victims" search out new ways of being rejected.

Although this engagement phase does not allow for more than gentle confrontation, therapists may counter dysfunctional role patterns in two ways.

First off, they may refuse to relate to given rules as definitive of the person before them. When, for example, the "baby" seeks the adult's advice about changing jobs, instead of offering any opinion, they may suggest that the client list known advantages and disadvantages of possible options. This recognizes the person's ability both to generate alternatives and to weigh their relative merits. Or when the "controller" persists in asking questions or requesting explanations that create distance between client and therapist, a decision not to respond will firmly, if quietly, reject this defensive ploy. And should the "victim" insist on cataloguing others' cruel actions, reflections on the client's strength under such adversity kindly rejects the helpless role. Indeed, for victims especially "it is crucial . . . [they] feel at ease and confident with their own basic positive qualities and abilities before they can start questioning the negative counterparts" (Van Deurzen-Smith, 1991, p. 131), like their dysfunctional stance as a permanent victim.

One may also gently challenge these unhealthy patterns by noting incongruencies in clients' self-presentation. When the "pleaser" smiles through tears or laughs dismissingly while recounting a painful event, an unsmiling therapist may simply reflect that he or she seems to be missing the humor in the account. Or when the "tough guy" chokes back tears as he announces his wife's filing for divorce, the therapist may note this controlling attempt when an emotional expression would be both appropriate and expected. Should the "rationalist" clearly present a vexing problem and its reasonable solution, a recognition of how confusing this must be for someone to be so clear and yet so helpless will call into question this unfeeling way of organizing one's life.

Always, therapists must relate out of a stance of shared interdependency. This means responding to clients not because of their expectations or demands or role patterning, but because the response authentically represents one's self at the moment.

In closing this section on engagement, it may be good to think back for a moment to the story that introduced this chapter. Of the two strangers, one was successful in helping the foolish people. Right off he accepted the helpless role they had assumed as real. He did not confront their self-defeating stance before they could assimilate his feedback; in fact, he went along with it by joining them in strict avoidance of the monster's field. He went into their town and lived in their houses, which emphasized the townspeople's worth and gave them a chance to exercise their talents at hospitality. He also taught them what he knew, which underlined their ability to change and grow. All the while he patiently bided his time. While he waited for the right moment to confront their monster directly, he quietly challenged their destiny as helpless victims at the mercy of such monsters. Why did he stay with them?—because he found his life to be rewarding and exciting as a Watermelon Hunter. He would have made a good therapist!

CONFRONTATION

The Real Relationship At some juncture both parties recognize and accept their involvement in a mutual endeavor. Both by then have firmly committed themselves to furthering the client's growth no matter how arduous the task. The relationship feels solid; it also seems more capable of sustaining directness and confrontation.

For the therapist this allows an increased emphasis on congruence, on genuinely sharing ongoing reactions to the client's self-presentation. Where previously direct contact would only have resulted in mobilizing childish defenses, now, at least, clients will attempt to deal with the fear such contact generates. For example, this bit of dialogue between myself and a fifty-year-old woman client struggling with her dependent personality could not have happened in the engagement phase of therapy:

Client: It was a horrible two weeks. I felt so abandoned and scared. My doctor was out of town; I didn't know whether to take the medicine for my bladder or the Xanax the psychiatrist prescribed, as I couldn't take both. And you too were away on vacation.

Therapist: And that was lousy!

Client: Well, I can't blame you for taking a break. You needed it.

Therapist: Dorothy, you're so nice! You drive me nuts! I'd be delighted if you just shouted at me, told me how angry you were to be left, told me how much you depend on me yet really can't trust I'll be there when you need me.

Client: Well, I did think a lot like that.

Therapist: But you didn't say that to me directly.

Client: No. . . .

Therapist: I'd be so bored living with you if you were so nice all the time. I know the "nice mask" already; there would be little to learn about you.
Client: You would! I've always thought that being nice is how you make people like you.
Therapist: Not me.
Client: Well . . . that's good to know . . . I guess.

Dorothy was trapped in a most unsatisfying marital relationship. She needed desperately either to divorce her emotionally abusive husband legally or, at the very least, to do so psychologically. Either way she would have to say "no" to him. This would require that she be able to bear both his anger and her own lack of niceness. As her self esteem depended upon others' acceptance of her, any unpleasantness, or even a small show of differentiation, made her quite uncomfortable. She had never been in an adult relationship in which difference and separation did not mean rejection.

For her to share her anger over my absence when she was desperate for my help, or for her to feel my exasperation with her, called up all her fears of abandonment and feelings of low self worth. Yet she needed to experience a mature relationship that allows anger and lives on healthy differentiation. In interactions such as this one she came to realize that anger and disagreement in themselves do not lead to a broken relationship. On the contrary, in the willingness to work through hard moments together they prove to be a potent way of building a lasting one. I judged in this session that our relationship was sound enough for her to deal with these negative feelings without calling our relationship into serious question.

Sometimes such genuineness can be quite difficult for the therapist too. Yet trust in oneself and in the strength of the relational bond can lead to growth for both client and therapist.

Billie, a 35-year-old mother of two preschool-aged boys, came into therapy because she was troubled over how she was frequently turning on them in anger. She seemed unable to control herself. This particularly disturbed her as she thought of herself as a fervent Christian.

As the problem unfolded it became clear that she was especially upset because these outbursts confronted her with personal imperfection. She should be perfect, which meant being always under rational control. This had been impressed upon her by her father, a fundamentalist preacher, who made his love conditional upon being blameless in his eyes. And she had married a man just like her Dad!

One day, well into this phase of therapy, at the end of a particularly intense session, she gave me a warm hug before leaving. In itself this spontaneous show of affection and appreciation was not unusual. What surprised me, however, was the sexual arousal it immediately generated in me, as this had never previously occurred. During the ensuing week I thought some about this reaction and decided to share this experience of mine with her at the beginning of our next session.

I did so . . . with some tinges of embarrassment. I told her I felt it incumbent upon me to share this, especially lest she had felt my excitement and it had disturbed her. Besides, I did not want this kind of secret between us. In return, she expressed some surprise that I had responded so strongly to her hug, especially as she had experienced no such reaction herself nor had she sensed mine.

We spent the entire hour discussing this incident. Billie realized anew how firm a lock she had on her feelings, not allowing any passion into her life. For her, life revolved around work and duty. She seldom played. Happiness, a kind of satisfaction rather than joy, resulted from a job well done.

She marveled most, however, that I had been willing to share with her this sexual reaction. In her world neither she nor I should have such feelings: they would be inappropriate and would manifest a lack of control. As such, they should be hidden, for revealed they could only earn disapproval and a withholding of love. But here and now she was reacting just the opposite to me after this revelation. She thanked me for sharing my experience and she expressed gratitude that I had not acted on those sexual urges. In fact, one reason she kept her own feelings so tightly controlled was because she presumed that if released they could only lead to unacceptable extremes. Finally, she commented how she even trusted me more now because she knew directly how genuine and non-self-serving my love for her was.

A therapist's self-revelation becomes increasingly part of the developing real relationship. This is necessary, as Yalom (1980) suggests, because

> a therapist who is to know a patient must do more than observe and listen; he or she must fully experience the patient. But full experience of the other requires that one

> open oneself up to the other; if one engages the other in an open and honest fashion, one experiences the other as the other is responding to that engagement.
>
> There is no way around the conclusion that the therapist who is to relate to the patient must disclose himself or herself as a person. (p. 411)

Traditionally, such person-to-person meeting was prohibited in the name of protecting the transference. The therapist should function as a "blank screen," a person *not* in relationship, so that the feelings and reactions toward the therapist might be seen in their uncontaminated state as transferential projections. However, as Rogers (1987) remarked, some of these feelings "are an understandable response to some of the attitudes and behaviors of the therapist" (p. 182). These attitudes manifest themselves throughout the whole therapeutic situation, nonverbally as well as verbally. The blank screen relationship is, indeed, a myth.

Existential psychotherapists do not question whether therapists should be self-disclosing. They ask rather when should this occur and how much should be shared.

Many years ago, at an early stage of an encounter group I was co-leading with him, Carl Rogers shared with the participants some personal facts about his life. They generated nothing in response. During a break, as we were reviewing the group's dynamics, he bemoaned that decision:

> I did that because nothing was happening and I thought by opening up I could induce others to follow suit. When I do that, it *never* works.

He taught me that day that self-disclosure must come from a genuine desire to share oneself with a client; it must not be a tactic to get something from another; it finally must be part of a real relationship and in the context of an active therapeutic alliance.

In a study relating therapists' self-disclosure to client perceptions of therapists' empathy, competence, and unconditional acceptance, Curtis (1981) concluded that

> findings confirmed the initial prediction: the greater the use of therapist's self-disclosure, the lower the subjects' impressions and evaluations of the therapist's empathy, compe-

> tence, and trust. The results raise doubt regarding the predictability of therapist's self-disclosure as a psychotherapeutic technique and suggest that, at least with respect to the type of self-disclosure used in this study, therapists who utilize self-disclosing techniques may risk adversely affecting essential impressions on which a therapeutic alliance is established. (p. 127)

Note Curtis' repetition of "self-disclosing *techniques*" and the negative effect such techniques may have on establishing a therapeutic alliance.

Curtis here simply reaffirms Rogers' reflection on his unsuccessful essay at self-disclosure. It occurred before the alliance was functioning and it was used as a technique to make that alliance happen. That does not work.

Yalom (1980) suggested this guideline for how self-revelation is appropriate in therapy:

> It is important to keep in mind the overriding goal—authentic relationship. One of the outstanding characteristics of "psychotherapeutic eros" is the care for the other's becoming. Rollo May suggests the Greek term *agape* or the Latin *caritas*—a love that is devoted to the welfare of the other. What is important, then, is that therapist self-disclosure be in the service of the growth of the patient. (p. 414)

Therapists do not speak about themselves out of some narcissistic need; they do so rather in the context of helping the client grow in and through the therapeutic encounter. Whatever one shares must serve that purpose. Moreover, this sharing depends upon the developed state of the relationship as to the content and the personal nature of the revelation.

Self-disclosure and confrontation do place a sometimes testing requirement on the therapist. Genuineness does not come easily especially when through vulnerability change occurs in *both* people. However, without it, and without the risk of meeting, psychotherapy becomes a waiting game played out between boredom and the healing power of time. Kottler (1990) makes this rather scathing observation about the process of psychotherapy directed by the "safe therapist":

> Therapists who play it safe in their work may remain basically satisfied with their moderate gains. They will do

> just enough to get the job done, but not enough to ever produce dramatic results. Under the excuse of protecting their client's welfare, they will avoid confrontation and conflict, preferring instead to move at a pace consistent with the client's own tolerance for boredom. They will wait and wait, knowing that waiting has its therapeutic value, and that most clients will get better on their own or in spite of what we do. They will say only what they have said before. They will do only what has been tried before. Any departure from the formula must be preceded by a consultation of the works of their favorite authority. (p. 89)

The Therapeutic Alliance DeBerry (1987) maintains that psychotherapy depends upon two necessary factors, the relationship and an expressed end or focus. The therapeutic alliance, "the sufficient factor for the occurrence of psychotherapy . . . reflects the particular combination of the necessary factors, viz., the *relationship* and *focus*" (p. 236). As Johnson and Greenberg (1989) note, this alliance arises "from the interaction between client and therapist; rather than being a therapist or client factor, it is an interactional product" (p. 98). A successful therapy process manages both factors without overemphasizing or underemphasizing either one.

In this second phase of therapy the alliance expresses itself differently in both factors. A shift from an emphasis on *Mitwelt* to *Eigenwelt* characterizes this change.

Van Deurzen-Smith (1991) describes *Eigenwelt* as follows:

> This private world is the land of intimacy. It includes intimacy with self as well as intimacy with others. It is the home world: the place where you feel at ease with yourself, because you feel surrounded by familiarity and kinship. The private world is the world of the I and the We. It encompasses everything that is felt to be part of oneself. (p. 87)

Clients now feel reasonably safe in the relationship and they look to the therapist as an active collaborator in their struggle for enhanced life. As they recognize some changes in themselves through this collaboration, the relationship becomes more valuable and more real. With this realization feelings in and about the relationship begin to develop in them and are sometimes hesitantly expressed.

In speaking about a person's self-presentation in stage four of his process scale of growth, Rogers (1961) reports that "Occasionally feelings are expressed as in the present, sometimes breaking through almost against the patient's wishes," and that "Though a closer relationship still seems dangerous, the client risks himself, relating to some extent on a feeling basis." Moreover, "There is a tendency toward experiencing feelings in the immediate present, and there is distrust and fear of this possibility" (pp. 137–138). Clients in the confrontation phase of therapy hesitantly dare to be themselves in relating to their therapist.

A woman in her late forties sought my assistance because of a generally unfulfilling marriage. Its emotional distance had propelled her into a troubling emotional affair with a younger man, himself in a suffocating marital relationship. She idealized their newfound love as "God given." But how might she square this "sacred" relationship with her desires either to leave her marriage and disrupt her home or to move into a sexually active, adulterous relationship?

Over some months Geri tussled with this dilemma, examining now the two relationships, exploring now her own moral values. On a practical level it resolved itself when her lover, Andy, started an intense affair with one of her dear friends. Many therapy hours dealt with her bewilderment, searing hurt, and feelings of rejection. She also searched deep within herself for the causes of the addiction that had so blinded her to the truth about his narcissistic love.

During these months I determined to relate to her as intimately as I could, so as not to replicate the abandonment she experienced with Andy and the distancing she endured from her husband. At the same time, I had to avoid any kind of symbiotic bond such as had fueled her addiction and was still causing her much distress. I could, of course, only express this intimacy as she was able to receive it as a love I have described as that of shared interdependency.

One day she entered my office quite upset by a new turn of events. The dilemma had resurfaced because of a possible meeting with Andy:

Client: My friend, Mary, called me yesterday. She announced, "I'm setting up a luncheon meeting for you, Andy, and me." I was *really* shocked! I told her that I wasn't seeing him any more, that it wasn't good for me. She said that she was sorry; she really didn't know. He seemed so down; she thought our being with him might help.

(Long pause) I feel so torn. I still love him yet I don't want to feel that heavy weight, that addiction in my chest again.

(Another pause) Do you think that I could see him without that happening?

Therapist: When you first mentioned the luncheon, I felt anger and fear . . . and I still do. I'm angry when I imagine you going back into a relationship with Andy, one that holds every possibility of bringing you intense pain, right at your core. . . . What do I fear? I shudder at the thought of you again losing yourself, of Andy once again taking over the center of you. I still experience that core of you as a barely healed scar, so vulnerable and so easily broken.

Client: (Silent tears. Finally looking up at me) I . . . love you, Bob.

Therapist: And I love you.

Client: (Long pause) I realize I've transferred on to you lots of the feelings I had for Andy. But that's O.K. I'm coming back to myself.

Geri began by describing a past conversation with Mary, much as a person might in the engagement phase of therapy. Then she reflected upon her present "torn" state and her ongoing love for Andy. This led her to a direct request for my opinion about her reopening the relationship. Instead of giving some abstract response, I shared with her my immediate feelings and my present experience of her. This allowed her to express her love for me, but she straightaway had to attribute this to "transference." She could not, at this juncture, allow her warm feelings for me simply to stand on their own. In these direct yet hesitant dealings with me in the present moment, Geri gives a clear presentation of the therapeutic relationship as it is joined by the client in this phase of therapy.

I did not challenge Geri's disowning of her love for me. At this point in therapy clients routinely find some protection against immediacy by psychologizing away their feelings. After all, attributing anger or love, possessiveness or dependency to transference protects both client and therapist from having to cope with the present reality of these factors in their relationship. I agree with Rogers (May, 1987) when he asserts that

> there is absolutely no need to make a special case of attitudes that are transferred to the therapist, and no need for the therapist to permit the dependence that is so often part of other forms of therapy, especially psychoanalysis. It is entirely possible to accept dependent feelings without permitting the client to change the therapist's role. (p. 184)

I just recognized that she still found it difficult to be present and vulnerable to herself and to me.

When Geri began therapy, she placed her concern, as most clients do, outside herself. She wanted either to figure out how to change her marital relationship or to come to a firm decision about how she would relate to Andy. As she grew to trust the healing potential of our relationship, she shifted her focus more to herself, to her own sexual values, to her tendency to equate her self worth with pouring herself out indiscriminately on behalf of others. Gradually she became at least as concerned about her co-dependent need to help others as about her unfulfilling male relationships. She looked at the "saving" behaviors in her family, explored how she interpreted her Christian faith to be consistent with them, and came to realize how crucial a role others' opinions of her took in her positive self-assessment. In Deurzen-Smith's words, she shifted her focus from the *Mitwelt* of her structural relationships with her husband and Andy to her *Eigenwelt*, her own private inner world.

This new focus upon self-exploration matches Rogers' (1961) observation that for clients in his stage four of therapy

> there are some discoveries of personal constructs; there is a definite recognition of these as constructs; and there is a beginning questioning of their validity. (p. 138)

Internal divisions between a positive and negative self worth, a strong adult and a dependent child, solidity and emptiness, these and other such splits in one's sense of oneself gradually become as critical to understand and to heal as troubling breaks in relationships with others. This means differentiating the constructs one has accepted as self-defining (for example, "My self worth depends upon me helping others") from feelings

("When I am urged to help others, I feel both satisfaction and irritation") and personal meanings ("I value the opportunity to spend some time each day visiting my invalid aunt"). As this happens, as each is identified with increasing exactitude, one's inner world becomes more known, decisions may be made concerning what one values there, and being with oneself grows into the possibility of truly being at home.

Therapeutic Interventions In her study on *The Existentialist Approach to Psychotherapy with Adults and Children,* Hanna Colm (1966) stresses a conviction close to the existentialist's heart:

> Healing does not result merely from greater *knowledge* of oneself but from *experiencing* oneself (as one *is*) in relation to another person and in the struggle toward mutual acceptance in spite of the humanness one finds in oneself and in one's partner. (p. 208)

This echoes Tillich's (1969) assertion that

> only in the continuous encounter with other persons does the person become and remain a person. The place of this encounter is the community. (p. 91)

One potentially powerful "community" is the therapeutic relationship.

Therapists may stimulate the experiencing of oneself in relationship and facilitate a direct encounter through reflecting with clients on what is currently transpiring between them. Superficial and defensive communication tends to highlight events other than those occurring at this place and in this moment. Trust in oneself and in relationships grow through meeting . . . here . . . now.

A woman with schizoid tendencies linked with a desperate fear of others' negative judgments was speaking to me; all the while, however, she was gazing fixedly at a point on the wall to my right. In the midst of her monologue, I turned and looked in that direction:

Client: What are you doing?
Therapist: I'm trying to find out what is so interesting to you over there.

Client: Why?
Therapist: Because you keep looking there and not at me. I'm losing out to something! You obviously don't wish to give your attention to me.
Client: I don't like people.
Therapist: Oh, I'm sorry. I've been under the impression that you liked me.
Client: I don't mean you! I mean . . . well, I don't trust you . . . you're so much smarter than I am.
Therapist: You're afraid I'll judge you.
Client: Yes.

A few sessions later she was complaining about a problem at home. This time she was facing me directly:

Therapist: Excuse me . . . I like this.
Client: What?
Therapist: You're talking right to *me*. You used to look everywhere else, especially over there. Remember?
Client: I trust you more. I feel pretty safe here.
Therapist: You're not sitting here worrying that I'll judge you.
Client: No.

Sometimes clients tend to discount the value of their relationship in therapy. But concern with immediacy,

> the current interaction of the therapist and client in the relationship . . . is significant because the client's behavior and functioning in the therapeutic relationship are indicative of his functioning in other interpersonal relationships. (Patterson, 1974, p. 83)

Moreover, healthy relating in this relationship may be generalized to other relationships. A typical dialogue runs like this:

Client: I don't have any friends.
Therapist: I find that disappointing.
Client: Why?
Therapist: I feel very friendly toward you and I have been understanding from you that you know that.
Client: I wasn't talking about you and me.
Therapist: This relationship doesn't count.

Client: You *have* to be friendly.
Therapist: You think I don't really care about you, that I'm just putting on an act because you're paying me.
Client: No . . . I know you like me. I just get so discouraged. I forget that I *can* relate openly and deeply with another. I do with you.
Therapist: Yes, you do. Like right now.

Obviously, as Patterson (1974) rightly asserts,

> while the relationship at every moment can be examined in terms of its immediacy, it is not always appropriate to respond to this, and it is, of course, impossible for the therapist to focus continuously on the immediacy of the relationship. (p. 85)

That said, in this phase of therapy this kind of immediate focus on our relationship carries great healing, learning, and growth potential.

As clients shift their focus inward, as previously noted they become concerned to identify conceptually how they experience themselves. This enterprise, sometimes an unfamiliar and confusing one, often requires expert assistance. Therapists will help most when they make the vague thoughts or feelings clear, when they push for concrete and specific verbalizations about the inner world. This type of clarifying intervention holds the promise of moving clients from rather obscure, tentative experiencing to direct action.

Marjorie, a recently married 22-year-old secretary, was caught in a dilemma. She was two months pregnant with their first child but she loved another man. When she married Jim, she did so only because David, the preferred man in her life, was engaged to someone else. Recently David had broken that engagement, they had spoken, the old love still burned fiercely. To make it worse, Jim had been spending long hours at the machine shop where he worked and seemed at day's end to enjoy the camaraderie of the guys rather than coming home to spend the remaining evening hours with her. By the time he arrived home she was ready for bed, so they had little time simply to talk with each other except on the weekends.

The mixture of loneliness and slow-burning anger, yearning for a lost love and guilt over these forbidden wishes had her paralyzed. How could she begin to address her internal confusion and tearing ambivalence? In abbreviated form, at one point in the session we entered into this dialogue:

Therapist: I think I may be able to help you get a little clarity about this. Besides being a therapist, I'm a magician, you know. Would you like to visit my magic shop?

Client: You are! Well, sure.

Therapist: Come in, come in. See my bottles . . . shelves and shelves full. Big ones, colored ones, shapely ones, lovely ones. They are filled with anything you may possibly want. Now, I hear you have a current problem relating to two men. Perhaps I could give you a precious bottle of some elixir that could resolve that problem for you. What will it be?

Client: I don't know. Let's see . . . how about a bottle of decisiveness?

Therapist: Fine, fine! A big one or a small one?

Client: Oh, a big one!

Therapist: Certainly. Now, for it to work you will have to drink it all. That means you'll have to make room for it inside you. What will you give me in return that will do that?

Client: Well, I could give you all my indecisiveness.

Therapist: Of course. That would be excellent. This means you will have to be very decisive this week with either Jim or David. If you aren't, it will dry up and you'll be worse off than before.

Client: Oh, I see. I better not take it then. I know . . . I'd like a little pink bottle of courage and I'll give you some of my cowardice in return. I'll use it to tell Jim how lonely I am, that I need him to spend some time during the week with me.

Therapist: Fine. It's a deal. Remember, you use it or you lose it. I'll check next week. Thanks for your visit.

Client: You're welcome. Glad to meet you.

In speaking afterwards about this encounter, Marjorie commented, "Gosh, this is hard. I'm not used to thinking deeply about myself."

Oftentimes, this movement inward in search of understanding and clarity must be set in a framework that gives firm direction because of the unfamiliarity of the endeavor. Then too, this support must lead clients to enlist capabilities other than their intellect. Most people in therapy employ their rational powers adequately but confusion and ambivalence still reign. They need to enlist other powers, like those of intuition or imagination or bodily sensing, in order to escape the intellect's ineffectual dominance and the confusion it is currently courting.

This interaction with Marjorie demonstrates how imaginative role playing might be used to clarify one's inner state. Chapters 7 and 8 will offer abundant examples of other such creative interventions: guided imagery, working with dreams, psychodrama, and meditative exercises, among others. In the present context, all of these interventions have the potential to create an internal focus. With their assistance clients may cut through intellectual confusion, confront ambivalence, and release the powerful healing power of images to overcome inner divisions.

EXPANSION

James Bugental (1965) divides his theory of Existential-Analytic Therapy into three distinct phases: analytic, ontogogic, and transcendent. The analytic (psychotherapy) "may be thought of as concerned with the removal of limitations on functioning with the intent of freeing the person for more satisfying psychological life." The second, the ontogogic phase, "is concerned with aiding a person to actualize or make real more of his potential once the grosser handicapping effects of his emotional disruption have been overcome." The final, the transcendent one, he suggests, "is one at which the person would move through and beyond many of the limitations on awareness and experience that are generally taken for granted and would then realize new oneness with all being" (p. 61). In describing this third phase of existential psychotherapy as a phase of "expansion," a therapy that is primarily an interpersonal therapy with Rogers' client-centered therapy, Satir's systemic view of interpersonal communication, and spirituality in its background, I intend to signify that during this phase experiences may occur that would fit under all three of Bugental's phases.

The Real Relationship For therapists congruence still predominates. It expresses itself, however, with much more spontaneity than previously. This happens for three reasons. Clients now do much more of their own inner exploring. They require less empathic assistance to catch the flow of their inner experiencing. This leaves stretches of silence in which therapists may more closely monitor the continual movement of their reactions to their clients' presence. Because these reactions are recognized less consideration needs to be given to the relative appropriateness of expressing them. Clients can listen to, reject, or integrate their therapist's feedback much more readily than before and with small possibility either of being unduly influenced or of distancing themselves from the relationship.

Because of this relative freedom to relate spontaneously and immediately and because of an increased ability to attend to oneself, the therapist's dual focus tends to alter ordinary awareness, first in the therapist, but through the quality of the therapist's responses, occasionally in the client as well. The relationship itself, the intersubjectivity, rather than the existence of the two individuals, becomes central to consciousness. For some periods it may so overshadow the separate reality of the two people that either or both may lose track of their ordinary perceptions of time or space. Their experience may approximate that described in Chapter 5 as one of contemplative incorporation. I believe this touches upon the description of unity in therapy described by Rogers (1961) in *On Becoming a Person*:

> The essence of some of the deepest parts of therapy seems to be a unity of experiencing. The client is freely able to experience his feeling in its complete intensity, as a "pure culture," without intellectual inhibition or cautions, without having it bounded by knowledge of contradictory feelings; and I am able with equal freedom to experience my understanding of this feeling, without any conscious thought about it, without any apprehension or concern as to where this will lead, without any type of diagnostic or analytic thinking, without any cognitive or emotional barriers to a complete "letting go" in understanding. When there is this complete unity, singleness, fullness of experiencing in the relationship, then it acquires the "out-of-this-world" quality which many therapists have remarked upon, a sort of trance-like feeling in the relationship from which both the client and I emerge at the end of the hour, as if from a

> deep well or tunnel. In these moments there is, to borrow Buber's phrase, a real "I–Thou" relationship, a timeless living in the experience which is *between* the client and me. It is at the opposite pole from seeing the client or myself, as an object. It is the height of personal subjectivity. (p. 202)

Or, as I would prefer to stress, "intersubjectivity."

In these times, intuition and imagination tend to have greater freedom of entrance into consciousness. A sudden disconnected thought may occur, a weird image appear, or a sudden impulse emerge to sing a song or tell a story or relate some personal experience. There may or may not seem to be some immediately recognizable referent in the client's world: that does not appear to matter. These have more of a quality of play or inspiration than of any linear thinking. These may come, indeed, earlier in therapy, as with my playful inspiration to escort Marjorie to a magic shop, but they surface less frequently then and are acted upon less readily.

Barbara, a young woman in the process of divorcing her husband, seemed particularly tense one session. She could offer no clear reason for her state. Something about her triggered in me the recurring thought that I should tell her a Pueblo Indian tale I had recently heard about a wild woman. So I did.

It recounts how an old Indian warrior spent his last days collecting the bones of animals that had died out in the desert. He would bring them to his cave dwelling and in the evenings attempt to reassemble the skeletons.

One day he came upon the bones of a large wolf, an unusual creature in those parts. Over a period of days he meticulously searched the area till he finally found the last bone, part of the wolf's foot. That night, while chanting a prayer, he put this last bone in place and then stepped back.

Before his eyes the bones slowly came together, flesh grew on them, until a wolf with golden-gray fur sprang up in the firelight and faced him. Then suddenly, as he continued singing, it metamorphosed into a strong, lovely woman, naked except for her flowing golden-gray hair. She smiled at him, laughed aloud, and then ran off into the dark night.

When I finished recounting the story, I asked Barbara where in her body the tension lay. Perhaps she could find the "missing bone," the key to *her* happiness. She closed her eyes and explored silently. Finally, she indicated her abdomen and especially her sexual organs. I wondered aloud what they might say, what they needed to express for her tension to subside. She did not know at the moment but on departing she said she would try to find out during the week.

Some minutes into our next session Barbara handed me a long letter, the words her vagina needed to say. She asked me to read it, silently. As I did she wandered restlessly about my office, till she finally settled down on the floor next to my chair. She took my hand, squeezed it roughly, or held it gently, as I slowly absorbed *this* story. Upon finishing, I could only say, "thank you." It undoubtedly is the most honest, most revealing, most passionate personal statement anyone has ever shared with me in therapy. After some minutes of silence, still letting her emotions out through clutching my hand, she smiled and thanked me. "I know you are not afraid of the wild woman in me. I'm grateful."

I gave her back the letter. She offered to make me a copy. I said, "No, it's your statement, not mine. You alone need to have and to heed the words of your life. But thank you, deeply, for your trust."

In the later stages of his growth process in therapy, Rogers (1961) points out that "Feelings are expressed freely as in the present" (Stage Five, p. 139), and "A feeling which has previously been 'stuck,' has been inhibited in its process quality, is experienced with immediacy now" (Stage Six, p. 145). He also notes that "There is an increasing ownership of [these] self feelings, and a desire to be these, to be the 'real me'" (Stage Five, p. 141).

Barbara was divorcing her husband because he lacked passion and because he found her emotional life too overwhelming for him. She had lived for years with this deep pain of rejection and with her own guilt about being "too much." She needed desperately to say to herself and to have someone accept the wild, passionate side of her being. In bits and pieces she had tried earlier in therapy, but she really did not know how to do so in that setting. Besides it proved consistently to be too frightening. With the inspiration of the "wild woman" she confronted that fear; through the voice of her vagina she found the vehicle to express the passion of her life.

A growing equality between therapist and client becomes also pronounced during this phase. It manifests itself, especially, in the client's disagreeing with and directly confronting the therapist. Such genuineness flows out of an increased self esteem, a lessened sense of dependency upon the therapist, and an established trust in their mutual commitment to the therapeutic process. This bit of dialogue between a client and me may illustrate this.

As she was beginning the termination process, I had mailed her a flier about a women's group starting up at our agency. I had commented on it that I thought it might be helpful to ease the transition time from now to the end of our work together:

Client: I received the notice of the group and your note saying I might like to join it. I'm troubled because we haven't talked about this previously. I wonder what it means about us.

Therapist: You wonder if I'm indicating some desire to change our relationship.

Client: Yes . . . maybe . . . I guess it's just me. But this is the anniversary of my heart operation, I'm in a new internship, and I'm getting ready to move.

Therapist: In the midst of all these separations, here I am suggesting another one, just when you need stability here at least.

Client: Yes, that's why I'm upset.

Therapist: I'm sorry. I have no intention of changing, or any desire to cease our relationship. I just wasn't sufficiently sensitive proposing it to you now. If I had been more in your shoes, I'd have realized how you might take this proposal, especially coming out of the blue.

Client: Bob . . . thanks for your love. I love you a lot, you know.

Therapist: I do. Thank you.

The Therapeutic Alliance In the Confrontation phase, clients tended to focus upon their inner world, the *Eigenwelt*, and the experience of "I" and "We." This continues into this Expansion phase but with the addition of what Van Deurzen-Smith (1991) designates as the concerns of the *Uberwelt* or "over-world":

> the ideal world with its spiritual dimension of beliefs and aspirations where the person is likely to refer to values beyond herself. (p. 68)

As clients continue to address their inner world, they become clearer and more exact in their recognition of what is occurring there. Among all the factors Rogers (1961) identifies in the later stages of therapy, I find the following aspects of his Stage Five most usually present here:

> There is a strong tendency toward exactness in differentiation of feelings and meanings.
>
> There is an increasingly clear facing of contradictions and incongruencies in experience.
>
> There is an increasing quality of acceptance of self responsibility for the problems being faced, and a concern as to how he has contributed. (p. 142)

Much of the earlier confusion has dissipated. In the resulting clarity internal divisions stand starkly revealed. Where they were previously blamed on others, clients now generally look to understand their part in causing and maintaining them. For the most part they can do nothing about their past experiences, nor does it help them to keep focusing on the negative impact particular people have had and continue to have on their sense of themselves. They want to identify, instead, how secondary rewards flow from their divided sense of self, and they seek to substitute healthier ways of getting what they need to sustain a reasonably healthy life.

This ongoing struggle to be responsible for one's own life takes much effort and does not readily assure success. As Yalom (1989) from his experience with his patients remarks,

> it is extraordinarily hard, even terrifying, to own the insight that you and only you can construct your own life design. Thus, the problem in therapy is always how to move from an ineffectual intellectual appreciation of a truth about oneself to some emotional *experience* of it. It is only when therapy enlists deep emotions that it becomes a powerful force for change. (p. 35)

The account of Barbara's battle over accepting the passionate, nonrational side of her being vividly concretizes Yalom's universal observation.

Some of the divisions highlighted, however, stem not from personal actions but from the human condition. As limited beings participating in a material existence, we humans face the inevitable diminishing processes of illness and death. This confronts us with the necessary separation someday from all those we love and the life we cherish, and it forces upon us the specter of loneliness and the sword of meaninglessness. Does human existence after all have any purpose to it? As we considered in this book's first section, some existentialists would respond in the negative, others would say its only purpose lies in living one's life with an integrity that includes one's destiny with death, others would assert that a positive answer may be found only in the realm of the spirit. Whatever answer one finds most compatible, according to the whole spectrum of existentialist thinkers our responsibility to life is served most deeply by expanding the limited possibilities of our existence even in the shadow of this basic uncertainty about the ultimate worth of all our efforts.

Yalom (1980) shaped his work on *Existential Psychotherapy* around this quartet of Death and Isolation, Freedom and Meaninglessness, as well as the existential anxieties that they generate. Bugental (1965) put these "existential neuroses" at the core of his ontogogic phase of therapy. As my clients take up the task of examining their life values and purposes, as they clarify their personal ideals and attempt to make choices consistent with them, these human realities step forward out of their accustomed background. Individual problems, personal ways of construing and living one's inner life fade before the impact of these universal truths. Not all clients address them explicitly; indeed, not every client moves into and through this phase of therapy before terminating the process. But with a growing emotional maturity and increased sensitivity to one's own life sooner or later they must be reckoned with.

As these facts about human existence cannot be dispensed with, the anxiety they leak into our lives can only be recognized, accepted, and integrated. Since clients do not experientially know the process of their final march toward death, and since they cannot by reason alone determine life's final meaning or explain away their ultimate aloneness, they must turn away from intellectual analysis in this integrative effort. Increasingly, they call upon the powers of their *other* cerebral hemisphere, the seat of their imagination and intuition, those guardians of the entrance to nonmaterial reality. Perhaps by advancing through their portals the human spirit may give direction and hope without at the same time discounting the material inevitabilities of their human experience.

Therapeutic Interventions If confrontation aims "to bring to awareness the presence of cognitive dissonance or incongruence in the client's feelings, attitude, beliefs, or behavior" (Patterson, 1974, p. 76), such interventions markedly diminish in this phase of therapy. Clients more readily confront themselves and challenge themselves to grow. In this enterprise they require support and facilitative structures that may aid this self-exploration.

The interventions associated with previous phases still have their function because therapy seldom moves in a linear progression. Rather, it ebbs and flows. The same pesky issues tend to crop up, old fears and anxieties revisit, the internal chorus of negative voices have a lifetime of practice and accept silencing most grudgingly. In this sense therapy could be dubbed "cyclotherapy" (Yalom, 1989, p. 115), yet the handling of these recurrent struggles takes progressively diminishing time and energy. Client and therapist may feel like they are going round and round, the former revisiting old ground, the latter having similar reactions and repeating familiar responses, but as with a cone both now move more swiftly toward the point.

As clients resolve interpersonal issues or at least find satisfactory ways to live with them, and as they become more at home within themselves, room opens up for more general life concerns. Therapists need to be alert to, and call attention to, emerging questions about the human condition. They often get triggered by thoughts about terminating therapy. The sense of impending loss may generate feelings of anxiety about being alone and may occasion questions about the ultimate purpose of all their mutual efforts.

Traditionally, psychotherapists have most often chosen to avoid tackling such concerns, leaving them more to the religious domain. One may speculate about the reasons for this nonattention to the anxieties connected with human existence: suffice it to point out that a secularized civilization that has crowned the material sciences king feels generally ill-at-ease facing that king's eventual demise.

With the emergence of these existential issues and their attendant anxieties, clients often express dismay. After all their work, they *still* are not happy. Two specific interventions may help at this juncture.

Therapists would do well, first, to reframe this anxiety as not only normal but even a sign of psychological maturity. Any sensitive and self-reflective adult concerned with personal growth will run into the inbuilt limitations of human existence. The insensitive may never approach these boundaries; the immature usually choose to avoid them by emphasizing the present and the everlasting search to procure immediate gratification. Their surfacing at this time signals both an increased self-presence and a willingness to face reality.

Patterson (1974) stresses this fact:

> *The condition for self-actualizing persons is an environment of self-actualizing persons.* The therapist, then, must be a self-actualizing person. (pp. 92–93)

As a corollary to that sobering requirement, in the present context I would suggest that only a mature therapist, one who confronts personally the existential realities of human existence and who accepts the attendant anxiety, will take this phase of the existential journey with clients. They need to know that their therapists experience the same anxieties and harbor the same concerns. They will profit especially from understanding how another human being finds happiness and peace in the midst of it all.

In Chapter 4 we discussed the existential concept of "joy." It does not equate with pleasure or the absence of pain. It rather comes from a dedicated responsiveness to the task of self-creation. It completes itself in the integrative acceptance of *all* personal reality, including death and the ultimate aloneness before its visitation. Clients need therapists who experience joy and who are willing to share how that happens in them. Bugental (1965) notes that

> A further evidence of growing maturity in the therapist is that he has an evolving set of constructions about himself, his world, the nature of psychotherapy, and what he means by the concept of personality. (p. 372)

Clients will profit most as their therapists identify themselves as fellow travelers walking humbly yet faithfully into the unknown.

As indicated in Chapter 3 existential psychotherapy stresses both the future and transcendence. Although we may speculate about the future and even plan for it, we can never *know* it, that is, experience it, through these intellectual maneuvers. Moreover, the intellect functions best at tasks requiring analysis and control; transcendence, indeed, happens only when we drop our controls and allow reality to influence and shape us. As they confront the ongoing call of self-creation in the face of death's promise, clients need tools other than intellectual ones. In Chapter 7 we will offer an abundance of such creative tools, which mainly employ the imagination. The final chapter will then explicitly consider the place of spirit and the spiritual, the living of the future and transcendence, in existential psychotherapy.

To conclude this chapter, note that the people in the Land of Fools discovered monsters behind every watermelon because they were afraid of life not immediately recognizable as their own. They did not understand that only by embracing such monsters do they become us . . . and we become spirit.

7

CREATIVITY IN THERAPY

A blind boy lived with his grandmother, an angry woman who resented him as a burden and who shared as little of her meager substance with him as she could.

One day she shouted for him to take down his father's bow as a mother bear and her two cubs were outside. Following her directions he aimed, shot, and to her dismay missed the bears each time. Angrily accusing him of being the reason they were starving to death, she stormed off.

That night a loon visited the troubled boy. The loon said, "I have come to help you as once you helped me. When you found me in a trap and I told you about my children, you let me go. Here, climb on to my back."

With that they flew through the night salted with stars, over the purple mountains, until they circled above a lake black as ink. Telling him to hold on tightly, the loon suddenly dove down under the water. The boy held his breath until the loon burst out of the lake and settled on the shore.

"Open your eyes," she said. "What do you see?" "Why, I see shapes, I see shadows." The loon replied, "I think we'd better do it again."

This time she plunged even deeper. The boy clung to her, held his breath, and shivered with the cold. Back again on land, the loon commanded, "Open your eyes. What do you see?" "I see birds and trees and the horizon line. Oh, thank you so much!" But the loon responded, "Get again on my back. That's not enough."

Flying as high as she could, she dove even deeper into the dark, silent lake. Down, down, down she swam. Then back up, up, until she exploded out of the water.

> *"Open your eyes, boy. What do you see?" "Why, I see 5,712 grasses on the far, far mountain. And in the west I see my grandmother dressing three bears, one of them large and two of them small, that I killed with my arrows today." Then the loon directed him, "Go home now and do what you must do." And he did.*[1]

What should we do when we cannot see? In this age of information we may readily access megabytes of data about every conceivable subject . . . except about ourselves. When a youthful poet wrote him a letter full of questions about growing into a mature poet, in words from another time that still hold much wisdom Rilke (1962) responded:

> I do only want to advise you to keep growing quietly and seriously throughout your whole development; you cannot distort it more rudely than by looking outward and expecting from outside replies to question that only your inmost feeling in your most hushed hour can perhaps answer. (p. 21)

To see, indeed, requires insight. But how, then, may we move inside ourselves. In another letter, Rilke counseled his young friend to

> be patient toward all that is involved in your heart and try to love the *questions themselves* like locked rooms. . . . Do not now seek the answers, which cannot be given you because you would not be able to live them. . . . *Live* the questions now. Perhaps you will gradually, without noticing it, live along some distant day into the answer. (p. 35)

When I was a boy, I too thought that seeing came from teachers. I pictured life as a castle full of dark rooms begging to be explored. If I should listen attentively to others and absorb dutifully a certain level of their wisdom, then lights would switch on and I would know how to live. Lights did come on at times, but invariably they lit up others' castles, not mine! As a young man, I came

[1] Adaptation of an Inuit story, "The Boy and the Loon," as related by Clarissa Pinkola Estes.

to suspect that the darkness surrounding life served as a kind of obstacle course, a necessary trial. If I should train myself to move carefully and patiently through the darkened rooms, I would eventually find a doorway leading into chambers radiant with light. That meant, as my eyes adjusted, developing the ability to see in the dark. Indeed, this did happen enough for me to avoid bumping into large sofas and overstuffed chairs, to limit the grosser mistakes in living. But life's finer beauties remained unavailable still. Now in my fifties I've come to realize that the darkness *is* the light. I have no other places to search out; I have nothing to do but to be here and now; insight comes not from some intellectual understanding about life, but from an inner conviction born in experiencing honestly the life that lives me. The ego, that persistent image pretending to be me, still strives for the answers that may rationally define, direct, and secure my life. My self, however, more clearly recognizes the fruitlessness of such pretentions.

The truth of his life became apparent to the blind lad only as he dared its depths. He had in and through his compassion formerly lived in nonintellectual ways, so he was somewhat accustomed to the risk of exploring in other realms. The loon, his vehicle into himself, knew his readiness and therefore came to his aid. We all, if we shall live fully, must look for our own ways into the experience of creating ourselves.

For the existentialist, life could not be revealed solely through intellectual explanations. Heidegger, after reading *Being and Time*, a monument of philosophical abstraction, "in his later work (which marks a radical shift in his thinking) . . . turned to the work of the poet: particularly to the work of Hölderlin, and, still more recently (in the *Holzwege*), to Hölderlin and Rilke" (Hopper, 1956, p. 151). Sartre, the author of *Being and Nothingness*, a landmark of modern philosophy, wrote five novels (including *Nausea*), short stories (*Le Mur*), and numerous plays (the most famous being *The Flies* and *No Exit*). After writing a series of dramas including *The Iconoclast, The Rebellious Heart*, and *The Broken World*, Marcel wrote his major philosophical works, *Being and Having* (a philosophical diary), and *Homo Viator*. But in the last, an essay on hope, he "devoted two of his happiest and most penetrating studies to the spiritual witness of Rilke" (Hopper, 1956, p. 152). Camus, the philosopher of the absurd, expressed his philosophy primarily through novels (*The Fall, The Stranger, The Plague*), plays (*Caligula, The Possessed*), and in his retelling of *The Myth of Sisyphus*.

Why did these philosophers resort to such unusual and nonscientific media as novels and plays? Michalson (1956) expresses it well:

> The biggest gap between existentialism and other current philosophies lies in its unwillingness to be bound by the standards of the sciences. Kierkegaard repudiated the scientific pretension in Hegel's system. In their philosophies of life, Nietzsche and Dilthey saw that man's life is history and not nature. While nature can be objectified and rationalized, history is too ambiguous to be grasped. It can only be lived through and reflected upon. The primary data of the life philosophies are therefore found in confessions and memoirs, private journals and autobiography, and these are considered more valuable philosophically than the tests and measures closer to the exact sciences. The natural sciences are fine implements for assessing the realm of objects and problems, the realm of things man holds. But how shall they interpret the realm which holds man, the ontological subtleties in a man's struggle for his very being? (p. 16)

To understand life we must enter it. Various intellectual systems may be developed through a process of deduction that leads to the solving of problems. The mystery of life, however, opens itself only inductively as we explore it from within. And growth occurs mysteriously, not through the correctness of answers, but through life itself which becomes the answer.

In existential psychotherapy people grow as the therapist walks with them into two distinct but contiguous worlds, one of the imagination, the other of the spirit. Think back to the story of the boy and the loon: we can well imagine the saving journey, though we may not understand it; we may, moreover, intellectually doubt the reality of the loon's spiritual assistance, but we may out of our own experience firmly believe in its truth. Let us, therefore, in this chapter consider how the imagination may be used in psychotherapy. In the final chapter we will address the place of the spirit.

THE WORLD OF THE IMAGINATION

People engage psychotherapists for a variety of reasons. Sometimes they need facts; other times they seek a forum for selves openly to one who cares and who will listen without judgment. Frequently the client, like Rilke's young friend, looks to the therapist for the answers that will bring peace; always the person feels incapable of handling life's problems alone.

When in reciting their stories of pain and frustration clients keep returning to the phrase "I don't know why I . . . ," they are underlining an unchecked view of themselves as a problem needing some reasonable solution. The existential therapist knows otherwise. Rarely do such people need information or problem solving or skill building. Ordinarily, they are neither ignorant nor unintelligent nor incapable of dealing with a world of objects. Rather, they require some way of entering into their subjective experience other than through intellectual analysis. The intellect is fashioned for dividing, for taking apart, for understanding separate bits of experience. These people instead must engage the imagination, the human being's preeminent power for uniting, for healing, for finding wholeness underlying the confusion of diversity. It alone among human abilities widens vision so that confusing smallness may be overcome and a return made to the process of growth.

It all depends on how one understands troubled people. Consider this admittedly homely analogy: After working strenuously outdoors under the summer sun, you prepare to step into a relaxing shower. When with a longing sigh you finally turn the shower on, you expect the immediate release of clean, warm water. But none is forthcoming. Try as you may, turning now this knob, now that, adjusting the shower's filter, now wider, now narrower, still nothing happens. "I don't know why . . . the shower doesn't work. . . . " What could be wrong?

In the most extreme scenario, the shower fails to perform as expected because of a serious drought. The water table is so low, the reservoirs are so empty, that only an act of God bringing rain will return the shower to normal functioning. Failing such divine intervention the only answer lies in moving to another region, buying a new home, and relying on an entirely new shower.

A less dramatic situation lies in a broken pipeline or a malfunctioning generating system. The water stands ready to be transported if only a plumber or electrician will correct the current malfunction. The problem is solved by finding the right expert and having enough money to pay for the requisite services.

But perhaps neither of these situations obtains. Plenty of water may be available and all of the systems may have maintained their basic integrity. The problem could, indeed, reside within a perfectly sound system. Over the years various minerals carried by the water have collected in the pipes until the buildup has constricted and finally obstructed the water's flow. What is required is simply some agent capable of moving deeply into the system in such a way as to break up the foreign material and widen the channel to a diameter suitable to the water's quantity and necessary pressure.

In a pathological model, psychotherapy depends on the skill of the therapist. The expert intervenes either to restructure a personality damaged beyond repair or to mend broken parts of an otherwise healthy personality. Psychotherapy in this model mimics surgery; the psychotherapist mirrors the medical surgeon.

Existential psychotherapy as creativity espouses a growth model, not a pathological one. In the latter the task demands bringing a noncapable person from a negative position to one of normal balance; in the former the therapist seeks to release a capable person's own powers so that arrested growth may continue on. The imagination is first and foremost among these powers.

In order to utilize the imagination's resources effectively, it sometimes requires discipline and strengthening. I therefore often give homework requiring its use. For example, people awakened during the night should record their dreams then; otherwise, it should be done first thing in the morning. Each day as quiet time presents itself attention should be directed to the ongoing flow of inner images and the feelings that cling to them. These too are most fruitful when written down.

After tussling with Betty Edwards' *Drawing on the Right Side of the Brain* (1979) and personally experiencing the shift from the brain's left to right hemispheres, I have recommended that some clients take up some of her exercises, especially those in Chapter 4 (pp. 46–59) that deal with that experience explicitly. More recently, following the suggestions of Lucia Capacchione (1991) in the *Recovery of Your Inner Child,* I have used drawings with the nondominant hand (p. 36) and dialoguing between the two hands (pp. 30–31). I will illustrate this technique by sharing my own experience working with it.

During a recent peer supervision group, Jean shared her dream about twin baby boys, one healthy and lively, the other malnourished and bloody. Although the dream appeared to hold small energy for her, I found it quite touching. After returning home from our meeting in Washington, I decided to engage these twins.

With my left hand, I first drew the robust twin. Although done awkwardly, I did feel rather free in doing it as I had little expectation of some aesthetic production. I then entered into dialogue with the child, writing with my right hand to question and respond to him, printing his responses with my left hand. The picture and dialogue are reproduced in Figure 7.1.

On subsequent reflection, I recognized how in the ongoing pressure of professional responsibilities I have been neglecting the spiritual, playful side of myself. I have resolved to make more room for this somewhat lonely child.

A few days elapsed before I turned to the other twin. I share the drawing and ensuing conversation in Figure 7.2.

Afterwards, I was puzzled by two aspects of the drawing: what had caused the red blood covering the boy, and what is signified by the closed space filled with wavy lines?

As I was pursuing some genealogical family research a couple of days later, a light went on. Although I was born first, before my birth my mother suffered a miscarriage. Could not the container represent her womb? Might not this baby with mongoloid features be my unborn older brother's participation in my life?

A second realization came a week later at a group psychotherapy conference in New Haven. During a gestalt training session, with the leaders' expert assistance I further addressed these twins. When I was suddenly asked if I had been physically abused as a boy, I answered, "No, but I was mugged here in New Haven three years ago today!" With that startling announcement, through much anger and tears, a good deal of leftover pain pushed its way to the surface, got expressed, and healing has happened at new levels within me. I gratefully acknowledge the assistance the wounded child is giving me.

I also find helpful some simple meditative exercises. If nothing else, they make the client stop and turn inward, and often they result in a release of stress as well as some degree of interior peace.

Emphasizing at first the discipline of keeping at the meditative task, I teach these meditations:

1. While breathing deeply and slowly, count your breaths in cycles of four. Should your mind wander from the exercise, when you become aware of it quietly and patiently resume

Figure 7.1
Drawing and Dialogue With Two Hands

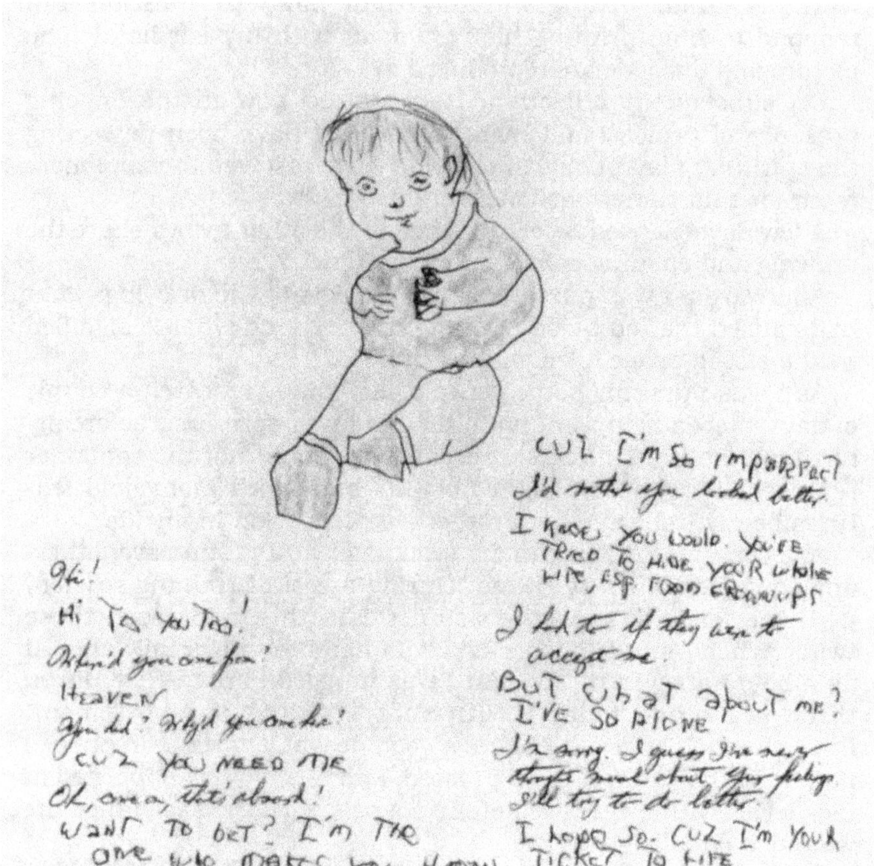

Figure 7.2
Drawing and Dialogue With Two Hands

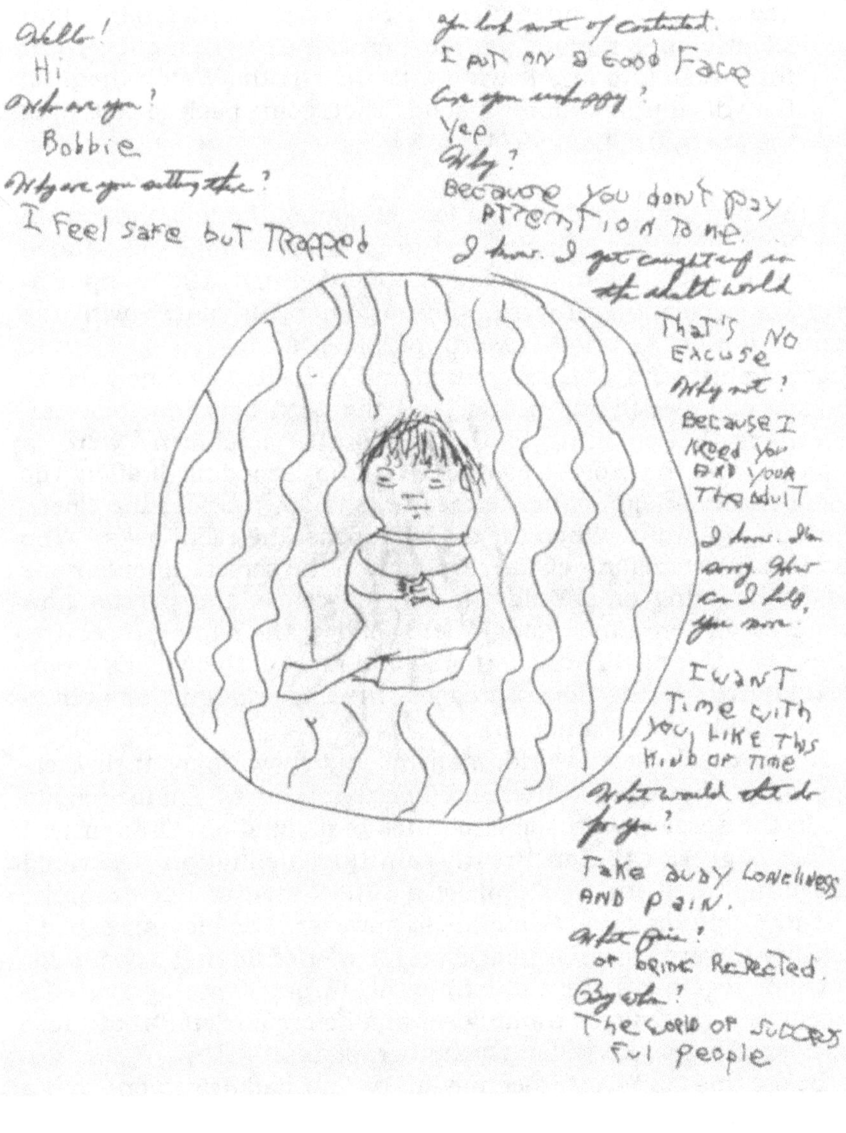

counting by returning to one. (LeShan, 1974a, pp. 19–20, 79–82)

2. Using the same breath counting, when you become conscious of thinking, "note different kinds of thoughts, whether 'planning' or 'imagining' or 'remembering.' This sharpens the focus of attention" (Goldstein, 1976, pp. 27–28).
3. Take yourself imaginatively to a peaceful meadow. Near it flows a small, quiet stream. Sit down on the bank and silently contemplate the moving water. As thoughts arise, turn them into logs flowing with the stream. Watch them till they disappear around a bend. Then come back to watching the water. (LeShan, 1974a, p. 84)

I use two other meditations for developing the imagination. In the first, the client is instructed to imagine a thousand-petaled lotus flower floating in a secluded pond (LeShan, 1974a, pp. 88–90). Some meaningful word, such as "man," is placed with the central flower. As another word, perhaps "strong," associates to that primary word, it is recognized and deposited as a new flower on one of the outlying petals, and the path between them acknowledged. Returning to the center, the anchoring word is repeated and the process continues. In the second meditation, the client enters an empty movie theater, sits down before the closed curtain, and waits. When the curtain opens, the client asks, "Who am I?" and waits for a visual response on the screen. Should none be forthcoming or should the images cease, the person now inquires "Where am I going?" and follows the same procedure. These two questions are alternated and most of the client's attention is given to the flow of images, the imagination's answer to these intellectual stimuli.

In our quick-paced world, many clients show up for their therapy stressed-out and scattered. When that occurs, I am inclined to begin the session with some minutes of meditation. Ordinarily, I either suggest the Zen breath-counting meditation described above or the silent repetition of a Hindu mantra (for example, *shanti*; *rama*; *hasam*). Sometimes, however, I employ an explicit turning inward through imagery as a way of finding a focus for our time together. Let me illustrate this through sharing a bit of a recent one-way mirror training session before our staff that I had with a colleague, herself a psychotherapist.

Before this 10:00 A.M. meeting, Mary Ann had driven one and a half hours on an interstate highway, spent an hour in supervision, and the following hour in a staff meeting. By the time we sat down she clearly needed the opportunity just to stop. She had brought with her a collage she had put together the previous week at an art therapy conference hoping to go into it more deeply through some kind of guided imagery. The moment she suggested this, however, she realized a strong resistance to following the plan that had seemed so right to her the night before.

Recognizing that the block could be coming from her already full morning or, if not that alone, from somewhere other than her conscious mind, I suggested that she close her eyes and let her imagination search throughout her body for the place where the resistance was residing. As she was breathing rather shallowly, I asked her to begin this inner journey with ten deep, slow breaths.

In a short time Mary Ann found a massive marble structure in her right arm. Because of some fear that it might collapse on her, she soon discovered a way of entering into it where she felt safe. Once inside, however, she was plunged straightaway into a kind of meltdown that turned the solid object into a raging river. Although quite afraid of being swept away by this torrent, she finally allowed herself to go with it. Eventually, having been hurled through boiling rapids, she ended up in a quiet pool in a protected cove. After floating silently for some time, she got out of the water, climbed on to a large rock overlooking the cove, and settled down into a spongy moss bed that covered it. She stayed there, peacefully, for three or four minutes. Then she opened her eyes.

Our ensuing conversation dealt not only with this hectic Monday morning but also with her stressful life, a life filled with the problems of beginning a private practice while continuing her work at our agency, caring for a rural home, and raising her teenage children, while striving constantly to improve her therapeutic skills. By the time we finished, she had realized more deeply how she must find some regular time to go into herself to maintain a necessary measure of interior calm. For the moment, indeed, any new learnings in and through the collage would have to wait!

These and similar meditative exercises, some structured and some unstructured, some employing the imagination and some not, used as needed by therapist and client, may assist both in coming home to themselves. Once a certain amount of self-presence has been gathered, then they each may have more of their inner resources potentially available for the therapeutic encounter.

Clients often consider therapy to be about generalized states—for example, low self esteem that calls for a miraculous infusion of confidence from the therapist, or specific problems that require this expert's brilliant solutions. But neither somebody else's saving action nor another's answers will suffice. The therapist must not do the clients' work or take over the clients' responsibilities. However, without doing this the therapist may assist clients by sharing his or her own inner experience of them so that it may serve as an explicit point of departure for further therapeutic exploration. As an example of how the therapist may use the personal internal flow of imagery to help clients touch and express their experience, consider this interaction that happened in a therapy group I was leading.

A shy young man, new to the group, had not spoken. As others revealed their lives, he appeared to be listening intently and following closely the rising and falling of others' feelings. With eyes, ears, and body he seemed present, but no words about his own life were forthcoming.

Whenever the conversation lagged, I found my attention turning inevitably to him. He *is* saying something, but what? And how?

I emptied my mind, opened my imagination toward him, and called out to my intuition: Listen, listen. . . .

Across my inner landscape a color drifted. As it filled me a word formed: "blue."

"Jim," I said, "I'm very aware of you. I feel you reaching out silently to us, to me. I want to respond but words fail me. In fact, all I can think to say to you is . . . 'blue.'"

This brilliant pronouncement was met with group chuckles, some head shaking, perplexity, or dismissal. After the murmuring died down, Jim quite logically requested, "What does that mean?"

I replied, "I don't rightly know. I'll try to find out."

I closed my eyes and turned to the blue inside me. As it began to shape itself I told its tale essentially in these words:

> I see a body of water. Light blue and gentle. A sudden storm lashes the surface, creating huge waves. I dive below, seeking safety. As I descend the blue deepens and expands, becoming an enveloping mass, like a giant blue-black blanket. I find peace here but also loneliness and fear. Ahead of me lies a long-buried and forgotten treasure ship. I wonder if I'm the only one who has approached it, who has discovered it, who

> values it. Perhaps . . . this world looks so strange, seems so far away, pulses with a life so unlike my own.

At that, the images faded away. Aware once more of the group's time and place, I opened my eyes. Jim, directly across from me, was gazing at me through silent tears. Self-consciously now he began to dab with his handkerchief, then discreetly he blew his nose. Busywork completed, he then reported, quite simply, "You heard me." From that time on, Jim trusted the group, and me, with many more words and much of his life (cf. Willis, 1989, pp. 81–82).

When I first became a therapist, I hesitated to share such "irrational" intuitions with clients. But as I have experienced over and over the power they have to unlock stuck places for clients, I have come to trust them and myself with them. So while I listen to the client's words I generally try also to keep a "third eye" scanning inside for signs of imaginative movement. When these signs occur—like a breeze charting a current through a field of wheat—I follow it till I see or hear something. Then I simply tell the other person what I am experiencing. This happened in a session with a young woman stuck in a stultifying marriage.

Barbara began by recounting the following dream she had had the previous night:

> I'm in a museum, looking at a sculpture of myself. From the waist up it's made of ice. A green light situated inside, below the navel, makes the torso shine an eerie green. Where the ice is cracked, the color is rich and beautiful. The shoulders, broad like a man's, taper down to a woman's waist. I can't tell my gender, however, because I can only look at the sculpture from the back.

We proceeded to unpack the dream using ordinary gestalt techniques (being different parts of the dream, speaking in the present, carrying on a dialogue between the various parts). Nothing seemed to click. Although the dream felt important to her, Barbara finally left it, still wondering about its present significance for her.

As she moved on to other topics, I listened but I continued to scan internally for some clue for her. Suddenly, sensing some inner shift, I turned all of my attention inside. I heard clearly two words: "Green back." I interrupted her then and repeated them to her. She at first looked puzzled at this strange communication. Then speaking slowly, thoughtfully, she tried the words aloud: "Green back . . . green backs . . . greenbacks . . . oh, my god, money! The hold of Jim's money is cracking and that's where my own richness and beauty are revealing themselves!"

Now, eight months after her divorce, Barbara considers that recognition a major step in her disentanglement from a well-to-do man whose uptight background and jet-set lifestyle were murdering her spirit.

How may a therapist help clients use their own imagination in therapy? I give different directions depending upon the person's ability to imagine, the degree of present defensiveness, and the strength of our working alliance.

In the previously mentioned session with Mary Anne, I judged that she was at the moment experiencing a good deal of resistance. I therefore gave her quite explicit instructions, which ensured my close involvement:

1. Find the place in your body where the resistance is located.
2. When you can envision the resistance, tell me where it is and how it appears to you.
3. When you wish to do something, tell me what you desire and whether you can do it.
4. When you find yourself stuck, inform me about the situation and then as you can follow my suggestions.

During sessions like that one, I am most interested that she is increasingly able to overcome her resistance as it is manifesting itself in her inability to imagine herself doing whatever she wishes. The content of what she experiences and what the particular images mean may be fascinating but they do not constitute the therapy. Therapeutic movement will happen as she chooses to take charge of her inner experience and its imaginative expression.

Some clients require less assistance from me. If so, I prefer not to interrupt the flow of images. By working out a system of nonverbal signals, like a nod for "yes" or a head shake for "no," one finger lifted for "I'm stuck and need your help" or two fingers for "I'm frightened," we keep in communication and we have to do only a minimal amount of switching back and forth from right to left hemispheric activity.

Sometimes—for example, when clients have a specific question or problem—I'll do the following: Using a combination of physical and breathing exercises, I will help them move into a state of deep relaxation. When that has sufficiently taken hold, I will request that in their imagination they leave my office to seek out a secluded meadow situated near a woods. I ask them simply to nod when they find it. I then direct them to explore the meadow, making it their own, and that they nod again when they are willing to move on. Finally, I suggest that they should now follow a path leading deep into the woods to the dwelling of a wise person, who is now willing to speak with them about their questions or problems. I instruct them only to signal if assistance is needed. Otherwise, when the conversation is concluded, they should make their way back to the meadow and nod to me when they wish to return. At that point I switch their attention back to their breathing. After counting deep breaths backwards from ten to one, they should then open their eyes. Only thereafter as they may wish and as it seems important to them will they share with me all or parts of their imaginary trip into the woods.

Think back to the tale that opened this chapter. The loon helped the blind boy move deeply into himself so that he might see. Because his vision remained clouded after each of the first two journeys into the dark waters, this spirit guide fashioned progressively more effective ways for him to go even deeper. The therapist's task lies in creating structures aimed at facilitating the client's seeing; what is seen and what results from the new knowledge has ultimate importance for the client. Once the boy saw he could then be dismissed: "Go home now and do what you must do."

During the past year, with a colleague's assistance I have experienced another imaginary methodology, a shamanic journey into the Lower World. Although similar in some respects to the method detailed above, it has some significant dissimilarities. Induction happens through ritual rather than internal focusing. Both methods expect the person to pursue a specific task. The only verbal direction is to find some opening in the earth leading to the other realm. Instead of client-initiated nonverbal signals, a series of directive rhythms (on a drum, with a rattle, through tapping, with a metronome) are agreed upon. And this rhythmic background is maintained by the leader throughout the client's journeying.[2]

---

[2] For anyone interested in understanding the context of such a shamanic journey, William Taegel's *The Many Colored Buffalo*, the book that initiated this series on the frontiers of psychotherapy, is rich in explanation and experience.

To give some sense of how this journey may be employed in therapy, let me share a condensation of a session I had with Barbara after her divorce. She was at that time in the process of termination.

When she entered my office, she sank down heavily onto the couch. Avoiding my eyes she told me that she had almost stayed home as she was hurting too much. She was uncertain about the cause of the pain but she guessed it had to do with our discussions about termination. She did decide to come, however, because last night in a dream she had seen a pregnant Indian woman floating down a river, the same woman she had dreamed about last summer when she was camping in Minnesota. She just knew she had to follow her today.

As she had never used imagery within a shamanic format, I explained this method to her. Then I asked her to find a place in the room that felt right for her journey. She decided to lie down on my rug with her feet facing southward, as that approximated the Indian woman's position. After she had prayed silently for some moments for spiritual assistance, I set up a steady tapping rhythm. She afterwards reported this experience:

> In her imagination she went immediately to a river cascading wildly through a desert landscape. For a time she rested in one of its quieter pools. Getting out, she started walking away from the river across the desert toward some low hills. Drawing near to them, she spotted a mountain lion on a ledge above her. When it turned away, she scrambled after it. As it strode surely back toward the river, she realized that it intended to hunt. When the mountain lion reached the water and began to search for prey, she suddenly became the animal and watched herself stealing stealthily along, moving in and out of the trees crowding the river bank. Then, most surprising to her, she reappeared and the animal became her. As this happened she felt a surge of strength and purpose.
>
> At once, transformed, she discovered a cave and entered it fearlessly. Its walls were decorated with huge trumpet flowers. As she moved deeply into the cave, it became filled with thousands of spirits composed of light. They buzzed around her and to her delight wove around her a cocoon of light. This brought great peace. When the spirits vanished, the wrappings of light melted away. She exited the cave through one of the trumpet flowers directly back into my office.

As our available time had almost expired, we did not speak much about the journey in detail. However, just before she left, she said, "Do you believe in all this stuff?" I countered, "How do you feel now compared to fifty minutes ago?" She thought a moment, smiled, and walked away in strong, unhurried strides.

Barbara started our next session announcing that she had discovered this week that the mountain lion in some cultures embodies the goddess. She also declared that she had finally decided that she was moving soon . . . to Arizona! As I write these words she has started a new life for herself in Tucson. When I last spoke with her, she was intending to spend some days in the desert looking for a mountain lion.

In selecting the kind of imagery to employ, I am guided by a geography of the imagination suggested by Michel Foucault (1986). If the client is attempting to reach a new stage of psychological growth, I have found imagery on a horizontal axis from near to far to be most helpful. It serves as a type of initiation ritual by which one leaves the realm of the familiar and journeys alone to encounter forces demanding the actualization of heretofore unused potential. The previously described wise person fantasy, where one moves from the open and safe meadow into the depths of a mysterious woods, illustrates well this type of work with guided imagery.

Should a person be more in search of transformation than growth, the vertical axis offers a descending movement into another world, a symbolic letting go of the ordinary, an encounter with transforming powers, and an ascent back into our usual reality. Such imagery holds the potential for new life. Barbara's shamanic journey where she and a mountain lion shared identities, where spiritual forces brought her peace in a cocoon of light, offers a somewhat dramatic example on this imaginary axis.

When, however, the client's task requires the reclaiming of disowned parts of oneself, no spatial movement is appropriate. Instead, the person needs to stay rooted in the self to be able to explore on a light/dark axis. One seeks through this imagery to gain not growth or transformation, but truth. The loon plunged the blind boy into the dark waters of himself till he could see clearly the truth of his relationship with his abusive grandmother; I needed to search the blue waters of my imagination before I could retrieve for Jim the truth of his inner experience; Mary Anne had to penetrate her granitelike resistance, let go of its protection in a raging torrent, so that she could discover the truth of her urgent need for interior peace.

When someone brings a dream to explore, I direct him or her to recount it in the first person and in the present tense. As the dream story unfolds, I listen for its primary challenge: does it ask for movement into areas left unexplored (the horizontal axis), or does it present some dilemma requiring a revisit into the dream (the light/dark axis), or, finally, does it hold promise of transformation through expansion (the vertical axis)? In the remainder of this chapter I will show how I work with the first two kinds of dream challenges; in the next chapter Jerry's dream fragment will be given and the transforming work we did with it illustrated.

When Marilyn, a student in her late twenties, was substantially along in her therapy, she brought the following dream. As it turned out, she had already shared it in a psychology class and had concluded that she had some unfinished business with her ex-husband, who had died in a motorcycle accident seven years previously, and only five months after their divorce:

> I'm standing with my son near our car parked in front of our condominium. We live on a quiet *cul de sac.* But today many people are rushing around trying to find my dead husband. I point to the woods behind our home and tell them that he's in there, lying under a fallen tree and covered with a pile of leaves. Nobody believes me.

I decided to engage both her imagination and her body through a combination of gestalt and psychodramatic techniques. I choose to do so because I judged that she was being invited by this dream to realize some new growth. To do this she needed to move from the protected *cul de sac* on a horizontal axis into the woods containing her ex-husband's corpse.

I keep in mind these general guidelines for discovering images with the most growth potential:

1. Do not choose images of people, especially well-known ones, as their expansion will come largely from memory or from fixed perceptions.
2. Avoid ordinary images as they generally already will have been so thought out that they have become objectified and fixed.

3. Select images that are imaginative or emotional opposites. This may bring out interior divisions in need of healing.
4. Choose images that occupy adjacent space or that touch each other as they have already some dream connection.
5. Look for images similar in kind. Together they may expand through slightly different viewpoints.
6. Identify images that will shift the client's perspective.

Following the first guideline, I did not choose the images of herself, her son, her husband, or the searchers. I also rejected the condominium/home, the car, and the dead body as probably too fixed for much imaginative expansion.

I selected the *cul de sac* as being the closed and known opposite of the open and secret-bearing woods. It also seemed appropriate because of Marilyn's emotional emphasis on its quiet nature as opposed to the hectic activity of the searchers. Moreover, it would shift the perspective, making it the foreground instead of the more usual context for the dwellings on that street.

The woods seemed potentially rich as the opposite of the *cul de sac*, as the hiding place for the body, and as containing the covering leaves. Finally, I chose the pile of leaves instead of the fallen tree because the leaves were adjacent to the woods, the same in kind as the woods yet not identical with them.

I instructed Marilyn to be, in turn, the *cul de sac*, the woods, and the leaves. As she spoke about herself, again in the first person and in the present, she came to realize how they represented three distinct parts of herself: the leaves represented her generally nonexpressive facade in just being there; the *cul de sac* stood for her intellectual defensiveness that kept her emotionally apart from others; these both served as containers for the passion and *joie de vivre* that surged deep within her but that even she had a difficult time accessing.

Through these autobiographical descriptions, the taking of various positions about my office, and imaginary interactions between these three aspects of herself, she concluded that she kept her creativity and self-expression controlled because she did not believe that they would be sources of life for her. And somehow her ex-husband's continued presence in her feelings contributed to this self-imposed emotional imprisonment.

Toward the end of our session, Marilyn brought her husband explicitly into the scene. She placed him in a chair in a far corner and with his back to her. After an emotional soliloquy (she refused to be him), she concluded by telling him with much fervor to leave her forever. With that, she turned to me and asked if I would keep the body and dispose of it. I said I would. Then she left.

At our next session, I gave her a small bottle of ashes and suggested that she probably needed to dispose of them herself so that she could be certain that he was really gone. She took it and kept in on her mantelpiece for some weeks, until one Sunday afternoon she scattered the ashes on a quiet stretch of Cape Cod beach.

Soon afterwards, I received in the mail this brief expression of Marilyn's therapy and where she now found herself:

> I am a fisherman, my face weathered by years of facing the salty blasts, my hands worn and calloused from endlessly working the nets.
> I search the sky for some sign, a flock of seagulls hovering overhead, to direct me where to cast my nets.
> The sea is rough, the water cold, the depths ominously impenetrable. . . .
> Mending my nets, I think and wonder and remember the small, simple chest I carry with me on all my journeys. A gift given to me at birth that still remains unopened, I remember Pandora. . . .
> Slowly, carefully, I take out my simple chest and caress the smoothness of the wood, the coolness of the latch.
> Hesitatingly, I lift the lid, holding my breath in anticipation.
> The contents are dark and glisten, not in reflection of the sun which is hidden behind the storm clouds, but from a light of their own.
> What is it I have been carrying with me for so long, too fearful to look at? Gently I dip my hand and pull out a palmful of tiny black orbs.
> What a wonderful treasure of potential, my cache of tiny roe, desperately in need of tender care and nurturance.
> New found joy to be able to cast out my nets and feed the turbulent waters around me with the gift from my simple chest. (M.C., 1991)

A body needed to be confronted and a bottle of ashes dispersed before a humble wooden box filled with living roe could be shared with others.

Marilyn also shared with me a paper that she wrote for her psychology class. She spoke about this dream:

> This idea of being aware was solidified in class during the Gestalt dream work. I thought I had complete understanding of the significance of that dream, but found that I was unaware of the possibility that there might be more. My experience during that class was like being on a rollercoaster. Once we started talking about the dream and becoming part of it, the rollercoaster zoomed down the levels of my awareness and being and brought out a lot of significant points that I needed to find. Having become aware of the potential, I brought the dream to my counseling session where we continued with the gestalt technique and worked through the rest of it. Bringing all of the aspects of the dream into my awareness was a powerful and moving experience, lifting an incredible load off of me. I see this experience as becoming aware, bringing what is already inside to consciousness and realizing its significance. (M.C., 1991)

She says so well what an existential psychotherapy seeks in helping the client remove the blocks to the life force constantly striving to express itself. And she witnesses to the powerful role of the imagination in realizing that goal. I thank her for allowing me to share her reflections with you.

When clients bring dreams in which they were thwarted from accomplishing some desired end, these dreams are more appropriate for exploration through guided imagery than through psychodramatic or gestalt interventions. Here the clients are blocked from realizing the whole truth of their present existence. In such instances the interpretation of the specific images and the overall understanding of the dream are nowhere as important as the overcoming of resistance and releasing of the ability to move freely in the imaginary world. The therapist seeks always to support the clients' freedom to choose and to confront them with the responsibility for their choices. In keeping with these tasks, I use the following guidelines to structure my interventions:

1. Focus on the imagery process, not the content of the images.
2. When the flow of imagery ceases, suggest the gathering of additional information through the person's dominant

sense modality (that is, seeing, hearing, feeling, touching, or smelling).

3. When a specific image stands out for the client, ask what he or she desires to do regarding it, then find out if the given action is possible.
4. Should the client wish to perform some action but be incapable of doing so, help overcome the resistance by making specific process suggestions.
5. Should the client begin rationally to explain the resistance or attempt analytically to explore various options for solving the problem, make a suggestion that calls the person back to sensing and feeling in the immediate imaginary context.
6. Some suggestions carry implicit meaning that seems generally true for people. For example, any action toward the left engages the past, toward the right addresses the future; searching for assistance in shadowy or distant corners asks for the calling up of overlooked personal resources; looking for something in a closed place and especially on one's person (for example, "in your left vest pocket") recognizes the resources as private and strictly under personal control; moving upward engages spiritual abilities while traveling downward enlists nonrational powers.
7. Make suggestions that either utilize the client's recognized and accepted strengths (a young robust man confronted with a roadblock may readily find an axe or a bulldozer nearby) or suggest the fulfillment of a strong desire (a short person may easily find a ladder to climb over a high wall).

By way of illustration, consider this summary of a therapy session with a middle-aged, overweight woman complaining of low self esteem and a lack of self confidence.

She arrived ten minutes late for our meeting. Traffic problems! She also announced that her usual pleasant anticipation of the therapy hour was today missing; indeed, on her drive over she had twice thought of turning around, going back home, and calling to cancel her appointment. Why?—a mystery!

After she had quieted down a bit, she reckoned that she felt better and did appreciate being with me. We sat silently for a while until, without any introduction, she blurted out this dream fragment: Alone in an antebellum mansion, she had walked up a magnificent marble staircase. At the top a locked door blocked her explorations. Try as she might she could not open it. She had then awakened, frustrated. Now she wondered: What did that door conceal?

When she indicated that she would like to return to the dream with my assistance, I agreed to lead her into it through guided imagery. After some moments of relaxing exercises and deep breathing, I suggested that in her imagination she leave my office and revisit her dream mansion.

She did so readily. She strode purposely through its open front door and proceeded directly up the marble stairway. But as previously she was stopped by the locked door on the top floor.

Since she was primarily a visual person, I suggested that she search around to her left and particularly into dark corners for something that could smash down the door. I did this for two reasons—she was physically big, and many of her personality problems stemmed from an oral dependency stretching back to early childhood. She found nothing useful. I then asked her to look in her left pants pocket for a key or some other instrument—this would appeal to her need to control as well as engage her secondary sense modality, her sense of touch. Again, nothing.

She went back to examining the door. When she noticed some light coming from under the door, I finally made the right suggestion; this overweight woman who desired so much to be smaller could perhaps, like Alice, become very small, and thus slip under the door. Immediately she found herself in a large, well-furnished but unoccupied sitting room.

After she had wandered about the room without hindrance and to her satisfaction, her attention was drawn to a lovely, alluring garden she could see through the two French doors. She declared, "I *must* visit there." But these doors, not surprisingly, were also locked.

Following up on the previous successful strategy, I suggested that she hunt for some small crack in the wall next to the doors because sometimes it would open up and reveal a secret cubbyhole. With this I was emphasizing her control over all access to this horticultural inner sanctum. Sure enough, she soon located a wall safe; in it she discovered an electronic button that controlled the doors. She pushed it; the doors opened straightaway. She then closed and locked the safe, entered the garden, and from the outside relocked the doors. Now she could explore this gorgeous place deep within her in safety and in privacy.

As she strolled along its paths, she was amazed at its beauty. The colors were radiant, the plants were full and lush, the garden was simply brimming with life. At one point she sat down on a bench and just drank in the garden's loveliness. As she did so, she realized that she was being transformed into a beautiful woman. She sat with this recognition for some time, then opened her eyes.

For three or four minutes she stayed quiet, reflecting privately on what she had experienced. Then, eyes glistening, she exclaimed, primarily to herself but for me to share, "I *am* beautiful! I've never been able to admit that, especially to myself."

This woman needed to overcome her resistance to meeting both herself and me before she could dare to face her own beauty. With the help of her imagination, with my staying with her even in her resistance, and with a couple of suggestions that validated her desires while assuring her privacy, she gradually was able to accept the truth of her own loveliness, one not dependent solely on culturally determined standards. That day she took a significant step towards becoming a self-confident woman (Willis, 1984, pp. 39–40).

Meditation and intuition, guided imagery and dreams; all open a passageway into our brain's other hemisphere, all give promise of our breaking out of the intellect's limited problem-solving propensities and gaining access to the mystery of creative transcendence. But mystery and transcendence in existential psychotherapy include not only the imaginative but also the spiritual.

8

Psyche and Spirit in Therapy

One day an atheist was walking along a cliff when he slipped and fell over the edge. As he plunged downward, he managed to grab the branch of a small tree that was growing from a crevice in the rock. Hanging there, swaying in the cold wind, he realized how hopeless his position was. Far below were jagged boulders, and there was no way to climb up. His grip on the branch was weakening.

"Well," he thought, "only God can save me now. I've never believed in God, but I might be wrong. What have I to lose?"

So he called out: "God! If you exist, save me—and I'll believe in you!"

There was no answer. He called again. "Please, God, I never believed in You, but if You'll save me now, I'll believe in You from now on."

Suddenly, a great voice boomed down from the clouds, "Oh, no you won't. I know your kind." The man was so surprised he almost lost his grip on the branch.

"Please, God, You're wrong, I really mean it, I'll believe." The man pleaded and argued.

Finally, God said, "All right, I'll save you. Let go of the branch."

"Let go of the branch!" the man exclaimed. "Do you think I'm crazy?" (Deikman, 1976, p. 65)

THE WORLD OF THE SPIRIT

The *Oxford English Dictionary* defines a spirit as "a separated, incorporeal being or personality, usually regarded as imperceptible at ordinary times to the human senses, but capable of being visible at pleasure, and frequently conceived as troublesome, terrifying or hostile to mankind." The phrases "usually regarded" and "frequently conceived" alert a psychologist to two different though related questions about the spiritual world as it impacts on psychotherapy: in the first place, do spirits exist as independent beings, and secondly, what kind of spiritual experiences do clients bring to and utilize in therapy? The former poses a philosophical or ontological problem while the latter points to individual perceptions and how they are personally understood and explained. When we are told that the desperate atheist held a conversation with a thundering God, we may quite legitimately wonder if that *really* happened. If so, it did not occur in our ordinary reality. Should we be further told that the atheist subsequently let go of the branch and that he was saved from death by the hand of God, our wonder would surely turn to amazement *that* it happened.

The Nature of Spirits Certainly, in the religious traditions of humankind belief in spiritual beings existing as separate entities is central. God (or the gods) is said to have created the universe, to have fashioned human beings in the divine image, to have clear expectations about appropriate human behavior, and constantly to exercise real influence in the course of human affairs. This influence may come directly, as when the Olympian gods swayed the tides of battle, now toward the Greeks, now toward the Trojans, or when Jahweh made a dry passage through the Red Sea for the Hebrew people fleeing the cruel Pharaoh, or when the Word of God became man in order personally to save humankind from the powers of sin and death. The divinity may also employ other spiritual beings as helpers or guardians armed with superhuman powers. They assist human beings especially when they are assailed by evil spirits intent on sabotaging the divine plan or when they are subjected to extremely stressful situations.

When Raymond Moody (1977) examined the case histories of one hundred and fifty people who had had near-death experiences, he reported that "What is perhaps the most incredible religious and non-religious backgrounds and, therefore, gave different names to this light,

> not one person has expressed any doubt whatsoever that it was a being, a being of light. Not only that, it is a personal being. It has a very definite personality. The love and the warmth which emanate from this being to the dying person are utterly beyond words, and he feels completely surrounded by it and taken up in it, completely at ease and accepted in the presence of this being. He senses an irresistible magnetic attraction to this light. He is ineluctably drawn to it. (p. 59)

This account of a beneficent spirit finds an echo in Stanislaus Grof's (1976) report of the experiences of LSD research subjects. Grof draws his observations together from over seventeen years of clinical research and hundreds of personally recorded LSD sessions. Among other aspects of these accounts Grof notes the following:

> The ancient theme of an encounter and interaction with spirit guides, teachers, and protectors is one of the most valuable and rewarding transpersonal experiences in LSD sessions. The subject perceives these beings as suprahuman or spiritual entities existing on higher planes of consciousness and higher energy levels. Sometimes, the spirit guides are a source of light or energy with or without concomitant vibrations of a high frequency. . . .
>
> Spirit guides appear in the sessions in various capacities; sometimes they give an explanation of what is happening or advice in regard to the desirable approach to the LSD experience. On other occasions, they accompany the individual through various difficult experiences, like Virgil in Dante's *Divine Comedy*, giving him intellectual and spiritual support, or even creating shields of positive energy that protect him from the destructive influences of evil entities. . . . Sometimes these spiritual helpers remain unrecognized; at other times the subject identifies them as various aspects of his higher self or as discarnate religious teachers and enlightened beings. . . . (pp. 196–197)

Under the unusual stress of physical near-death and the disorientation of an LSD altered consciousness, people report interacting with spiritual beings. Theologians and believers may well attribute these experiences to personal, concerned entities; transpersonal psychologists may, however, simply recognize these spirits as

> transcendent aspects of the psyche "above and beyond" the ego. . . . Western examples include the higher self; the transpersonal witness; the Jungian Self which is the center of the psyche; and the inner-self helper that is a helpful and apparently transcendent personality that occurs in multiple personalities. (Walsh, 1990, p. 96)

The ego, that enduring image of oneself composed of the names with which one identifies ("intelligent," "spontaneous," "happy," "middle class," "young"), is an artifact of intellectual recognition. We human beings often think of ourselves as being coextensive with it, and it furnishes some sense of personal stability. But the ego and the person are not identical: "to be me" is not "to be ego," just as "to be thinking" does not exhaust "to be experiencing." Indeed, when we move out of the ego's analytical realm and gain access to our imaginative and intuitive capabilities, we often obtain "wisdom from inner sources that seem wiser than the ego or personality" (Walsh, 1990, p. 96).

In his memoirs, Carl Jung (1989) shares with us a series of personal fantasy figures—Elijah, Salome, Philemon, Ka—who originated in dreams or in guided imagery. Although he speaks ambivalently about whether these entities had existence separate from his own, Jung clearly considered them to be bearers of information not known by his ego:

> Philemon and other figures of my fantasies brought home to me the crucial insight that there are things in the psyche which I do not produce, but which produce themselves and have their own life. Philemon represents a force which was not myself. In my fantasies I held conversations with him, and he said things which I had not consciously thought. For I observed clearly that it was he who spoke, not I.
>
> Psychologically, Philemon represented superior insight. He was a mysterious figure to me. At times he seemed to be quite real, as if he were a living personality. I went walking up and down the garden with him, and to me he was what the Indians call a guru. (p. 183)

Such an inner experience is not unique. A friend of Gandhi told Jung that he himself had a "ghostly guru. . . . Most people have living gurus. But there are always some who have a spirit for teacher" (p. 184). And Wilson Van Dusen (1972) speaks about his dream maker as "The Other Me." He enumerates these qualities about this part of himself that differs from and surpasses the ego in knowledge:

> (a) It lives and does things.
> (b) It exists in some kind of polar relationship to ego or self-awareness. The less self-awareness, the more the activity of The Other Me becomes apparent.
> (c) It has total intimacy with the individual.
> (d) It has a central concern with the quality of the life.
> (e) It knows far more than the individual. There are intimations that it knows more of history and may be able to see the future.
> (f) It knows both the inner and outer realities and tends to treat these as one.
> (g) Its natural mode is representation or symbolizing in which something higher or more inner is illustrated by a dramatic arrangement of elements from a lower level. (pp. 180–181)

After an extended discussion of The Other Me, Van Dusen concludes:

> In any event, The Other Me has to lie beyond the accepted bounds of the individual as he is ordinarily conceived. Either the conception of the limits of the person has to be greatly expanded or we have to concede that higher processes are reflected in us. In a real way it would be vain pretension to claim The Other Me as our own since he is known so little and we have no control over him. It would seem more modest and fitting to concede that higher processes are reflected in us. (p. 184)

We may also explain the experience of an independent spiritual entity acting in and through ourselves by referring to the common defense of dissociation. Under stress of a nature or quantity surpassing our ordinary coping power, aspects of the psyche may split off from conscious awareness to function independently and to all appearances separately. In multiple personality disorders, these dissociated parts become more or less separate personalities; in less extreme instances they may function as subpersonalities contained within our ordinary experience of ourselves. Indeed, the "research on dissociation . . . suggests that all of us live with some degree of dissociation. . . . The implication is that anyone—ancient shamans, modern channelers, and all the rest of us—may be capable of receiving information from aspects of our own psyches that lie outside conscious awareness" (Walsh, 1990, p. 94).

Some aspects are overworked and readily available. They speak to us almost constantly. Anyone who has attempted to meditate will recognize immediately the interminable chattering and debating that goes on between opposing pairs of interior voices. "I should" is quite readily countered by "no you shouldn't"; the disappointment of "I can't" struggles against the hopefulness of "you can too!" Other voices have been pushed to the margins of our awareness and only rarely are they heard and recognized. When they speak out, it usually happens suddenly and rather surprisingly, as when chronically ambivalent people hear themselves saying almost unwillingly "I will." Still other voices have never burst into consciousness. They will ordinarily only become audible during some radical change in life circumstances—for example, a life-threatening illness, the demands of a completely foreign environment, or the intense internal focusing occasioned by psychotherapy. Taegel (1990) calls these different groups of voices the "overidentified aspects," the "disowned selves," and the "unknown selves." He notes that "the journey of the transforming selves begins with the recognition of the many selves" (p. 20).

Some of these selves speak to us about spiritual things and urge us on to explicitly spiritual activities:

> Some are lively energies that want to lead us toward spiritual ecstasy; they love religious experiences. Some want to lead us to discern the meaning of life. Others prefer magical experiences, like Elijah on his famous chariot or Moses and his burning bush or Mary and her angels or Buddha by his tree.
>
> Others remain quiet and like us to listen to the still small voice of God. Still others are quite extroverted and love us to tell their story to the outside world. Some like belonging and give us a spiritual charge each time we experience community. Many that are in my view the most basic, perhaps the

> most important, are nature lovers and long for stimulation by majestic skies, wondrous mountains, and rushing rivers. (Taegel, 1990, p. 111)

Any of these dissociated voices, but especially those urging us to move in explicitly spiritual directions, could be experienced as inspirations offered by separately existing spirits.

At this point, we may accept from religion and from experiences occurring when the intellect is not in control that spiritual beings exist independently of ourselves. Or we may conclude instead that they simply are parts of ourselves, dissociated parts that break through into consciousness only in certain situations where our imagination and intuition exercise control over our awareness. Faced with almost sure death, the atheist could have been visited by God, or in the trauma of the situation he could have experienced an interior godlike voice breaking through into his consciousness for perhaps the first time. Finally, we may rather agree with Walsh (1990) that

> it cannot be decided definitely because the available information or observations can be interpreted in many ways, and we have no absolute method by which to determine which interpretation(s) may be best. (p. 98)

And we may further conclude with him that

> at the present time, we may simply not be able to decide definitely between these various interpretations. Consequently, an agnostic view of spirits and channels in which we confess their indeterminacy and our ignorance may be the only intellectually honest position. (p. 98)

For an existential psychotherapist the ability to prove abstractly the existence of God or spirits or even human beings matters little. We grasp the reality of beings through our relationship to them, not through some universal understanding of their essential nature. "Do spirits exist as separate entities?", an essentialistic inquiry, must be altered to "What experience of a spiritual being do our clients bring to therapy?" In this latter question "spiritual" means not explainable through our ordinary sense processes, which are tied down to the time and space limitations of material reality.

Think back to the teaching story that began this chapter. Which would be crazier for the man barely hanging on to his life—to refuse the proffered help of the divine voice because of a philosophical position that such a Being could not exist, or to accept it as at least a preferable option to dying without the possibility of any assistance at all? Certainly, for him to let go of the branch would take an act of faith, but confronted with a sure death faith just may be a reasonable choice. The canard that "there are no atheists in a foxhole" may not only be true but also a sign of sanity. Faced with death human beings do not look for rational certainty; they rather reach out for help.

The Experience of Spirits Psychologically, the experience of spirits is felt to be an interaction between a living human being and an intelligent, nonmaterial entity separate from (but not necessarily "outside of") the person's ego or self. This interaction takes on at least three recognizable forms: spiritual visitation, communication, and assistance. Let us consider in turn each of these kinds of interaction. Perhaps through this examination we may understand spiritual realities and how they may be integrated into the therapeutic endeavor more immediately.

Some years back I received a panicky phone call from a stranger. A woman had been told by a close friend who happened to know me that I could surely help her. When I inquired as to the nature of her problem, she would only say that she was consumed by fear and that she simply could not speak about it on the phone. I agreed, therefore, to see her for an assessment session in which she could fill me in on what was happening and I could determine whether I could be of assistance to her. A decision on any possible course of therapy could only come later.

Christine showed up exactly on time. She appeared to be in her late thirties. She was rather thin and wiry, ordinary looking, but quite intense. After the usual introductions I told her that I would be happy to hear whatever she might wish to share with me about what was troubling her.

She became quiet and her body alternated between stern rigidity and spasms of shaking. Fear drained the color from her face and appeared to be paralyzing her ability to speak. Finally, however, like steam cascading out of a ruptured pipe, she exploded: "I'm being haunted by my two dead great aunts!"

Over the next half hour, in fits and starts she complained about the hateful spirits who had taken routinely to harassing her during those precious unwinding moments just prior to sleep.

Standing together at the foot of her bed, they would accuse, berate, and threaten. Only when all hope of sleep had vanished from Christine would they depart. Separated from peace, fearing for her sanity, she implored me to give her some powerful rite of exorcism that might free her.

As I knew next to nothing about this person, I could only form some working hypotheses: she could be hallucinating, in which case medical interventions might help her and indeed might be necessary; she could be letting a hyperactive imagination run away with her and this would require a shift into some more objective reasoning; she could be experiencing sense distortions because of the low-lit darkness in her pre-sleep bedroom; or she could be entertaining a return of two shady ladies.

Whatever . . . she needed to establish some immediate control over the situation. I opted therefore for the least intrusive interventions: in the two lamps guarding her bed, she would put powerful 3-way bulbs; should the shades reappear, at once she was to turn up the lights to 200 watts, and then sternly command: "Go to Hell where you belong!" I suggested these strategies because they would give her some immediate active response; they also would validate her firm belief in this spirit visitation and relieve her worry about possible insanity. Indeed, she had been terribly afraid to speak with anybody because she was certain she would be hospitalized. In her own mind she needed to be certain that she could assert firm control over these apparitions and also maintain her personal freedom.

Christine called to cancel our next appointment scheduled for four days later. She reported herself now in charge of the situation. She had done as I had directed; her evil visitors had returned that first evening and the next but had stayed only briefly. They had not appeared since. She wished now to carry on by herself just as long as she could call me if she again began to lose control. I never spoke to Christine—or, by the bye, any of her family—from that time on.

Were her relatives *really* visiting her? I don't know, but that question seems irrelevant to the crisis and the interventions created to resolve it. Christine thought that they were plaguing her, and I needed to intervene strongly to assist her in the psychological trauma threatening to engulf her. I had to accept the situation as described because she was experiencing it as factual. Only by going into her experience and helping her to engage her own capacity to direct her life could she reestablish some sense of personal space and integrity. (cf. Willis, 1991, pp. 59–60)

A client recently described another family visitation, not by dead aunts but by a dying mother.

Joan's mom had suffered a severe heart attack. The family had been taking turns watching by her hospital bed just in case she might come out of a coma and need their presence. This stress-filled vigil had been going on for three weeks; everyone was exhausted.

Joan left the hospital at 1:00 A.M. She simply could not stay there another moment; she desperately wanted to sleep in her own bed. She did not call anyone to replace her because the other family members were equally in need of an uninterrupted and restful night.

At 2:00 A.M. Joan sat upright in her bed when she was awakened by someone calling her name. She saw her mother's face hovering over the end of her bed. It smiled at her and then seemed to split: part of the face stayed gazing at her, the other part turned from her as if to leave. After some moments the vision faded.

Joan thought about hurrying over to the hospital, but she knew that would be a futile endeavor. Her mother was dead; she had come to tell her so. So she settled back down and tried to sleep, without much success. At 6:00 A.M. the phone rang. The head nurse explained that Joan's mom had passed away just after two, but that the staff had agreed not to wake Joan until now. Joan thanked the nurse, hung up, and then thanked her mom for making the effort to say goodbye.

Joan told me about her mother's leavetaking in the context of a series of losses that had culminated recently in her loss of a job. She recognized how important goodbyes are and also how physical absence does not in itself mean separation. Whether her mother had actually appeared in her bedroom, she could not prove or disprove; yet neither of us doubt that Joan's experience of that night is still living on in her. Moreover, it was at this time influencing the way in which she left her colleagues. Indeed, as I am writing this account, she is today having a joyous going-away party at her home for anyone in her agency wishing to share a goodbye.

Spiritual communication often happens at the moment of a loved one's death. Just as concentration and personal involvement cause us to lose track of passing time in such a way that time both expands and contracts, so love may overcome physical separation by de-emphasizing location (*locus*), a physical and material reality, and stressing position (*situs*), a relational and spiritual one. *Objects* obey the rules of material reality as regards passing time and material distance; *subjects* may move into a nonordinary reality where those rules do not apply. In Chapter 3 I shared how passing time became a vastly altered personal time in an Indian sweat lodge as I moved deeply inside myself to a center of quiet and rest. In such a position (*situs*) all time may be changed; from such a position (*situs*) love may overcome material distance. Consider a couple of examples of this phenomenon.

A sophisticated and well-to-do woman in her late fifties was referred to me because of a family tragedy. A beloved brother, recently divorced, had out of his loneliness and depression murdered his ex-wife and their 4-year-old son. Then, after carefully arranging the bodies and cleaning up the area around them, he killed himself. A Roman Catholic raised with strict moral prohibitions concerning suicide, Diane needed to deal both with her grief and with her confusion over this otherwise "good" man's actions.

As she shared this tragic story, she spoke of this, for her, extraordinary experience. Her brother lived in the midwest, in the Central Time Zone, one hour different from her East Coast time. As she and her husband were celebrating a wedding with friends in a rustic Connecticut inn, she suddenly felt a burning pain shooting through her chest and around her heart. This was followed by a stabbing pain in her neck and shoulders. She then became nauseous. When she informed her husband of this, he initially chided her about her liquor intake. After she showed him her barely touched champagne glass, they both fell silent. Some minutes passed before she was able to continue eating her dinner.

On arriving back home, they found a message on their answering machine from a brother who lived in Jack's hometown. She was urged to call immediately as Jack had died suddenly that afternoon. As she later learned, he had shot himself in the head while they had been dining with their friends.

Diane now knows that because of their closeness she had experienced some of the pain of Jack's physical death. She does not question this even though she has not known such nonordinary communication previously. As her therapist, I accept her explanation and simply share with her that love as a supramaterial form of communication overcomes distance. We do not talk about spirits or spiritual communication, but clearly she judges that she has touched that reality. Could it be simply a coincidence? Of course. Could it be a spiritual communication channeled through love? Certainly, many other people have reported similar communications at the moment of a beloved's death . . . like Dottie.

She started our session this way:

Client:	You must help! I think Mom's going crazy. I don't understand.
Therapist:	All right. If possible, quiet down a bit. Tell me what's so upsetting to you.
Client:	I'm sorry. . . . I went home to Mississippi last week for my brother's funeral. The Army had returned his body from Vietnam. After the funeral, Mom pulled me into her room, away from Dad and the others. She was pretty hysterical. She begged me to listen to what happened and to assure her that she's O.K. Here's the story she told me:

> It's early Wednesday morning. I'm awakened by the alarm clock falling off the night stand. It shows 3:00 A.M. I have a tough time getting back to sleep mainly because of a sharp stomach pain on my left side. After taking some Alka-Seltzer I do finally drift off. At breakfast I mention it to your father. He says, "Oh, forget it. Just something you ate."
>
> The next night much the same events occur. The clock falls again; it's 3:00 A.M.; my stomach hurts like crazy in the same place. But this time your father wakes up. As we're talking a sudden wind blows through our bedroom. He goes over to the window and shuts it. When he climbs back into bed, perplexed-like he comments, "It's sure calm outside. Clear as a bell and quiet. No wind to speak of." We don't talk about it anymore that night or the next day.
>
> Early Friday morning I awake with that pain. It's so bad I wake Jim. As we're considering calling Doc Samuels, we hear a knocking on the bedroom window. It startles us because it's in the same rhythm your brother used when he was locked out: "tap, tap/ tap, tap, tap/ tap, tap/ tap, tap, tap, tap." Jim rushes over and flings open the window, half expecting to see Bobbie just sitting there in the oak tree. No one's there. No wind's blowing either. And you know what?—it's three o'clock.

> The next week we get a visit from an Army lieutenant. He informs us that Bobbie died last Saturday afternoon, Vietnam time, about 5:00. A grenade was thrown into his foxhole; he fell on it to save the others; it tore out his stomach and abdomen, on the left side. When we figured out the time difference, he probably died about 3:00 A.M. our time, Friday morning. Oh, Dottie, I think your brother knew he was about to die, was trying to warn us, and was begging for our help.

Finished with her mom's account, she just sat, looking at me. Without removing the possibility that her mother *is* disturbed, I assure her that such events as these do happen to people, that they are ordinarily signs of a strong loving bond, that in itself the experience need not alarm her. I suggest she call home, tell her mother not to worry, and relate our conversation. If she wants an explanation, just share with her that we know that time and space don't always act the way we are accustomed to expect. How they can change so, we don't clearly understand. We do know, however, that in intense moments we humans have this capacity to communicate with people with whom we are close. Indeed, all we can say for sure in this instance is that it reveals Bobbie's deep love for his family. (cf. Willis, 1989, pp. 84–85)

Tales such as Dottie's do not get shared a lot, inside or outside the therapy room. They are just "too weird," "too spooky," "a sign I'm going nuts." Yet when they are revealed, the storyteller invariably swears to the truth of it all, even if that condemns her or him to a judgment of insanity.

For many of the same reasons, people hesitate to share how they receive comfort and assistance from the spirit world. Can you imagine the confirmed atheist letting go of the branch, being caught by a heavenly hand, and then going home to tell his buddies about his new-found faith? He would not only be afraid of losing a lot of friends; he would most likely be quite concerned that he would be trundled off to some psychiatric ward for a professional assessment of his mental stability! Well, let me begin this discussion of spiritual assistance by accepting these risks myself.

After being mugged back in 1988 I spent a number of hospital days drifting in and out of ordinary consciousness. During one of these periods of reverie, no doubt drug-enhanced, I became aware of two sheltering animals. Standing on a rock above me, a magnificent stag shook his antlers, looking now here, now there, like a living radar. Down next to me a panther, black as coal, circled, now rubbing against my leg, now patrolling in ever-widening circles. I realized that they had come to aid me. As vulnerable as I felt, I was most grateful.

Now, six years later, they still guard me. Soon thereafter, a white stallion with sharp, flashing hooves and a high-soaring eagle joined them.

Where did they come from? Joan Halifax (1979) writes extensively on the spirit world of the native shaman. She notes that "The stag, reindeer, and deer, the medium of magical transport for the shaman, is believed to be a mediator between heaven and earth and a messenger of the gods. The antlers, symbols of regeneration and growth because of the way they are renewed, are often associated with the Sacred Tree and the mysteries of death and rebirth" (p. 82). The stallion appeared suddenly during a therapy session. It reminds me forcefully of the granite horse outlined on the slopes of Mt. Adams. This great animal overshadowed and protected my boyhood years in Central Washington. As for the panther and eagle, I do not know. At any rate, because of my own experience with these spiritual assistants I agree with Norman Cousins (1979) when he approvingly quotes Albert Schweitzer as saying:

> The witch doctor succeeds for the same reason all the rest of us [doctors] succeed. Each patient carries his own doctor inside him. They come to us not knowing this truth. We are at our best when we give the doctor who resides within each patient a chance to go to work" (pp. 68–69)

An example of how they assist me in my work may be illustrated by an imaginary journey I took during a supervision session. A supervisee, Mary Ann, expressed a desire to learn more about the place of imagery in therapy. She knows methods of deep relaxation and has some familiarity using gestalt methods with dreams; she had not, however, used guided imagery with her clients.

Instead of abstractly discussing imagery and therapy, I decided to give her an experience guiding me on an abbreviated shamanic journey to the Lower World. In this way she would get experience in assisting imaginary exploration and also expand her knowledge of the imagination through contact with this particular world of the shamanic tradition.

I gave her three simple instructions: if I should suddenly become silent, ask where I am; if I should become blocked, tell me to look around for assistance; if I should be afraid or in danger, tell me to find protection or leave.

Using a combination of physical and breathing exercises, she relaxed me and then suggested I find some way to travel to another world. I did so through a cave. After I shared some initial indecision and wandering, she suggested that I look around for help. Immediately, my animal guardians appeared. The stag set off directly into some hills so I followed. On a mountain top I discovered a stone sacrificial altar. When I indicated some fear, Mary Ann told me to look under the altar. To my relief my panther was crouched there, attentive and protective.

We left the hills and entered a desert landscape reminiscent of the Pacific Southwest. I walked on a faint path winding through the sagebrush. Suddenly coming upon a rattlesnake, I stopped. Mary Ann said, "I'm with you." With that the stag lashed out with his hooves, severing the rattler's head from its coiled body. I continued on. Twice more the path was blocked, once by a scorpion, another time by a giant tarantula. Both times she instructed me to leave. I did so, detouring through the sagebrush, but coming back to the path further on.

At last, the path ended in a clearing. There stood a stately bush, surrounded by a garden of trumpet flowers. As I fell silent in wonder at this floral display, Mary Ann asked what I wanted to do. Straightaway I picked a gorgeous flower. With that action I somehow knew the journey was complete. Feeling both secure and happy, I flew back to my office . . . holding the trumpet flower firmly in my hand.

After discussing the effectiveness of her interventions, we talked about some of the more salient learnings about travel in this Lower World: the cave entrance, the appearance of power animals, the need to trust these spirit guides, the natural landscape, the risks of such journeying, the prudent avoiding of evil forces, the bringing back from that world some aid for oneself and others. Familiarity with, and the charting of, this inner landscape stood out, indeed, as the most significant of learnings.

I keep in contact with these spiritual helpers through periods of quiet meditation, through guided journeys like this one, and through drawing. I am including here as Figure 8.1 a recent attempt I made to picture these spirit guides concretely for myself.

FIGURE 8.1
Medicine Wheel

Some years ago, a professor of sociology introduced me to this world of spirit animals. It all started with a dream fragment of a bus that kept dematerializing. Taking this to mean that he was being directed to embark on a spiritual journey, I helped him with this guided imagery:

> Jerry took the bus on an interstate highway heading southwest from the East Coast. He exited in Oklahoma and immediately found himself on a Cherokee reservation. After spending some time in a teepee speaking with the Indians gathered there, he wandered to the banks of a small creek. As he stood there, a small rabbit came up to him, stopped, and looked at him. It then hopped over to a clump of bushes and seemed to indicate that Jerry should look there. Indeed, the underbrush concealed a silver flute. When he played it, the rabbit changed into a beautiful woman. She told him: "I am ready to help you. If you need me, just play the flute."

This began an extraordinary therapeutic journey. Intrigued by the Indian setting, Jerry did some genealogical research on his family. Sure enough, an early white settler on his mother's side had married a Cherokee woman. After other dreams had introduced him to a bison and an eagle, he felt this trio of animals to be incomplete; there should be a fourth guide. One day he exultantly produced a copy of a Plains Indian medicine wheel: in the East an eagle, in the South a rabbit, in the North a buffalo, in the Wear a bear. His intuition had been correct. From that time on these four became almost daily companions. Jerry even got to consulting with them about taking speaking engagements, going to particular conferences, writing research projects. He reported these meditative encounters as immensely valuable to him.

The manner in which these animal guides affected his therapy may be illustrated in one particularly profound session. Jerry appeared to be quite agitated. Earlier in the week, when he had meditatively sought out his totemic guides, he had discovered an intruder. There, perched near his eagle (intelligence), rabbit (humility), bison (friendliness), and bear (wisdom), was a repulsive vulture.

As he raged about this carrion bird, Jerry finally admitted that it represented the sexual scavenger in him. Although married, when he went to his numerous out-of-town conferences he quite readily orchestrated one-night stands with disposable partners.

He disliked this in himself; he violently hated its devouring representative.

Taking account of his Cherokee ancestry, I suggested that he summon a council meeting right here and now. Relying on techniques pioneered by Moreno and Perls, I soon had the seven of us suitably situated about my office.

Jerry got right into the action, moving swiftly from role to role—questioning, demanding, imploring. A real shift occurred when, sitting in the bear's wise skin, he quietly suggested to the assembly: "Why don't you let the bird stay? You know, he, like us, only gets one vote."

With that compromise, Jerry visibly relaxed. His frustration and distress drained away. Suddenly, with a shout he jumped up, strode to the vulture's perch, and symbolically gave this new guide a welcoming hug!

In subsequent months, Jerry often showed up, vulture in tow. But now the dark side of himself was owned. His extramarital assignations diminished and his marriage flourished. (cf. Willis, 1991, pp. 60–61)

Spiritual assistance in therapy may come in many forms, including those more closely approximating the symbols of white Western civilization. Meet, for example, Veronica, the descendant of wealthy New England gentry.

A middle-aged, somewhat compulsive activist, over the past month she had been fearfully moving inside herself into a seemingly bottomless well of pain. Some of it could be attributed to a present estrangement from her mother, but otherwise her present life situation was satisfying. She speculated that this aching must be coming from childhood experiences, perhaps linked to her mother. However, she could not recall any specific incidents that could be generating such distress.

On this particular day Veronica felt heavy—"like weights hanging from my arms and legs"—and she was experiencing an intense ache in her chest. Although she wept and expressed her inner feeling of desolation and abandonment at some length, she remained quite distressed.

Determining that she needed to move inside to find some source of personal solace, I guided her in the wise person meditation described above.

When Veronica was once more consciously back in my office, she told me that her wise being was Jesus, not the historical human person, but an enveloping being of warmth and light. After some initial struggle with herself to "do this right," she had quieted down and just let herself be in his presence. When she had finally asked him why she was hurting so much, Jesus simply responded, "Because I love you." At that point she had felt a profound peace flowing through her. Then, having lost track of me and my voice, she had opened her eyes.

She was initially quite puzzled with this interior response to her question. As we talked about it, however, she came to realize that her pain could well be one of yearning. She had unquestioningly assumed that her pain was issuing from some childhood deprivation or injury; the pain, therefore, could only be bad. But a deep love desiring oneness and wholeness could also be experienced as intense pain, like St. Augustine's "My heart is restless till it rests in Thee." That pain, far from signifying some unknown trauma, rather could be heralding for her the hope of eventual fullness. It could be flowing from her goodness as the potential of love.

Veronica left that session much lighter. Most likely, some of her pain will be discovered to be leftovers of childhood rejections and alienation. But a significant portion of it, she now knows, is accounted for by her human condition of being separated from Love. Her spirit guide, Jesus, had helped her understand; he also now existed in her as a comforting source of guidance in a new and potentially strengthening fashion.

How may we explain Veronica's experience? Existentialist philosopher and theologian Paul Tillich (1948) says this about the experience of grace:

> Grace strikes us when we are in great pain and restlessness. . . . It strikes us when we feel our separation is deeper than usual, because we have violated another life, a life which we loved, or from which we are estranged. . . . It strikes us when, year after year, the longed-for perfection of life does not appear, when the old compulsions reign within us as they have for decades, when despair destroys all joy and courage. Sometimes at that moment a wave of light breaks into our darkness, and it is as though a voice were saying: "You are accepted. *You are accepted,* accepted by that which is greater than you, and the name of which you do not know. Do not ask for the name now; perhaps later you will do such. Do not seek for anything; do not perform anything; do not intend anything. *Simply accept the fact that you are accepted!*" If that happens to us, we experience grace. . . . And in the light of this grace we perceive the power of grace in our relation to

> ourselves. We experience moments in which we accept ourselves, because we feel that we have been accepted by that which is greater than we. (pp. 161–163)

Tillich's description of the experience of grace remarkably parallels Veronica's situation and experience of spiritual assistance during that therapy session. Tillich would undoubtedly equate grace with love, and love with God. With God's help Veronica will some day dry up the overflowing well of her pain. As an existential psychotherapist, I accept Veronica's experience as reported and use its power for healing, for self acceptance, and for a return to the hope of her own life force. Although I may also agree with her interpretation of her experience, as her therapist I need not do so. What we both do agree on is the undoubted power of the assistance she received in that interior forest clearing.

Before concluding this discussion of how spiritual experiences may be integrated into an existential psychotherapy, it seems necessary to consider one other spiritual reality: how the spiritual life of the therapist may affect the process of therapy. This life may be described in many ways, but one that is marked by purpose in the face of meaninglessness, humility in lieu of guilt, and love in the midst of separation will be most effective in helping the client overcome the existential anxieties of the human condition.[1]

Viktor Frankl (1984), the founder of logotherapy, is the existentialist of meaning. For him, "striving to find a meaning in one's life is the primary motivational force in man" (p. 104). He goes so far as to maintain

> that mental health is based on a certain degree of tension, the tension between what one has already achieved and what one still ought to accomplish, or the gap between what one is and what one should become. (p. 110)

And no matter the desperation over or the hopelessness about a given situation, we all must answer for our own lives as

---

[1] Irvin Yalom, in his study of the existential anxieties, presents extensive case material as he demonstrates a variety of therapeutic strategies that may assist people confronting such life experiences. He does not address the topic of the therapist's own spiritual life as perhaps *the* most effective antidote to these spirit-wrenching anxieties.

"responsibleness [is] the very essence of human existence" (p. 113).

Frankl does not take this position easily. His existential philosophy was forged around the fiery furnaces of the Holocaust. If anyone should know about the response to meaninglessness, this survivor of Auschwitz should. But rather astonishingly Frankl finds even a Nazi concentration camp experience a possible source of meaning:

> As logotherapy teaches, there are three avenues on which one arrives at meaning in life. The first is by creating a work or doing a deed. The second is by experiencing something or encountering someone; in other words, meaning can be found not only in work but also in love. . . . Most important, however, is the third avenue to meaning in life; even the helpless victim of a hopeless situation, facing a fact he cannot change, may rise above himself, may grow beyond himself, and by so doing change himself. (p. 146)

In our modern age we have become accustomed to equate pain with failure and hopelessness, pleasure with success and purpose. Pain must therefore be avoided as evil, its opposite pursued as good. But this position treats the human being as a closed system, as a narcissistic entity whose meaning revolves solely around one's perception of personal satisfaction. As Frankl says in countering this position,

> the true meaning of life is to be discovered in the world rather than within man or his own psyche . . . I have termed this constitutive characteristic "the self-transcendence of human existence." (p. 115)

This transcendent aspect of our existence does not depend on pleasure or pain; it depends on immanence. Indeed, an intense experience of pleasure (as in love) or pain (as in despair) may be the catalyst that drives one into the depths of oneself to "the still point of the turning world" (Eliot, 1943, p. 15) from which transcendence springs. Joy flows from the experience of an immanent centeredness expressing itself in a transcendent love of existence.

Faced with the desperate nature of many lives, in the name of existentialism some therapists choose nihilism as the antidote to pain. And they teach a kind of learned meaninglessness to their clients. Frankl relates this interaction between George Sargent and his therapist:

> "George [said the therapist], you must realize the world is a joke. There is no justice, everything is random. Only when you realize this will you understand how silly it is to take yourself seriously. There is no grand purpose in the universe. It just *is*. There's no particular meaning in what decision you make today about how to act." (pp. 152–153)

We can well imagine that George's therapist was attempting to lessen his client's pain by saying, "It's no big deal!" But a hurting person knows that it is. The therapist has the task of "immunizing the trauma against nihilism rather than inoculating him with the cynicism that is a defense mechanism against his own nihilism" (p. 153). What is needed is a path to transcendence through pain, not a steeling of oneself against its meaning.

I found myself facing a kind of nihilism in one period of my life. Following the ordinary identity struggles of one's twenties and early thirties, especially when they came to a head during the societal upheavals of the 1960s, I was bereft of the comfortable God of my Christian upbringing. God as family (a caring Father, a self-sacrificing Son and Brother, a forgiving Spirit of Love) seemed to me more a human creation modeled on some idealistic experience of family life than some objective revealed truth. In my hard-won adulthood, I could no longer believe easily in this construction of God that found no continuing basis inside me. Instead I now experienced God more like a context, a power in which I lived. I had no image of this God; I simply knew Its presence surrounding me. I wished to know more about It, and I was open to Its action in my life. I could, however, only wait. Then Ann walked into my life. No one has taught me more about this God and the spirituality of meaninglessness than she.

Three months before the phone call that began our pain-filled journey together, Ann and her husband, a well-to-do and important executive of an international corporation, had journeyed to their son's graduation ceremonies at a prominent midwestern university. Upon arriving at his apartment that graduation morning, they found him dead, his brains splattered about his bedroom. In his right hand he still grasped tenaciously the service revolver, his Dad's, that had killed him.

The parents gradually pieced together what lay behind the tragedy. The school tuition was being paid by the boy's natural father, a businessman living in the Far East. They discovered a stack of uncashed checks from his father in Ted's drawer. By their dates, it became obvious that Ted had not been attending school for the past two years, even though he had kept up an elaborate charade of doing so. Finally, on this supposed day of graduation, the truth could no longer be avoided. Instead of facing it and his parents, Ted had chosen suicide.

When Ann came to see me, she was nearly catatonic with despair. Her husband drove her to my office as she could not drive, and anyway he feared that alone she would purposely kill herself. Her intense depression covered a storm of emotions: anger at the boy's father for his financial sloppiness, guilt over her failure to penetrate Ted's skillful facade, overwhelming grief at the loss of this her only son, and rage at a God Who had failed to protect the life He had given and Who had callously allowed its despairing destruction.

Over the course of four years of four hours of weekly therapy, Ann and I had frequent conversations about God. The God of her Roman Catholic childhood lay forever shattered next to her son's body. How could she believe in a personal, loving, providential, and all-powerful God in light of the incredible horror of her son's lonely and desperate life that culminated in such despair! Either God does not exist, or He is not in charge of the universe, or He does not give a damn about human life. She dared me—or anyone—to justify God's request for her faith and obedience before the sacrilege of her son's death.

Together we searched for meaning, for any purpose behind this tragic aborting of Ted's life. We found none. And rarely did a session go by without Ann yearning desperately for her own death. Indeed, I did not know from day to day if she would be alive for our next meeting. With his suicide, Ted had destroyed not only his own life but also her purpose for existing. Ann now doubted both the existence of God and the worth of life itself.

When Ann provoked me to defend her God, I did not. As she challenged me to explain in any rational way Ted's death, I did not. With her, I found it meaningless; with her, the loving and personal God of her Catholic faith lost all sense; with her, doubt and meaninglessness remained as a kind of indictment against this God.

Yet I did not give up on her, and, incredibly, she did not give up on her life. In spite of my helplessness before her pain, in spite of her hopelessness before a purposeless life, we both accepted each other. And when she asked, I told her about my God, one so different from the one of both of our younger years. Gradually this God took a stronger position in both of our lives: a God without any name other than Being. We knew next to nothing about this God. We could not expect that It loves us or cares about us. We could not pray to It in thanksgiving or praise; we could not beg for Its assistance. It is nothing except that It is, but somehow It grounds our very being.

Without articulating this faith except in and through her pain, we came to the God that Paul Tillich (1969) calls the "God beyond God." As he explains it:

> Theism in all its forms is transcended in the experience we have called absolute faith. It is the accepting of the acceptance without somebody or something that accepts. It is the power of being-itself that accepts and gives the courage to be. (p. 185)

In this absolute faith we believed in a nameless, faceless Being beyond all personal relationships, beyond even the experience of mystical union. What grounded this faith?—only the tremendous worth of existence even in the depths of despair. This faith alone has the "courage which takes doubt and meaninglessness into itself" (p. 188).

As Tillich further amplifies, the state of being grasped by the God beyond God is a

> situation on the boundary of man's possibilities. It *is* this boundary. Therefore it is both the courage of despair and the courage in and above every courage. It is not a place where one can live, it is without the safety of words and concepts, it is without a name, a church, a cult, a theology. But it is moving in the depth of all of them. It is the power of being, in which they participate and of which they are fragmentary expressions. (1969, pp. 188–189)

Together Ann and I traveled beyond all explanations and all excuses to the recognition of Being in Which we dwell and from Which we draw life. As her therapist I had to dare the ruthless glare of her pain and rage; in naked honesty I had to give up all lingering authorized versions of God and familiar rational premises arguing for God's existence. When only doubt and meaninglessness seemed to be left, still the courage to be struggled in their merciless embrace and eventually won out. It alone is the experience of the God beyond God.

One day Ann announced that she was beginning a training program for hospice volunteers. Soon after, we cut back our therapy sessions to an hour each week. She still missed her son terribly; she still longed for death so that her pain would cease; but now she was willing to live. And she was determined to help others live and die with dignity.

I have not seen Ann in seven years. Yet whenever I am meeting a client screaming out against the cruelty of life, she is with me. And whenever a client wrestles with hopelessness and despair, with a life without known purpose or meaning, I remember her. Then I summon up my courage to walk with yet another person to the nowhere and nobody of the God beyond God.

During the years that prepared me for the encounter with this God, I entered into psychotherapy with a neo-Freudian psychiatrist. One night, after nine months of intensive psychotherapy, the depths of a terrifying inner world opened up for me. For five hours I sat with a friend: speechless, paralyzed, swallowed up inside. A deep, black well became my only habitat. I fell . . . fell . . . and kept falling. Though terror urged me to stop the descent by reaching out with arms and legs, my gut somehow realized that I must dare even death. And I did. Then, about 3:00 A.M., I fell into light. Exhausted, but strangely peaceful, I thanked Tom and went to bed.

In the months that followed I came to realize what had occurred. Previously, I had structured my life around meeting others' expectations. If I could do whatever others demanded perfectly, then I could win their acceptance. In this way I could make my life secure. I could control their responses to me as well. Moreover, this security would extend past this life into any future one. By doing whatever others portrayed as the Will of God, I could also force the Divinity to accept me for eternity. That night, I had relinquished the psychic structures erected to protect me from death. In doing so, I also gave up a lifelong effort to control God. That meant, however, bowing humbly to the imperfection of my life and drawing to myself the guilt of human existence. I had to assume sole responsibility for my life, even if that meant being rejected. I even had to dare the Gates of Hell in this decision to take charge of my own life. Unwittingly, I had been trying to fashion my life, others' lives in relation to mine, and even God's life in my own image and likeness.

Since that night of existential crisis, I have found these realizations rooting themselves in my being and expressing themselves in my behavior:

1. I cannot escape either imperfection or guilt. The true response to each is, simply, "I'm sorry."
2. I cannot reasonably place expectations on myself or others. I may *hope* but given our imperfect existence I cannot *demand.*
3. I cannot control Life. Instead, I am constantly urged within to get out of Its way and let Life live me.
4. Confronted by the certainties of death and human imperfection, I may find no security other than in the risk of transcendence.
5. Transcendence happens only through the humble relinquishing of my life to the power of Life.
6. Whatever turns out to be the answer to the ontological question about God's existence, I can only allow spiritual realities to touch me as I forsake reliance on rational controls.

These personal convictions were sorely tried by Richard. He came to see me when it appeared that his obsessive behavior was endangering his job. A security guard at a local bank, he kept arriving late for work because his twenty minute drive from home on an interstate highway on some mornings was taking as long as two hours. It seems that whenever he hit a noticeable bump in the asphalt, he would quickly glance in his rearview mirror to see if he had by any chance hit somebody. Although he could see no signs of unusual commotion, he would reason that perhaps he just could not see the body. He then would exit as soon as possible, get back on the highway going the opposite direction and seek an exit prior to the site of the supposed accident. Another exit, another entrance, and then he would painstakingly retrace his original drive, making sure that no body was lying along the road. Finally satisfied, he would continue on . . . until the next big bump!

As it turned out this symptom was not alone. Almost at once, for example, I noticed how red and cracked his hands were. He soon told me how he was scouring his hands almost constantly in order to make certain that he was not passing potentially deadly germs from himself to others.

What fueled this bizarre behavior? Richard came from a rigid, fundamentalist Christian home. He had been raised to believe that we must love one another and that we must show that love in deeds. And if we disobeyed this commandment, God would punish us forever in Hell. Over the course of years, this belief had transformed itself in him into this expanded one: If I do something that could possibly hurt another when I could still take another precaution, then I am not *really* loving that person. And God will punish me, then, by hurting someone I love. And that will be my fault too.

Richard was caught in the agonizing grip of an obsessive compulsive disorder masquerading as God. I challenged it with a variety of strategies (Prozac to treat the underlying depression that was energizing the obsessive defense, *in vivo* desensitization to provide positive countering experience, relaxation exercises to overcome his spiraling anxiety). These all helped. However, what finally convinced him intellectually that he must change were these dilemmas with which I kept confronting him: if God is a loving God as you say, then how could He want you to be so miserable in trying to serve Him; if God is all-powerful, then how can you possibly control Him by making certain that you are blameless in every way; if you say that you love God, then how can you be so proud as to try to force God to love you? And as I shared with him a spirituality based on humility, he began to see some alternative way of relating to God.

I have not seen Richard for some time now. He no longer works as a security guard; he is pursuing a college career in business administration. Perhaps a quest for learning has replaced that panicked search for security! I do not know Who God is for him now, though I am reasonably certain that he is no longer attempting to play at being God to the same extent as previously. I hope for him that someday he will have enough courage to get out of his own way to allow Life to live him, to experience God in the act of transcending his waning need to control.

In the late 1970s I had the opportunity to train in a method of psychic healing taught by Lawrence LeShan (1974a & b), a parapsychologist and a researcher in the phenomenon of nontraditional healing. He employs the imagination as the primary instrument of healing. Through strict meditative discipline and a defined series of meditations, the healing person, in an altered state of consciousness, becomes one with the person seeking healing. The results in my healees vary from the cessation of physical symptoms ("my diarrhea stopped that evening"), from the immediate experience of bodily sensations ("waves of energy, starting at my head, moved down my body"), to subliminal communication ("I felt such love in this room") and emotional change ("I feel incredible peace and joy"). My experience invariably involves a trance state, vivid imagery, a strong emotional response, some exhaustion, and even occasional physical pain. (cf. Willis, 1979, p. 110)

I may illustrate this kind of healing meditation with a synopsis of one I recently experienced while directing my attention toward a dear friend who is suffering from an autoimmune disease that has caused numbness from her waist down. On the day of this meditation she was visited her parents in the South, always a stress-filled time.

After I spent a few minutes centering myself with a breath-counting meditation, I gazed nonreflectively and with as much presence as possible at a picture Lynn had given me of herself. Again after some minutes, when I felt a strong tension between myself and the picture, I closed my eyes and had the following experience:

> We are walking side by side. Gradually our bodies merge, sideways, till we are one. I become aware of red blood circulating through our common body. Soon it becomes fire. It grows in intensity. Suddenly, a beam of light enters through the top of our head and floods the body with light. Too much to contain, the body's pores open, light explodes through them, the body is consumed in the fire-light. As this happens I gasp for breath and tears flow down my face, the outward manifestations of a kind of ecstatic pain. Then the fire-light becomes the sun and fills the universe. I/she no longer exist except in unity with this massive fire-light. Deep within our nothingness that's true. After some moments the light diminishes and the altered state of consciousness recedes. I am once more in my office, alone, emotionally drained, but peaceful and deeply quiet.

As I have worked with these meditations, I have come to some firm conclusions. In the first place, I am not always able to achieve the kind of unity exemplified here. I fail when I am distracted by my own needs, problems, life. Locked in my own little world, I am unable to touch others in any significant manner. And even when I think I have become one with the other, I do not always get a response that the other has been in any way affected. Secondly, the feeling associated with this meditation is love. The focusing exclusively on another, the reaching out to that person, the giving of myself to the other's life, the transcending of my own boundaries without seeming to lose my sense of myself, the ecstatic experience of oneness: I recognize them all as familiar qualities of love in a relationship. Thirdly, I am able to sustain the intensity of this love only briefly. It feels like a massive power flowing through me, one I can barely contain. To my self I seem quite small and insignificant in its presence. Fourthly, any healing that happens appears to come about as the healee gets taken up into this Love. I do not do anything to the other person. Fifthly, the unity of love happens in personal time and it readily overcomes physical distance. Isolation and separation occur in the realm of sensory reality; in this clairvoyant reality they disappear (LeShan and Margenau, 1982, pp. 161–165). And finally, as in sensual attraction this love may influence the emotions and generate physical sensations in either or both of us. The heart and the body may participate in it. However, through the power of the imagination this love flows most essentially from the core of the self. It engages the whole of one's being rather than specific parts to make the healer totally available and present to the other person. This presence of another to one's life seems to hold the most meaning for the healee.

Under the impact of such meditative experiences, I have realized that healing in psychotherapy also happens through love. When I attend to another's life, I am loving him or her; when I go inside myself to find a word or to retrieve a feeling, to capture an image or recognize an intuition, I am loving myself; when I put my ego aside and allow the power of my life to break out of my human isolation, I know my self is being taken up into a Life greater than my own; when another person becomes whole in the power of our interaction, I can only attribute that to an energy far surpassing my well-meaning but halting attempts to join wholly and vulnerably another's life. And so, the God beyond God, Tillich's Ground of Being, has become for me identical with Life and Love. When I am truly present to another in psychotherapy, I am living and acting in the power of that Love. In that power I may bring the possibility of new life that is necessary for health. I agree with Ludwig Binswanger (1986) when he remarks that

> it would be rather unfortunate if our patients had to understand Heraclitus or Hegel in order to get well; but none can

> attain to genuine health in his innermost being unless the physician succeeds in awakening in him that little spark of spirituality that must be awake in order for such a spirit to feel the slightest breath. (p. 99)

In this chapter I have recounted a number of incidents not explainable in our ordinary sensory reality: Dottie's brother attempted to contact his parents before he died in Vietnam, Joan's mother appeared to her in a goodbye gesture just before she died, Diane felt in her body the physical pain of her brother's suicide. When clients share such accounts, they ordinarily do so with some trepidation, as if they are in danger of ridicule or a judgment of insanity.

Most usually these extrasensory communications happen between people who have a great deal of emotional involvement in each other's lives. Common sense would expect that. LeShan and Margenau (1982), when putting forward researchable projects concerning group cohesion and psychic phenomena, offer these working hypotheses:

> 1. Psi occurrences are most frequent between people who like each other than between people who do not.
> 2. People who identify themselves as members of the same group, which is important to them, will report psi occurrences between them more frequently than those who do not.
> 3. Psi occurrences are more likely when the stability of an important relationship is threatened and communication is necessary to maintain it, but sensory modes of communication are blocked. (pp. 219–221)

In the three examples cited above all psychic communication occurred between family members, when ordinary contact was impossible, and the people involved were emotionally quite close. My experience over many years of listening to such accounts fits both our common expectations and these research hypotheses.

In therapy, therefore, instead of manifesting ridicule or making judgments of mental incompetence, I simply explore with my clients the kind of relationships they have had with the psychic communicator. It soon becomes apparent that a deep, emotional unity of some duration exists there. I then reframe the experience as one of love, as one taking place in a reality not tied down by the ordinary rules of passing time and physical location. Personal time expands into past and future; personal space or position (*situs*) overcomes distance.

This takes a special shape in instances of prolonged grief. Sometimes it is assuaged by reaching back into the past and completing something left naggingly unfinished.

Many years ago Pat showed me quite dramatically the strong relationship between love, personal time, and healing. We had recently met and were in the process of becoming good friends. This session occurred as a kind of crisis intervention after seeing the late-60s film rendition of Erich Segal's *Love Story*. Like the heroine, Pat too had lived on and off in Manhattan, a transplanted Midwesterner. And someone she loved deeply, not a wife but a mother, had also fought a soul-etching battle with cancer. And lost.

She had sobbed her way through the film and could not stop crying afterwards. Between tears she was able to tell me about her mother's death. I was struck by the obsessive signature that underwrote disconnected sections of her rambling account: "And to think," she would say, "for all her family, she died alone." She spoke painfully about the days spent lovingly at her bedside, about the decision to go home from the hospital for some brief relief from her fatigue, about her hurrying back to the hospital after a call that her mother was dying, seeing a roadside clock pointing to 8:00 o'clock and knowing she had died.

What gouged most painfully, I came to realize, were two related, unfinished, flapping strands of memory: "I yearn," she might well say, "to tell her one final time, as she dies, that I love her so much; in saying good-bye I want to assure her of our ultimate reunion, sometime, somewhere." Recognizing that she needed to do that now if she were to get any relief from her grief, I told her I would help her go back to speak with her mother.

As I held her strongly but gently, through volcanoes of sorrow Pat returned, then, in her imagination to the hospital, to the room, her mother's bedside. Words of long-held love poured out, surrounding her and the dying woman with warmth and light. As the suffering ended, her final goodbye merged with her mother's last breath.

The tears slowed, then ceased. The tapestry appeared finally to be whole, complete. Pat and her mother, though apart, were together again.

Twenty-four years have now passed. I still have contact with Pat as she subsequently became my wife. She assures me that her pain has never returned. Today she lives with a settled hope, a calm memory of the future, that a reunion awaits them. If remote memories may overcome the barriers of passing time, if healing may touch an inflamed division of the past, then healing may also embrace a future uniting. (cf. Willis, 1989, pp. 80–81)

In other instances grief must specifically address the future. The relationship to the loved one has been altered by the physical separation. How will it continue, what shape will it assume, and what may be done to strengthen the new relationship?

After Ted committed suicide, Ann was plagued by two related wonderings: Did he still somehow exist, and is he now happy? The first addressed her own grief and her hope someday to reestablish contact with her son; the second flowed from her guilt over not recognizing his despair as well as her earnest wish for his peace.

These questions were emphasized when Ann had a series of extraordinarily clear dreams in which she met with her son and talked with him about his present state. In these conversations he appeared to be quite content. As she recounted them to me, she wondered if they could be taken as reliable answers to her questions.

I shared with her the kind of research and anecdotal evidence we have of nonordinary communication between loved ones, especially around the time of death. In those instances the common realities of passing time and physical location do not prohibit communication. I knew no philosophical or psychological reasons for denying such communications coming through dreams. Indeed, French philosopher Michel Foucault (1986), in discussing the dream reality, speaks about "lived space" and the "space of encounter" as opposed to "geographic space":

> In geographic space, motion is nothing but displacement: a concerted change of position from one point to another according to a previously established trajectory. The path is thus no more than the indispensable intermediary, reduced as far as possible, the lower limit of time which is indispensable for going from one point to another. In lived space, the displacement preserves an original spatial character; it does not cross, it travels along; until the very moment it stops, it remains a proffered trajectory of which only its point of departure is known for certain; its future is not prearranged by the geography of the setting, but is awaited in its authentic historicity. Finally it is the space of encoun-

> ters; not merely the intersection of lines which trace the shortest distance between two points, but overlapping of journeys, paths crossing, roads which converge to the same place on the horizon. . . . (pp. 60–61)

Be that as it may, we still cannot *know* that Ted now exists in a spiritual reality, although we may choose to *believe* that is so. We do know, however, that Ted's life in these dreams continues to influence her life. How should this influence be interpreted and how should she be responding to it?

One immediate problem in understanding this dream connection lies in the legacy of Freudian dream interpretation. Although Freud restored psychological legitimacy to dream images by making them communications from the unconscious, he misunderstood the therapeutic task to be the uncovering of the rational meaning hidden in the dream images. For, as Foucault (1986) explains,

> Freudian psychoanalysis of dreams never gets a comprehensive grasp of meaning. Meaning does not appear, for psychoanalysis, through recognition of a linguistic structure, but must be extracted, deduced, gleaned from a word taken by itself. And dream interpretation, naturally, becomes a method designed to discover the meaning of words in a language whose grammar one does not understand: it becomes a method of cross-referencing of the sort used by the archaeologist of lost languages, a method of probabilistic confirmation, as in the deciphering of secret codes, a method of meaningful coincidings as in the most traditional arts of divination. (pp. 35–36)

Freud failed to recognize that the dream is primarily and most importantly an imaginary experience. Indeed, as Foucault pithily remarks, "The aim of psychotherapy should be to free the imaginary that is trapped in the image" (p. 72).

Our imagination frees us for transcendence. It opens out the possibilities of our life before us, calling us to strive for the self we may be. And that life will realize itself, complete itself only in death. Indeed, in dreams

> death then carries the meaning of reconciliation, and the dream in which this death figures is then the most fundamental of all: it no longer speaks of life interrupted, but of

> the fulfillment of existence, showing forth the moment in which life reaches its fullness in a world about to close in. Hence, in all the legends, death as reward of the wise man, as happy declaration that henceforth the perfection of his existence no longer requires the movement of his life; in announcing death, the dream exhibits the fullness of being which existence has now attained. (Foucault, 1986, p. 55)

In his love for her, Ted was calling his mother from the fullness of his existence to the fullness of her own. She alone could make of herself whom she may become. Every moment lived, every decision taken, every potential realized created anew the existence she will be at the conclusion of this life. If she hopes for continued life after her earthly death, and if she believes that it will be shared with her son, then she is charged with living it resolutely now. Ted summons her to that out of the world of dreams.

Love in psychotherapy takes diverse forms. I experience each quite differently.

As a therapeutic alliance is established and begins to function, clients trustingly share their inner worlds, and I join them in a mutual striving for their growth of transformation. I love them for allowing me this intimate contact with their life. This love feels most essentially like excitement and gratitude.

With time this alliance strengthens to the point that I can freely share my changing perceptions of our relationship. I open myself vulnerably to them and touch them directly. As they take into themselves my feedback, I become a growing part of their inner reality. Love wells up in me as I recognize the courage of their openness and feel their acceptance of me. Love here is experienced as risk and vulnerability.

As I become privy to their erstwhile private struggles and yearnings, I am increasingly able to enter into the process of their self-creation. In time I come to recognize in their self-reports and in their behaviors the fruits of our common efforts. Like an artist who sees himself mirrored in his art, I find myself participating in my clients' sense of self. I love what we are becoming together; this love is experienced as concern for their growth and a deep caring for their life.

In any significant psychotherapeutic endeavor I know myself loving my clients in these three ways. As such journeys conclude I will miss the excitement of our regular encounters, but I readily send them off with best wishes for their happiness and continued growth. I appreciate what we have shared and value what we have accomplished together. I am glad we met. But as our lives move now along divergent paths, I do not mourn their absence nor do I find myself wishing for periodic updates on their life. We have met, shared, parted; now life goes on.

With some clients, however, love also becomes a strong magnetic power. It often begins as sexual attraction. This feels like a desiring to possess, a seeking for a special relationship, a striving for a deeper, sustained unity. Although it may be expressed only within ethical limits, this attraction needs to be accepted as a real part of our relationship. With an increased ability and willingness honestly to recognize and own this love, it may change into a more generalized force field which energizes us both. When we are in a session together life is enhanced, it flows in exciting ways and takes unexpected leaps. In such relationships the termination process deals with the specter of loss and with real grieving. Life will not be the same for either of us when we part. A certain richness and delight simply will disappear when we say goodbye. Apart, we each must find other loves, other energy sources, to enliven us.[2]

Finally, with some clients love grows into a union of spirits. We each have touched the other's life so profoundly we have been transformed into a new being through the exchange. Each exists now as "we" even though each continues on in a separate physical existence. When we come home to ourselves in our innermost reality, as we approach the center of the self, we find the other's life there too. The cessation of therapy will bring physical distance and only infrequent contact, but we will neither miss each other nor mourn our disrupted life together. This love and the unity out of which it flows cannot be broken for it exists as a

---

[2] In this era of excessive fear about sexual malpractice, many therapists pretend that sexuality, one's own and the client's, somehow never finds its way into the therapeutic relationship. Moreover, sexuality becomes naively equated with activities leading up to and including genital expression. How refreshing and how real is this brief reflection by existential psychotherapist James Bugental (1990) on his psychotherapeutic relationship with Louise:

> We had an affair, Louise and I. We didn't go to bed together; does that make it less an affair? We didn't take off all our clothes. We didn't have sexual intercourse. So, it would be said, we didn't "consummate" our affair. Nonsense. There was more of consummation to our relation than there is in many a heavy breathing, genital congress.

Reference is also made here to Ami Rokach's balanced article, "Psychotherapy: Close Encounters of the Intimate Kind," on the relationship of intimacy and sexuality in psychtherapy.

position (*situs*) taken in the ever-present experience of personal time.

In the months before Barbara left New England for Arizona, we both felt the approach of the inevitable separation. Both of us, however, found it difficult to face the loss and to allow ourselves to share the range of feelings it stirred up. From the first time we met, we had been unusually present to each other. She and her husband had not been fifteen minutes in my office when I quietly announced, "I don't know where it is coming from, but one of you is screaming out to me that your spirit is dying." The scream was Barbara's. After the couple separated, she stayed on in individual therapy. As the months passed by and our relationship strengthened, Barbara would often stop in the middle of a sentence, gaze silently at me for a moment, and then ask quite simply, "What?" Most usually this occurred as some shift of intuition or imagination was happening inside me. The energy between us grew to the point that one day in the quiet space following upon an intense presence to her inner experience she said in her refreshingly direct yet blunt way, "Boy, we just made love, big time!"

When Barbara stopped her therapy, I did not find myself missing her especially or mourning our separation. Nor did she. As she shared in a note, she at first found this quite surprising. But as she sought for an inner explanation, she realized that I simply had not gone away, that I was existing there as before . . . in her heart. Instead of pain she experienced only joy. Love, when it flows from the core of the self, participates in a spiritual reality that even death cannot destroy.

As I prepare to conclude this discussion of existential psychotherapy, I realize that it too has been a work of love. In attempting to share with you my experience as a therapist I have known much excitement, and I am grateful for the challenge of this exploration. At times, indeed, as I debated within myself whether I should "tell it as it is," the risk seemed great. But when I imagined you open and vulnerable to hear the truth as I have lived it, I could take the dare. In doing so I have grown as a therapist and as a person. I feel confident that you may share in that growth as you read about, grapple with, and experiment with this way of being a therapist. I hope that comes true for you. When the last word is written, I will miss the hours spent struggling to be with you.

Many of you, I know, will read this book, find some ideas interesting and realize that some of the life experiences I have shared may be incorporated into your own journey. I am pleased we have met. I can well imagine others of you, moreover, being energized and enlivened as you grow professionally and personally through our meeting. I have felt your presence and the life tension between us for many months. I have tried to be sensitive to your life and striven to touch your spirit with the truth of my own. I do not find it easy to say goodbye to you.

Some of you will, perhaps, recognize in my way of being a therapist a kindred spirit. Names and places and situations—the material of our lives—are inevitably quite different. But as we have met in these pages, we have done so deep within:

> What is the knocking?
> What is the knocking at the door in the night?
> It is somebody who wants to do us harm.
> No, no, it is the three strange angels.
> Admit them, admit them. (D.H. Lawrence, 1966)

As we do, we experience a union of spirits that alone overcomes the human legacy of meaninglessness and guilt, isolation and death. Ultimately, in love we know joy.

REFERENCES

Aristotle. *The physics, I* (P. Wicksteed & F. Cornford, Eds.). New York: The Loeb Classical Library, G.P. Putnam's Sons.

Bannan, J. (1967). *The philosophy of Merleau-Ponty*. New York: Harcourt, Brace and World.

Barnes, H. (1956). Introduction. In J.-P. Sartre, *Being and nothingness*. New York: Random House.

Bentov, I. (1977). *Stalking the wild pendulum*. New York: E.P. Dutton.

Bibring, E. (1937). Symposium of the theory of the therapeutic result of psychotherapy. *International Journal of Psychoanalysis, 18*, 170–189.

Binswanger, L. (1986). Dream and existence (J. Needleman, Trans.). In a special issue of the *Review of Existential Psychology and Psychiatry* (K. Hoeller, Ed.). (Originally published as *19*(1), 1984–1985.)

Boss, M. (1963). *Psychoanalysis and daseinanalysis*. New York: Basic Books.

Boss, M. (1990). The unconscious: What is it? In K. Hoeller (Ed.), *Readings in existential psychology and psychiatry*. (Originally published as *Review of Existential Psychology and Psychiatry, 20*(1, 2, 3), 1986–1987.)

Buber, M. (1947). *Tales of the hasidim: Early masters*. New York: Schocken Books.

Buber, M. (1958). *I and thou*. New York: Charles Scribner's Sons.

Buber, M. (1965). *Between man and man*. New York: Macmillan.

Bugental, J. (1965). *The search for authenticity*. New York: Holt, Rinehart and Winston.

Bugental, J. (1990). *Intimate journeys*. San Francisco: Jossey-Bass.

Camus, A. (1946). *The stranger*. (S. Gilbert, Trans.). New York: Knopf.

Camus, A. (1948). *The plague* (S. Gilbert, Trans.). New York: Knopf.

Camus, A. (1955). *The myth of Sisyphus and other essays.* New York: Random House.

Camus, A. (1958). *Caligula and three other plays* (S. Gilbert, Trans.). New York: Knopf.

Camus, A. (1960). *The possessed* (J. O'Brien, Trans.). New York: Knopf.

Camus, A. (1961). *The fall* (J. O'Brien, Trans.). New York: Knopf.

Capacchione, L. (1991). *Recovery of your inner child.* New York: Simon and Schuster.

Carruth, H. (1964). Introduction. In J.-P. Sartre (1964), *Nausea* (L. Alexander, Trans.). New York: Random House.

Colm, H. (1966). *The existentialist approach to psychotherapy with adults and children.* New York: Grune and Stratton.

Conkling, M. (1990). Sartre's refutation of the Freudian unconscious. In K. Hoeller (Ed.), *Readings in existential psychology and psychiatry.* (Originally published as *Review of Existential Psychology and Psychiatry,* 1986–1987, *20*(1, 2, 3.)

Corey, G. (1991). *Theory and practice of counseling and psychotherapy.* Pacific Grove, CA: Sage Publications.

Cousins, N. (1979). *Anatomy of an illness as perceived by the patients: Reflections on healing and regeneration.* New York: Norton.

Curtis, J. (1981). Effect of therapist's self-disclosure on patient's impressions of empathy, competence, and trust in an analogue of psychotherapeutic interaction. *Psychological Reports, 48,* 127–136.

DeBerry, S. (1987, Winter). Necessary factors in psychotherapy: A model for understanding iatrogenic disturbance. *Journal of Contemporary Psychotherapy, 17*(4), 235–249.

Deikman, A. (1976). *Personal freedom.* New York: Grossman/Viking.

Dostoevsky, F. (1864/1974). *Notes from underground* (M. Ginsberg, Trans.). New York: Bantam Books.

Edwards, B. (1979). *Drawing on the right side of the brain.* Los Angeles: J.P. Tarcher.

Eliot, T.S. (1943). *Four quartets.* New York: Harcourt, Brace and World.

Estes, C. (1989). The boy and the loon. In *Journey into manhood.* Boulder, CO: Sounds True Recordings.

Foucault, M. (1986). Dream, imagination, and existence (F. Williams, Trans.). In a special issue of the *Review of Existential Psychology and Psychiatry* (K. Hoeller, Ed.). (Originally published as *19*(1), 1984–1985.)

Frankl, V. (1984). *Man's search for meaning.* New York: Simon and Schuster.

Freud, S. (1925). A note on the unconscious. *Collected papers, 14.* London: The Hogarth Press.

Freud, S. (1961). The ego and the id. *The standard edition of the complete psychological works of Sigmund Freud, 19.* London: The Hogarth Press.

Friedman, M. (1985, Winter). Healing through meeting and the problematic of mutuality. *Journal of Humanistic Psychology,* 25(1), 7–40.

Friedman, M. (1986, November). Carl Rogers and Martin Buber: Self actualization and dialogue. *Person-centered Review, 1*(4), 401–435.

Fromm, E. (1967). *Escape from freedom.* New York: Avon.

Gelven, M. (1970). *A commentary on Heidegger's being and time.* New York: Harper and Row.

Goldstein, J. (1976). *The experience of insight.* Santa Cruz, CA: Unity Press.

Greenberg, L. (1985, April). An integrative approach to the relationship in counseling and psychotherapy. *The Counseling Psychologist, 13*(2), 251–259.

Grof, S. (1976). *Realms of the human unconscious.* New York: E.P. Dutton.

Halifax, J. (1979). *Shaman.* New York: Crossroads.

Heckler, R. (1981). Reaching for the sun: A phenomenological approach to the therapist's experience of healing in psychotherapy. Ann Arbor, MI: University Microfilms International.

Heidegger, M. (1949). Hölderlin and the essence of poetry. In *Existence and being.* Chicago: Henry Regnery.

Heidegger, M. (1962). *Being and time* (J. Macquarrie & E. Robinson, Trans.). New York: Harper and Row.

Hopper, S. (1956). On the naming of the gods in Hölderlin and Rilke. In C. Michalson, *Christianity and the existentialists.* New York: Charles Scribner's Sons.

Huxley, A. (1932/1969). *Brave new world.* New York: Harper and Row.

Jackson, S., & Chable, D. (1985). Engagement: A critical aspect of family therapy practice. *Australian and New Zealand Journal of Family Therapy, 6*(2), 65–69.

Jacobson, N. (1989). The therapist-client relationship in cognitive behavior therapy: Implications for treating depression. *Journal of Cognitive Psychotherapy: An International Quarterly, 3*(2), 85–96.

Jaspers, K. (1991). The way of wisdom. In D. Raymond (Ed.), *Existentialism and the philosophical tradition.* Englewood Cliffs, NJ: Prentice Hall.

Johnson, S., & Greenberg, L. (1989). The therapeutic alliance in marital therapy. *Journal of Contemporary Psychotherapy, 3*(2), 98–110.

Jourard, S. (1968). *Disclosing man to himself.* New York: Van Nostrand Reinhold.

Jung, C. (1989). *Memories, dreams, reflections* (A. Jaffe, Ed.). New York: Vintage Books.

Kaufmann, W. (1966). *Existentialism from Dostoevsky to Sartre.* Cleveland: World Publishing Company.

Kierkegaard, S. (1944). *The concept of dread* (W. Lowrie, Trans.). Princeton: Princeton University Press.

Kierkegaard, S. (1969). *The journals of Kierkegaard, 1853–1854* (A. Dru, Trans.). London, Collins Fontana Books.

Kierkegaard, S. (1849/1989). *The sickness unto death* (A. Hannay, Trans.). New York: Viking Penguin.

Kopp, S. (1972). *If you meet the Buddha on the road, kill him.* New York: Bantam Books.

Kottler, J. (1990). *On being a therapist.* San Francisco: Jossey-Bass.

Lawrence, D.H. (1966). *Selected poems* (K. Rexroth, Intro.). New York: Viking.

LeShan, L. (1974a). *How to meditate.* Boston: Little, Brown and Company.

LeShan, L. (1974b). *The medium, the mystic, and the physicist.* New York: Viking.

LeShan, L. (1976). *Alternate realities.* New York: Evans.

LeShan, L., & Margenau, H. (1982). *Einstein's space and Van Gogh's sky.* New York: Macmillan.

Marcel, G. (1949). *Being and having* (K. Farrer, Trans.). Westminster: Dacre Press.

Marcel, G. (1951). *Homo viator* (E. Craufurd, Trans.). Chicago: Henry Regnery.

Marcel, G. (1963). *The existential background of human dignity.* Cambridge: Harvard University Press.

Marcel, G. (1974). *The existentialist drama of Gabriel Marcel: The broken world and the rebellious heart* (F. Lescoe, Trans). West Hartford, CT: St. Joseph College.

Margolin, M., & Goldman, S. (1974). Beyond reinforcement: Integrating relationship and behavior therapy. *Clinical Social Work Journal, 2*(2), 96–106.

May, R. (1967). *Existence.* New York: Simon and Schuster.

May, R. (1979). *Psychology and the human dilemma.* New York: W.W. Norton.

May, R. (1990). Will, decision, and responsibility. In K. Hoeller (Ed.), *Readings in existential psychology and psychiatry.* Originally published as *Review of Existential Psychology and Psychiatry, 20* (1, 2, 3), 1986–1987.

Michalson, C. (1956). *Christianity and the existentialists.* New York: Charles Scribner's Sons.

Moody, R. (1977). *Life after life.* New York: Bantam Books.

Needleman, J. (1963). *Being-in-the-world: Selected papers of Ludwig Binswanger.* New York: Basic Books.

Nietzsche, F. (1883–1891). *Thus spake Zarathustra* (T. Common, Trans.). New York: The Modern Library.

Paolino, T. (April, 1982). The therapeutic relationship in psychoanalysis. *Contemporary Psychoanalysis, 18*(2), 218–234.

Patterson, C. (1974). *Relationship counseling and psychotherapy.* New York: Harper and Row.

Rilke, R. (1947). *Selected letters of Rainer Maria Rilke, 1902–1926* (R. Hull, Trans.). London: Macmillan.

Rilke, R. (1962). *Letters to a young poet.* New York: W.W. Norton.

Rogers, C. (1957). The necessary and sufficient conditions for therapeutic personality change. *Journal of Consulting Psychology, 21,* 95–103.

Rogers, C. (1961). *On becoming a person.* Boston: Houghton Mifflin.

Rogers, C. (1969, June). The emerging person: A new revolution. Commencement address, Sonoma State College.

Rogers, C. (1980). *A way of being.* Boston: Houghton Mifflin.

Rogers, C. (1987, May). Comment on Schlien's article "A countertheory of transference." *Person-centered Review, 2*(2), 182–188.

Rogers, C. (1987, Winter). Comments on the issue of equality in psychotherapy. *Journal of Humanistic Psychology, 27*(1), 38–40.

Rokach, A. (1986, Fall/Winter). Psychotherapy: Close encounters of the intimate kind. *Journal of Contemporary Psychotherapy, 16*(2), 161–181.

Sanford, J., & Lough, G. (1988). *What men are like.* Mahwah, NJ: Paulist Press.

Sartre, J.-P. (1947). *No exit and the flies* (S. Gilbert, Trans.). New York: Alfred A. Knopf.

Sartre, J.-P. (1956). *Being and nothingness* (H. Barnes, Trans.). New York: Philosophical Library.

Sartre, J.-P. (1957). *Existentialism and human emotions.* New York: Philosophical Library.

Sartre, J.-P. (1964). *Nausea* (L. Alexander, Trans.). New York: Philosophical Library.

Sartre, J.-P. (1965). Excerpts from being and nothingness. In *The philosophy of Jean-Paul Sartre* (R. Cummings, Ed.). New York: Random House.

Sartre, J.-P. (1966a). Being and nothingness. In *Existentialism from Dostoevsky to Sartre* (W. Kaufmann, Ed.). Cleveland: World Publishing.

Sartre, J.-P. (1966b). Existentialism is a humanism. In *Existentialism from Dostoevsky to Sartre* (W. Kaufmann, Ed.). Cleveland: World Publishing.

Sartre, J.-P. (1966c). Portrait of the antisemite. In *Existentialism from Dostoevsky to Sartre* (W. Kaufmann, Ed.). Cleveland: World Publishing.

Sequin, C. (1965). *Love and psychotherapy*. New York: Libra.

Sterba, R. (1934). The fate of the ego in analytic therapy. *International Journal of Psychoanalysis, 15,* 117–226.

Shah, I. (1967). *Tales of the dervishes*. New York: E.P. Dutton.

Shah, I. (1968). *The way of the sufi.* New York: E.P. Dutton.

Snyder, D. (1982). Perspective and engagement in counseling and psychotherapy: The phenomenological approach. *International Journal for the Advancement of Counseling, 5,* 95–107.

Sonnemann, U. (1954). *An introduction to phenomenological psychology and existential analysis*. New York: Grune and Stratton.

Stewart, D. (1991). A look at the self-righteous defense. In J. Travers (Ed.), *Psychotherapy and the self-righteous patient.* New York: Haworth.

Taegel, W. (1990). *The many colored buffalo.* Norwood, NJ: Ablex.

Thom, J. (1989). *Panther in the sky*. New York: Ballantine Books.

Tillich, P. (1948). You are accepted. In *The shaking of the foundations*. New York: Charles Scribner's Sons.

Tillich, P. (1969). *The courage to be.* New Haven: Yale University Press.

Tolstoy, L. (1887). Confession. (1991). In D. Raymond, (Ed.). *Existentialism and the philosophical tradition.* Englewood Cliffs, NJ: Prentice Hall.

Travers, J., & Stern, M. (Eds.). (1991). *Psychotherapy and the self-righteous patient.* New York: Haworth.

Van Deurzen-Smith, E. (1991). *Existential counselling in practice.* Newbury Park, CA: Sage Publications.

Van Dusen, W. (1981). *The natural depth in man.* New York: Swedenborg Foundation.

Walsh, R. (1990, Fall). Shamanic cosmology: A psychological examination of the shaman's worldview. *ReVision, 13*(2), 86–100.

Wilber, K. (Fall, 1980). The pre/trans fallacy. *ReVision, 3*(2), 51–71.

Willis, R. (1979). Meditation to fit the person: Psychology and the meditative way. *Journal of Religion and Health, 18*(2), 93–119.

Willis, R. (1984). The many faces of the hesitant patient. In J. Travers (Ed.), *Psychotherapy and the uncommitted patient.* New York: Haworth.

Willis, R. (1984, Spring). Growth and religious diversity. *Human Development, 5*(1), 19–30.

Willis, R. (1989). The healing of there and then. *The Psychotherapy Patient, 6*(1/2), 73–90.

Willis, R. (1991, Fall). A light shines in the darkness. *Voices: The Art and Science of Psychotherapy, 27*(3), 59–65.

Yalom, I. (1980). *Existential psychotherapy.* New York: Basic Books.

Yalom, I. (1989). *Love's executioner and other tales of psychotherapy.* New York: Basic Books.

About the Author

Robert Willis is the executive director of the Pastoral Counseling Center of West Hartford, Connecticut. After completing his doctorate under the direction of Carl Rogers at United States International University in San Diego, he has concentrated his professional efforts in teaching, supervising, and writing about the relationship of psychology and spirituality. His extensive experience in psychotherapy—at a college counseling center, in private practice, and in a private clinic—has stimulated his interest in expressing a systematic understanding of existential psychotherapy. In a modern world struggling with the pathology of inner emptiness and the anxiety it produces, he seeks through the therapeutic relationship to awaken the core of the Self waiting patiently within those who request his assistance.

AUTHOR INDEX

J

K

L

M

N

P

R

S

T

V

W

Y

SUBJECT INDEX

www.ingramcontent.com/pod-product-compliance
Lightning Source LLC
LaVergne TN
LVHW011757200926
848484LV00003B/726